LABOR MOVEMENTS
AND LABOR THOUGHT

LABOR MOVEMENTS AND LABOR THOUGHT
Spain, France, Germany, and the United States

Sima Lieberman

PRAEGER SPECIAL STUDIES • PRAEGER SCIENTIFIC

New York • Philadelphia • Eastbourne, UK
Toronto • Hong Kong • Tokyo • Sydney

Library of Congress Cataloging in Publication Data

Lieberman, Sima, 1927—
    Labor movements and labor thought.

    Includes bibliographies and index.
    1. Trade-unions—Europe—History. 2. Trade-unions—United States—
History. 3. Labor and laboring classes—Europe—History. 4. Labor and
laboring classes—United States—History. 5. Social conflict—Europe.
6. Syndicalism—Europe. I. Title
HD6657.L54 1985   331.88′094   85-16859
ISBN 0-03-002604-0 (alk. paper)

Published in 1986 by Praeger Publishers
CBS Educational and Professional Publishing, a Division of CBS Inc.
521 Fifth Avenue, New York, NY 10175 USA

Printed in the United States of America on acid-free paper

INTERNATIONAL OFFICES

Orders from outside the United States should be sent to the appropriate address listed below.
Orders from areas not listed below should be placed through CBS International Publishing, 383
Madison Ave., New York, NY 10175 USA

Australia, New Zealand

Holt Saunders, Pty, Ltd., 9 Waltham St., Artarmon, N.S.W. 2064, Sydney, Australia

Canada

Holt, Rinehart & Winston of Canada, 55 Horner Ave., Toronto, Ontario, Canada M8Z 4X6

Europe, the Middle East, & Africa

Holt Saunders, Ltd., 1 St. Anne's Road, Eastbourne, East Sussex, England BN21 3UN

Japan

Holt Saunders, Ltd., Ichibancho Central Building, 22-1 Ichibancho, 3rd Floor, Chiyodaku, Tokyo,
Japan

Hong Kong, Southeast Asia

Holt Saunders Asia, Ltd., 10 Fl, Intercontinental Plaza, 94 Granville Road, Tsim Sha Tsui East,
Kowloon, Hong Kong

**Manuscript submissions should be sent to the Editorial Director, Praeger Publishers, 521
Fifth Avenue, New York, NY 10175 USA**

to Erik and to Marcel,
with love

Contents

LABOR MOVEMENTS
AND LABOR THOUGHT

Introduction: Society, Economy, and the Trade Union Movement

A brief study of labor movements in the industrial, "capitalist" world at the start of this decade reveals a great diversity in the structure and goals of such movements. In some countries, such as the United States and the German Federal Republic, most trade unions had organized under a single labor federation, a federation that accepted the existing politicoeconomic system and that strove to achieve for its members a higher standard of living through lawful efforts. In these countries, the cohesive labor movement tended to embrace a politically conservative position and generally supported its government in its opposition to communism. In the United States, Samuel Gompers, John L. Lewis, William Green, Philip Murray, Walter Reuther, and George Meany rejected ideological Marxism and were critical of labor leaders who were influenced by the dictates of the Communist Party of the Soviet Union.

In Germany, in the 1860s, Marxists and Lassalleans vied to place their ideological stamp on the nascent labor movement. August Bebel, Wilhelm Liebknecht, and Ferdinand Lassalle accepted the Marxian concepts of the class struggle and of the coming proletarian revolution. All of them agreed with the following thoughts in Karl Marx and Frederick Engels' *Communist Manifesto* of 1848:

Of all the classes that stand face to face with the bourgeoisie today, the proletariat alone is a really revolutionary class.... The proletarian is without property; his relation to his wife and children has no longer anything in common with the bourgeois family-relations; modern industrial labour, modern subjection to capital, the same in England as in France, in America as in Germany, has stripped him of every trace of national character. Law, morality, religion, are to him so many bourgeois

1

prejudices, behind which lurk in ambush just as many bourgeois interests.... In depicting the most general phases of the development of the proletariat, we traced the more or less veiled civil war, raging within existing society, up to the point where that war breaks out into open revolution, and where the violent overthrow of the bourgeoisie lays the foundation for the sway of the proletariat. (Marx and Engels 1980, pp. 25, 26)

Yet, as early as 1914, most of the leaders of the German Socialist party and those of the German trade unions stood behind the military plans of their imperial government. At its founding congress in 1949, the German Trade Union Federation, the Deutscher Gewerkschaftsbund (DGB), demanded centralized planning of the national economy, but not government or state control of the latter. The 1949 program of the DGB stated:

Planning on national economic lines is thoroughly reconcilable with the principles of human freedom. The most important freedom for the majority of the people, the freedom from need and from the fear of need, will only be achieved in this way. Planning along national economic lines and free consumer choice, the right to change one's place of work and the freedom to choose one's vocation are not antitheses. Considerable leeway for private initiative and for competition among managers with regard to achievement remains within these guidelines. (DGB 1973, p. 82)

At its 1963 congress, held at Düsseldorf, the DGB approved a program that read in part: "The DGB and its trade unions express their support for the inalienable rights of man to freedom and self-determination.... Free and independent trade unions can only exist and work in a democracy. The DGB and its trade unions thus defend themselves decisively against all totalitarian and reactionary endeavours, and combat all attempts to limit and rescind the basic rights anchored in the constitution" (DGB 1973, p. 94). The program was totally silent on key Marxist concepts, such as the class struggle and the future proletarian revolution. The very language of the program opposed the desirability of a "dictatorship of the proletariat."

The labor scenario was quite different in Spain in the early 1980s. After four decades of dictatorship, during which free and independent trade unions were prohibited by law, organized labor emerged divided by differences in political ideology and by distinct ethnic or regional identification. Once independent trade unions were again legalized following the death of General Francisco Franco in 1975, separate labor federations were lawfully established in 1976 and in 1977.

A Communist-led Labor Confederation of the CCOO claimed to fight for the economic, social, and political welfare of all Spanish workers. It asserted that its long-term political reform objectives were nonrevolutionary and that it was quite willing to cooperate with the post-Franco era government in order to rescue the economy from severe crisis. It acted, however, as an economic arm of the Spanish Communist party.

It was only in 1977 that the Unión General de Trabajadores (UGT), a labor federation with close ties to the Spanish Socialist Workers' party, acquired the legality it had lost with Franco's victory in 1939. In 1978, its secretary-general, Nicolás Redondo, asserted that "the U.G.T. declares itself to be socialist; U.G.T. believes that labor's apolitical stand is impossible or is a fallacy. Every organization representing collective interests opposed to those of another collectivity has an indubitable political content. Consequently, the trade unions which do not aspire to the total transformation of the capitalist society into a classless society do not deserve to be known as such" (Lieberman 1982, p. 335).

In the same year, the other pre-1939 major labor federation, the Confederación Nacional del Trabajo (CNT), once a strong anarchist organization, also obtained legal status. It still professed to reject bourgeois democracy and advocated the organization of society into free, but federated, "communes." The CNT claimed to be completely apolitical since "all political parties, regardless of their nature, only attempt to conquer power in order to rule the community" (Lieberman 1982, p. 337).

Other labor federations, reflecting religious, regional, and ethnic interests, fragmented the Spanish labor movement in the late 1970s into a number of organizations whose goals and policies did not harmonize. For many of these organizations, political aims commanded the same priority as the pursuit of economic gains for their members or for all Spanish workers.

The French case in the early 1980s was an intermediate one between the highly fragmented and disunited structure of the Spanish labor movement and the apolitical and strongly united German labor movement. Two major French labor organizations, the Confédération Générale du Travail (CGT) and the Confédération Française Démocratique du Travail (CFDT), followed very different strategies in response to the economic crises of the 1970s and to the political defeat of the Left in 1978. A few other labor federations, such as Force Ouvrière (FO) and the Fédération de l'Education Nationale (FEN), constituted small, independent organizations following their own course of action.

A majority of the Communist-dominated CGT leadership opted for the political strategy of "fundamental opposition" to the economic policies of the government and of the employers. These CGT leaders took the position that the economic crises of the 1970s had been caused above all, by the policy choices of government and of the private monopolies. They blamed the government, the employers, and the Socialists for having supported policies of international specialization and of national industrial "redeployment" that resulted in enormous job losses. They rejected the view of a minority in the CGT that the labor organization should become a "proposition force" that could offer France new ways of solving its economic difficulties and that would induce the nation to move in the direction of social transformation. The majority felt that the CGT should be mostly concerned with building up the political strength of the French Communist party.

The CFDT followed a very distinct policy course. Its leadership gave emphasis to a pure "contractual" policy—to a return to exclusive labor-market action and to negotiation with employers and government without regard for political considerations. Some of the organization's leaders advocated the use of the economic struggle to move in the direction of *autogestion*, that is, employees' self-management. But, on the whole, the strategy of the CFDT was one of unconditional participation in government economic policy, the federation supporting the participation of labor unions in the national planning process.

The exhortation of Marx and Engels appearing at the end of the *Communist Manifesto*, "Working men of all countries, unite!," failed to materialize in the course of the following 130 years. Even at the national level, time did not make it easier for various labor organizations in a single country to cooperate and to reconcile policy objectives. The historical development experience of various national labor movements reveals that in some cases labor came very close to achieving a united, cohesive nationwide organization, whereas in other instances, organized labor was unable to set aside divisions based mostly on political and social ideologies.

The following chapters attempt to study the evolution of labor movements in four countries from their beginnings to the present day in order to illustrate the variety of national structures organized labor developed in the course of more than a century following the publication of the *Communist Manifesto*. The reader will not only note major differences in the historical development of these labor movements but will also wonder why the thoughts of the men and women whose voices and writings shaped the evolution of these movements were often so distinct. What explains these differences?

The French Revolution and the economic revolution that began in England during the last quarter of the eighteenth century were the battering rams that weakened surviving feudal institutions and resulted in their eventual collapse. The Industrial Revolution did not penetrate the various European and non-European countries at the same time and was not equally pervasive in the various economies in which it acquired a foothold. In some nations, traditional institutions resisted better the challenge of modernization than in other countries.

It was only in the 1960s that something akin to an "industrial revolution" established itself in Spain. The process of industrialization was slow and gradual in nineteenth-century France. In Germany, on the other hand, industrial investment banks and the formation of Bismarck's empire gave a major stimulus to rapid industrialization, starting in the 1870s. Industrialists, bankers, and state and imperial government officials joined efforts in the creation of a large heavy industry base that allowed Germany to produce more steel than Britain by 1910. The establishment of this base allowed the German Empire to build an efficient railway system and a powerful mercantile fleet. It also allowed the empire to become a leading producer of machinery and a strong military power. Equally important, the rapidly growing German economy started offering jobs to large numbers of workers who would otherwise have emigrated in order to survive.

An even faster pace of industrialization characterized the American economy with the United States becoming the leading manufacturing power in the world in the early 1890s. Net capital formation in the period 1866–96 was higher than it had been at any time prior to 1865. It has been estimated that output of all commodities per worker-hour increased by 64 percent in this period (Kenen and Harris 1961, p. 72). Gross national product on a per capita basis nearly doubled during this same time.

Ninety years after the *Communist Manifesto*, Leon Trotsky recognized that

> The error of Marx and Engels in regard to the historical dates flowed, on the one hand, from an underestimation of future possibilities latent in capitalism, and, on the other hand, an overestimation of the revolutionary maturity of the proletariat. The revolution of 1848 did not turn into a socialist revolution as the *Manifesto* had calculated, but opened up to Germany the possibility of a vast future capitalist ascension.... Meanwhile, the prolonged period of capitalist prosperity that ensued brought about not the education of the revolutionary vanguard, but rather the bourgeois degeneration of the labor aristocracy, which became in turn the chief brake on the proletarian revolution. (Marx and Engels 1980, p. 7)

Technological change in the pre–Industrial Revolution era affected only a few classes or castes within society. Only those who possessed wealth or political power were able to reap the benefits of new knowledge and of better methods of production and distribution. The masses of the people did not experience a great change in their living conditions during the centuries that lapsed from Antiquity to the eighteenth century. The fundamental characteristics of human society remained anchored to the immutable pillars of traditionalism; and the large majority of the people in every nation continued to earn a livelihood in the primary sector of the economy, following the example set by earlier generations.

Modern industrialization brought major social changes. It was accompanied by an exodus from the fields and by a rapid expansion of industrial urban centers. It was in the crowded, unsanitary, and ugly "coketowns" that mushroomed during the early phases of modern industrialization that a recently formed urban industrial proletariat became aware that the promise of the new industrial society benefited only a small bourgeois class that attemped to maximize its wealth by exploiting workers without mercy. The bourgeois employer lacked a feeling of responsibility for the welfare of its workers, a sense of charity, a personal rapport that had characterized relationships between master and wage earner in the preindustrial society. It was in the industrial cities where workers could best compare their misery with the standard of living of their employers, where they became aware of who was paying the price of industrialization. It was only natural that they should feel that they had been unjustly deprived of the economic benefits of industrialization and of the freedoms promised by the French Revolution.

A proletarian class consciousness started forming in the minds of workers who still had no thoughts of organizing as workers. The formation of a workers' class consciousness and a spirit of rebellion against the injustices of the new industrial society developed fastest and most strongly among those workers who felt that the propertied classes had deliberately kept the proletariat from sharing in the expanding output of the industrial society and refused to give industrial and rural workers a meaningful role in the nation's political life.

A study of the patterns of development of national labor movements will provide empirical validation of the hypothesis that wherever workers perceived no likely change in their political, social, or economic status, the awareness of their increasing degradation induced them to place as much or even more importance on the social transformation of their society than on the attainment of a higher material standard of living within the existing society. In those countries in which workers believed that they were not allowed to share in the fruits of industrialization or in which they felt that they were condemned to pariah status by an inflexible and unchanging politicosocial system, their organizations were shaped by their wish to effectuate a political transformation of society.

During the second half of the nineteenth century, this situation existed in the agrarian, traditional societies of southern Europe, societies still tied to resilient neofeudal institutions. It was not by accident that the masses of rural and urban workers in Spain, Italy, and southern France embraced the philosophy of anarchism at that time. These were economically backward societies in which poor transportation and communications left groups of workers regionally isolated from each other. This isolation favored the establishment of a sense of local or regional identification among workers and left them indifferent to national or international labor organizations.

The situation was quite different in countries that experienced rapid economic advance during the latter half of the nineteenth century. In those countries, workers entertained the hope of being able to improve their economic conditions through the formation of labor organizations. In such cases, good means of transportation and communications helped workers to unify into nationwide organizations whose principal goal was obtaining immediate economic gains for their members. When the scenario was one of rapid economic growth, the revolutionary interests of the proletariat weakened as its purchasing power expanded. In the case of the United States, democratic political institutions further limited the interests of workers in social change. The hypothesis can be advanced that in countries where workers had reason to believe that their standard of living could rise with the general growth of the national economy, their interest in political and social change was lessened by their eagerness to share benefits brought by economic advance. The hypothesis appears to be verified by the history of the German and the American labor movements.

It is therefore suggested that the attachment of certain contemporary labor movements to different political ideologies and their consequential fragmentation are directly related to the degree of relative economic backwardness of the countries in which these labor movements developed. Extending the "Alexander Gerschenkron thesis" to the case of organized labor, it may be asserted that organized labor faced highest "tensions" in those societies that imposed on the workers the greatest obstacles to their political, social, and economic advance (Gerschenkron 1962). The greater the strength of traditional institutions in a particular society, the greater that society's relative social and economic backwardness, the greater appeared the potential benefits of social transformation to its proletariat, and the greater were the latter's efforts to do away with the perceived obstacles to change. Under such conditions, workers necessarily planned or attempted to overthrow the existing sociopolitical system in accordance with guidelines provided by different political and social ideologies.

The following chapters will give the reader the opportunity to evaluate this hypothesis.

NOTES

DGB. 1973. *The German Labor Movement.* Düsseldorf, West Germany.

Gerschenkron, A. 1962. *Economic Backwardness in Historical Perspective.* Cambridge, Mass.: Harvard University Press.

Kenen, P.B., and S.E. Harris. 1961. *American Economic History.* New York: McGraw-Hill.

Lieberman, S. 1982. *The Contemporary Spanish Economy: A Historical Perspective.* London: Allen & Unwin.

Marx, K. and F. Engels. 1980. *The Communist Manifesto.* New York: Pathfinder Press.

1

The Anarchist-Socialist Polarization of the Spanish Labor Movement: From Its Origins to the Beginning of World War I

THE DAWN OF SPAIN'S LABOR MOVEMENT

Spain's economy was essentially an agrarian one as late as the mid-nineteenth century. Decades after the so-called Industrial Revolution in Britain, the small, middle-class industrial groups of Catalonia and Vizcaya were nothing but precapitalist nuclei located on the periphery of a tradition-guided mass. The neofeudal, preindustrialist characteristics of Spanish society in the 1830s are easily revealed when we compare the size of the ecclesiastical population, a population probably exceeding 150,000 persons, to a population of about 21,000 textile workers for the entire Catalan textile industry, Spain's major industry at that time. The resilience of Spain's feudal institutions is also well established by the fact that wealth at this time was still based on the ownership of large landed estates; the most important landholders were still the nobles and the high church officials. At that time, 1,323 noble families owned 16.9 million hectares of land, ecclesiastics possessed about 1.4 million hectares, and 390,000 members of the lower nobility, the hidalgos, owned nearly 9.2 million hectares (Tuñón 1972, vol. I, p. 21).

The great majority of Spanish workers were still rural workers, receiving mostly food and shelter as remuneration for work that often lasted 12 hours a day during the planting and harvesting seasons. Needless to say, their living standards were dismally low. Living conditions were not much better for the Catalan textile workers, who had to endure low daily wages, sudden unemployment, and the hardships resulting from a total absence of any protective labor legislation. Unable to sustain their families on the basis of a wage of 5 to 7 *reales* per day, they were often forced to seek employment for their minor children in the same factory. The records of the Hospital of Barcelona reveal that a large number of these children, some of them as young as eight years of age, were treated for severe injuries suffered while working in the textile mills.

In spite of hunger and misery, and in spite of rising food prices during the 1830s, Spanish workers were slow to organize. One reason for the slow development of workers' organizations was the government's ban on all types of such groups. The only way Catalan workers were able to protest recurring unemployment and rising food prices during the 1830s and the early 1840s was by resorting to "luddism," that is, the violent destruction of machinery and of factories. A true "lumpen-proletariat" put to the torch in a single day a number of public buildings and El Vapor factory in Barcelona in 1835. Textile machinery was destroyed in Sabadell the following year.

It was only in February 1839 that a royal decree finally authorized the establishment of workers' mutual aid societies. Taking advantage of this executive order, the weavers of Barcelona founded, on September 26, 1840, a Mutual Association of Weavers, a mutual aid society designed to camouflage the activities of a true trade union. This organization rapidly encountered changing fates in the insurrectionary Barcelona of 1842 and 1843. Depending on what group controlled the city during those turbulent years, the association was either accepted or barred, tolerated or prosecuted. Its establishment in 1840, however, marked the beginning of the industrial trade union movement in Spain.

The association still existed in 1845, as shown by the reports of a commission established by the governor of Catalonia to settle disputes between workers and their employers (Tuñon 1972, vol. I, p. 65). Five years later, this governor complained about workers' organizations that had been established without previous permission by the authorities.

By the end of the 1840s, Carlist warfare in northern Catalonia, political unrest, rising prices, and the fear that the new textile machinery would produce serious unemployment induced workers to form illegal unions, generally under the disguise of mutual aid societies.

The year 1854 witnessed the beginning of a drastic increase in the cost of living, as well as a military revolt in Madrid that resulted in the adoption of a new constitution in the following year and in the formation of a new government, a government constituted principally by lawyers and large landowners. In the words of Stanley G. Payne, "The 1854 revolt was in a sense the Spanish '1848.' " (Payne, 1973, vol. II, p. 459). The revolt extended to Barcelona where it was joined by the workers who gave it a social tone. The workers of Barcelona went on strike, demanded the closing of factories, and proceeded to destroy some *selfactinas,* the "self-acting" spinning machines recently imported from Britain.

It was in Catalonia that a Spanish labor movement was born. By the mid-nineteenth century, Catalonia, although a relatively backward region in the totality of Western Europe, was ahead of the other Spanish regions in many ways. It had produced imaginative intellectuals, dogmatic Carlist populists, industrial entrepreneurs, and courageous industrial workers. The latter had not yet embraced any socioeconomic ideology. They tried to obtain modest but immediate improvements in their conditions of work by grouping into illegal associations and by participating in poorly planned strikes and political demonstrations.

The Spanish social critics of the time had little influence on the Catalan proletariat. These writers, generally of low middle-class, radical background, can be regarded as "utopian socialists," heavily influenced by such Frenchmen as Saint-Simon, Fourier, Cabet, and Proudhon.

As of 1835, a Barcelona daily, *El Vapor*, started publishing articles recognizing the unfairness of the distribution of the national product, which was largely attributed to a coalition of capitalists and scientists calculated to deprive ignorant workers of the just fruit of their labor. Fourier's idea of groups of people engaging in collective work and living in cooperative communities was acclaimed, although the articles' author was careful to present the Fourier scheme prudently, pointing out the "ignorance" of workers, invoking God, and trying to present Fourier's solution to social problems in ways that would be acceptable to the Spanish traditional elites.

Saint-Simon's ideas appeared in the review *El Propagador de la Libertad*. In this journal, José Andrés de Fontcuberta published a number of articles emphasizing associationism, industrialization, and the new social ethic advocated by the French writer.

Most of the early Spanish utopian socialists appeared, however, to be guided by the works of Fourier, and this may be quite natural in an economic environment in which agricultural and handicraft labor were still predominant. Joaquín Abreu, an ex-deputy who was exiled in 1823, presented a detailed explanation of Fourier's thoughts in the Madrid daily *El Correo Nacional,* and Manuel Sagrario de Veloy attempted without success to establish a phalanstery in Tampul, near the city of Jerez.

The decade 1844–54 witnessed a blooming of utopian socialist literature in Spain. Its authors, most of them intellectuals, came from the lower stratum of the middle class and sincerely felt the hardships of the *misérables.* Fourierism triumphed again in the newspaper *La Atracción,* founded by Fernando Garrido in 1847, which appeared for three months only. Garrido and Sixto Cámara then published the newspaper *la Asociación* in 1850, whose life promptly ended with the imprisonment of Garrido.

Cabet's ideas were propagated in Barcelona in the newspaper *La*

Fraternidad, which was published by Narciso Monturiol in 1847 and 1848. In 1848 and 1849 appeared the two widely read works of Sixto Cámara, *El Espíritu Moderno* and *La Cuestión Social*. In these works, Cámara advocated, in a Saint-Simonian fashion, a society in which capitalists, scientists, artists, and workers would cooperate to maximize the prosperity of the nation.

Barcelona was again the center of worker protest in 1855. While in other Spanish cities workers took spontaneous action to protest rising food prices and unemployment, it was the workers of Barcelona who gave priority in their petitions to their right to organize and to the legalization of such right. The emphasis they placed on their right to bargain collectively disturbed both the employers and the traditional socioeconomic oligarchy.

How much the workers' demands regarding the legalization of trade unions disturbed the privileged classes of Spanish society is well evidenced by the quick reaction of the political and military authorities. An order of the governor of Barcelona, Cirilo Franquet, of April 30, 1855, prohibited both the closing down of factories by employers and collective work stoppages by their employees; and workers' associations were forbidden to operate without previous permission by the authorities. An order of the captain-general of the region, General Juan Zapatero, prohibited on June 21, 1855 any activity by workers' unions.

In spite of the position taken by the authorities, on July 2, workers in Barcelona, Gracia, Badalona, Sans, and Igualada abandoned work and petitioned for the legalization of trade unions and for the establishment of hearing commissions composed of representatives of both employers and employees. The strike became a general one in Barcelona. The government took immediate harsh action against the workers, and many were transported to Cuba. The strike ended on July 11 after a deputy sent from Madrid by Espartero promised the workers that mixed hearing commissions would consider the workers' demands.

The Madrid government promptly forgot the promises made to the workers of Barcelona. Early in October, it introduced legislation specifying that any employers' or workers' organization, including mutual aid societies, necessitated for the legality of its operations previous governmental permission. These organizations were not to be allowed a membership exceeding 500. The proposed law limited the duration of the workday for children 12 to 18 years of age to ten hours.

Although the legislation was eventually rejected by the parliamentarian hearing committee, labor unrest continued in Spain throughout the year, and rising prices exacerbated the situation until the summer of 1857, when workers' insurrections in Vallodolid, Burgos, and Palencia forced the fall of the Espartero government. These uprisings were to implant in the social and political history of the county for the following 100 years a permanent and definite characteristic: a major fear of the proletariat by the possessing, bourgeois class and a resulting alliance between this class and the traditional oligarchy.

Rural insurrections, generally caused by hunger, were spontaneous and of short duration. These incidents took the form of peasant marches, theft of foodstuffs, and the *jornaleros'* shouts of *viva la república*, the peasants naturally associating the formation of a republic with a redistribution of land.

The first significant insurrection by rural workers took place in Andalusia in 1861. A veterinarian from Loja, a village near Málaga, Rafael Pérez del Alamo, succeeded in forming an army of rural workers and in taking control first of the village of Iznájar, near Córdoba, and then of the city of Loja. The armed *jornaleros*, however, were quickly routed by the army, and some were promptly executed by the military. Rural workers, deprived as yet of any true labor organization, still depended on the liberal bourgeoisie to defend their interests. A real rural workers' organization was still a matter of the future.

Fate was kinder to the trade unions in the early 1860s. Although the Narváez government in Madrid had expressly forbidden their existence in 1857, a royal decree of 1861 authorized once again the operation of mutual aid societies as long as the latter did not have more than 1,000 members and operated only locally. The order explicitly forbade these organizations to engage in any activity relating to the work conditions of its members.

Two years of trade union toleration by the military authorities started in Catalonia during the summer of 1864, when the captain-general of Catalonia, General Dulce, gave de facto authorization to the operation of trade unions. The improved atmosphere for Catalan trade unionism allowed the publication of two new workers' newspapers and the celebration of a Workers' Congress.

On September 4, 1864, Antonio Gusart y Vila produced the first issue of *El Obrero,* a paper that advocated the legalization of trade unions as well as workers' production and consumer cooperatives. This newspaper called for a Workers' Congress, which indeed took place on December 25 and 26 of 1865 in Barcelona. The congress agreed to form federations of trade unions in cities in which there would be more than a trade union and embraced cooperativism. It adopted *El Obrero* as its official publication. More importantly, the congress decided to petition the executive part of the central government instead of the Cortes for the legalization of trade unions. The government suspended *El Obrero* in the summer of 1866, following a military insurrection in Madrid.

Between April 1 and July 8, 1866, José Roca y Galés published another workers' newspaper, *La Asociación,* which also advocated worker cooperativism. During the period 1864–66, the first Circles of Catholic Workers were established.

1866 brought an end to two years of de facto government acceptance of trade unions. From then until the revolution of 1868, government persecution of trade unions surfaced again.

As yet, Spanish workers were not conscious of the connections linking economic to political life. Most workers distrusted the central government regardless of the people in power and generally felt that a republic would be to their advantage. The workers' distrust for the central government largely explains why Bakuninism was to acquire an easy headstart over Marxism during decades to come. The typical Spanish labor leader of those years had been influenced "a little by Proudhon, a little by Fourier and a lot by Pi y Margall" (Droz 1979, p. 300). In 1864, Pi y Margall still proclaimed as the ultimate social goal the sovereignty of the individual.

The International Workingmen's Association (IWA), generally known as the First International, had been founded in London on September 28, 1864. In 1866 it celebrated its first congress in Geneva, a meeting clearly marked by Proudhonian views. This congress launched the idea of an eight-hour workday and the motto "eight hours of work, eight hours of recreation, eight hours of rest."

The First International only penetrated Spain in 1868, even though its General Council authorized on November 22, 1864 a certain L. Otto "to correspond in the name of this Association with the friends of progress in Spain" (Minutes 1962, p. 50). There is no information about Otto's actions in Spain. We know that Paul Lafargue, Marx's son-in-law, was elected a member of the General Council of the IWA on March 6, 1866, and secretary for Spain on March 26. The General Council learned of the Workers' Congress in Barcelona in 1865 through a French newspaper. There appeared a Spanish delegate at the Brussels congress of the IWA in September 1868; his name has been reported as "Sarro Magallán," acting for the Iberian Labor Legion; the real identity of this man was that of a machinist from Barcelona, whose name was Antonio Marsal Anglora (Droz 1979, p. 301). Thus it appears that before the revolution of 1868 and Giuseppe Fanelli's arrival in Spain, the influence of the IWA on the Spanish labor movement was insignificant.

Following the revolution of September 1868, the new provisional government of Serrano and Prim had allowed the formation of trade unions. A Central Directorship of Trade Unions was established in Barcelona and celebrated a congress in December 1868; the congress changed the name of the organization to the Federal Center of Trade Unions. Most of the trade union delegates to the congress supported the formation of a republican national government. The two secretaries of the newly formed Federal Center, Marsal Anglora and Rafael Farga Pellicer, also declared themselves in favor of a republic.

It was at that time that Mikhail Bakunin's emisssary, the Italian Giuseppe Fanelli, arrived from Geneva in Barcelona. Fanelli's mission was to obtain Spanish support for the First International. In Barcelona, Fanelli met Elie Réclus, a distinguished French anthropologist and a supporter of Bakunin. In the company of Fernando Garrido, another disciple of Bakunin, Fanelli visited first Tarragona, then Tortosa and Valencia. He then left alone for Madrid, where he arrived on November 4, 1868. There, in the home of Julián Rubau Donadeu, he met 21 persons, among them four typographers, five painters, two tailors, two engravers, two shoemakers, a carpenter, a gilder, a lithographer, a ropemaker, a journalist, and a bookkeeper. In this group were Anselmo Lorenzo, Tomás González Morago, and the brothers Francisco and Angel Moraga. After hearing Fanelli, this group declared itself ready to support the IWA. Fanelli left Madrid for Barcelona on January 24, 1869.

In Barcelona, Fanelli met the painter José Luis Pellicer, who arranged a meeting between Fanelli and a mostly middle-class group. Only a few of those present at the meeting, mostly young university students, became interested in Fanelli's proposals. One of these young men was Rafael Farga Pellicer.

Before leaving Spain, Fanelli had given his audiences the statutes and programs of both the IWA and Bakunin's International Alliance. These were studied by the two groups that had heard Fanelli, but these "Internationalists" appeared not to notice significant differences between the two organizations. The Madrid Internationalists started corresponding with Bakunin; their group expanded rapidly as it was joined by mutual aid societies, economic liberals, Masons, and intellectuals. The Madrid group constituted itself into the Central Spanish Section of the IWA, and by the end of 1869 it had established 23 trade associations in Madrid. It started publishing *La Solidaridad* on January 15, 1870.

The Barcelona group, operating in a city with a larger industrial working class, had even greater success. The moving spirit was Rafael Farga Pellicer, whose efforts were backed by Gaspar Sentiñón, a physician, José García Viñas, a medical student, Antonio González Meneses, an engineering student, and Trinidad Soriano, another student. In May 1869, this group simultaneously founded the Barcelona Section of the IWA and the Barcelona Section of Bakunin's Alliance. It demanded socialism rather than a federal democratic republic as had been advocated by the Federal Center of Trade Unions. Farga Pellicer took advantage of his position in the Federal Center to orient its publication *La Federación* toward the dissemination of Bakuninist ideas. This paper quickly became an Internationalist organ. in 1870, the Federal Center opted to ally itself—not to unite—with the IWA. This, however, was to place thousands of Barcelona workers under an anarchist-inspired leadership. The Federal Center was to permeate the Catalan labor movement with anarchist ideas, even though the rank and file were hardly revolutionary anarchists at the time. The Federal Center of Palma de Mallorca then joined the IWA, and sections of the IWA were formed in Alcoy, Málaga, Valladolid, Jerez, and elsewhere.

The February 12, 1870 issue of *La Solidaridad* called for a national congress of all sections of the IWA in Spain. The congress met on June 19 in the city of Barcelona under the presidency of Farga Pellicer. The most important matter under discussion was the policy the Spanish sections should follow regarding participation in the existing electoral system. The declaration of the majority of the delegates, most of whom were Bakuninist *Aliancistas*, stated that no alliance should be entered into with liberal bourgeois parties for the sake of obtaining desirable reforms or for the purpose of defeating politically members of the elite classes. This view was probably not shared by many delegates; they did accept, however, the thesis advanced by the Bakuninist group formed by Farga, Sentiñón, Morago, Meneses, García Viñas, and others. It appears that the Bakuninist position appealed especially to the delegates from Barcelona.

Murray Bookchin (1977) has explained the triumph of the anarchist view in Barcelona:

> It was these *Aliancistas*—this hidden Anarchist faction in Spain, known perhaps to only a few hundred initiates—that guided the proceedings at the Teatro del Circo. They prepared the agenda of the congress, staffed its key commissions, and provided the most articulate and informed speakers at its sessions. The *Aliancistas* had little need of manipulation for they enjoyed enormous prestige among the delegates to the congress. They were the actual founders of the International in Spain. So closely were the origins of the International linked to the Alliance that Fanelli's disciples had initially adopted the Alliance's program for the Madrid and Barcelona sections. . . . Perhaps the sharpest conflict within the congress centered around the attitude of the Spanish section toward politics. The *Aliancistas* advocated political abstention. . . . Abstention from politics amounted to unconditional support for "direct action oriented toward the suppression of the State. . . ." (pp. 52, 53)

In the end, the congress decided to take an abstentionist and antistatist position, leaving it to individual members to act politically.

Another important matter passed on by this congress was the form or organization of the Spanish sections. The Spanish Section of the International, or the Spanish Regional Federation as it became commonly known, was to be organized on the basis of a dual structure. Organization was to proceed on the basis of trade and on the basis of locality. *Secciones de oficio* were local trade unions whose members were workers in a common vocation; these local unions were in turn organized into occupational federations, or *uniones de oficio*. The goal of these federations was to improve conditions of work and solve workers' grievances. A *sección de oficios varios* organized workers of different skills whose numbers were too small to justify the formation of a *sección de oficio*. The various vocational unions in a community or region were in turn grouped into *federaciones locales,* whose function was the eventual administration of social and economic life in the new, postrevolutionary society. Workers were to elect committees that would administer these various organizations; they also elected the delegates who were to attend the annual congresses of the Spanish Regional Federation.

The Barcelona congress ended on June 26, having elected five persons to form the Federal Council of the Spanish Regional Federation: Anselmo Lorenzo, González Morago, Enrique Borrel, Francisco Mora, and Angel Mora. All of these had known Fanelli during his visit in Madrid and were strong disciples of Bakunin.

In September, Farga and Sentiñón attended the worldwide congress of the IWA in Basel, and it was in that Swiss city that Bakunin admitted the two Spaniards to his secret "International Brotherhood," a group made up of Bakunin's confidants that was to serve the Russian anarchist as his revolutionary general staff.

This was a time of political uncertainty in Spain. Isabel II had left the country in September 1868; General Francisco Serrano became the head of the provisional government. In 1869, after a new monarchist constitution had been approved by the Cortes, Serrano was elected regent, and Juan Prim, the head of the progressive party, became prime minister. The constitution of 1869 retained a monarchist form of government.

The end of the Isabeline regime did not bring political harmony to Spain. Absolute Monarchists opposed the Federal Republicans, who tried to do away with the elective, democratic monarchy and who wanted to end military conscription. The reformist Liberals were not united; they were divided between the Moderates, representing the wealthy upper classes, which wanted a government based on property and were willing to allow the church to retain most of its privileges and part of its landed property, and the Progressives, who took an anticlerical stand and advocated fiscal reform. Military officers feared the church's ambition of turning Spain into a theocracy, while Carlists were ready to fight for the restoration of the church's wealth as it existed before the appropriations of church lands in the 1830s by the Mendizábal government.

However, all of these propertied factions had one common view:

They all agreed on limiting as much as possible the political activity of industrial and agricultural workers. A fear of the masses united the wealthy landowners, the Catalan textile manufacturers, the priests, the military officers, and the titled nobility, as well as the nascent upper bourgeoisie. All of them were willing to keep Spain's working class tied to a harsh life and in a political vacuum.

At the end of the 1860s, the workers were presented a choice: They could support the limited reforms offered by the Liberals; they could listen to the socialist ideas offered by a few middle-class republicans, or they could embrace the Bakuninist ideology preached by a proletarian leadership. Most Catalan workers and the *jornaleros* opted for the anarchist solution.

It is worth noting that, unlike the situations in other countries, in Spain, no member of the propertied classes ever became a leader of the labor movement. There were already two Spains. There was a propertied Spain and there was also another Spain—that of the masses of workers who felt that they had no participation whatever in the institutions, interests, and values of propertied Spain. The "have-not" Spain was that of industrial and rural workers who felt betrayed by the church, by the military, by the politicians, by the noble and bourgeois landowners, and by the industrial employers.

The founding of the Spanish Regional Federation gave Spanish workers the opportunity to have a political organization of their own. They could now feel free to ignore the liberal parties that for so long had ignored them. As of the start of the 1870s, the workers also had their own press: *La Solidaridad* in Madrid, *La Federación* in Barcelona, *El Obrero* and *Revolución* in Palma, and *La Voz del Trabajador* in Bilbao.

And yet a very small percentage of all the workers of Barcelona joined the Internationalists in 1870; perhaps only 9 percent of the Barcelona proletariat joined the new federation (Bookchin 1977, p. 68). It was not only the yellow fever epidemic that struck Barcelona at the end of 1870 that accounted for a membership of only about 2,500 one year after the establishment of the Barcelona section of the IWA. The masses of industrial workers still lacked a social ideology; many who applauded the new ideas coming out of the speeches of Farga Pellicer also supported the efforts of the bourgeois republicans. The average Spanish worker of the time responded principally to economic opportunity, not to social ideology.

Even the labor leadership showed great uncertainty about abandoning the safe and traditional plank of cooperativism for the more uncertain goal of social revolution. Farga Pellicer, the loyal disciple of Bakunin, still showed his attachment to the bourgeois federal republican cause, when, in a letter to the Russian anarchist of August 1, 1869, he wrote:

Here socialism is not as developed as one could wish; the Federal Center has only busied itself with the organization of workers' associations of all vocations and crafts and to motivate them so that the federal republic shall triumph in the great battle we wage against the monarchists and other conservatives of all the other tirannies.... *La Federación* will actively work to reassure some and to convince all to be rational, socialists and federal republicans. (Droz 1979, p. 306)

Many Spanish sections of the IWA were actually controlled by pragmatic trade unionists, who, despairing of the intransigent position taken by the employers, allied themselves with the anarchists in order to engage in apolitical, "direct action" strategies. The skilled urban workers of Barcelona generally supported reformist syndicalism. The anarchists drew their main support from the hordes of poor, hungry, rural *Murcianos*, who came to Barcelona from the Catalan countryside, from the Levant (Murcia, Alicante, Valencia, Castellón), and from Aragón (Zaragoza), in search of work. As described by Bookchin (1977)

Pariahs in a strange, hostile urban world, the *Murcianos* encamped by the tens of thousands in squalid, miserable shacks. Their hovels ringed the great seaport and penetrated its suburbs, providing a huge reservoir of unskilled, menial labor exploited by the Catalan bourgeoisie. Disdained by nearly all the factions of the Liberals, later manipulated by such Radical demagogues as Lerroux, the *Murcianos* also provided a reservoir for the most volatile recruits of the libertarian movement in Catalonia. Without this transitional proletariat, Anarchism would have lost its mass base in a broadly syndicalist labor organization.... (p. 69)

1871 brought to Spain the constitutional monarchy of Amadeo I, a younger son of the Italian house of Savoy, who was supported by the conservatives led by General Serrano and by the moderate faction of the progressives who followed Práxedes Mateo Sagasta.

The conservatives in the Sagasta ministry reacted with panic to the news of the Paris Commune. The fear generated in government circles by the Paris revolt induced the governor of Barcelona to prohibit strikes and any meetings of workers' associations. When, on May 22, the republican deputy Baldomero Lostau demanded a parliamentarian condemnation of the conduct of the civilian governor of Barcelona, Sagasta replied that the Spanish sections of the IWA included more than 300 foreign agents whose mission was to disturb the public order. A few days later, Sagasta granted all civilian governors ample powers of repression against activities of the IWA sections.

On June 14, Sagasta accused the First International of trying to "destroy the family, destroy society, erase the homeland and to cause, through force, the disappearance of all known characteristics of civilisation" (Tuñón 1972, vol. I, p. 174). At the same time, the government ordered the suspension of *La Federación*, and Gaspar Sentiñón and Clemente Bové, the president of the Catalan textile union Las Tres Clases del Vapor, were arrested. Publication of *La Solidaridad* had been suspended by government order in January of the same year. It was replaced by *La Emancipación*, which came out in June under the direction of José Mesa Leompart.

A secret congress of the Spanish Regional Federation met in Valencia from September 10 to 18, 1871, with only 13 delegates present, representing about 2,000 members. The congress adopted the Bakuninist position that "the true democratic, federal republic connotes collective ownership, anarchism and economic federation, that is, the free, universal federation of free agricultural and industrial workers' associations." A new Federal Council was elected consisting of Francisco and Angel Mora, Valentín Sáenz, Inocente Calleja, Hipólito Pauly, José Mesa, Anselmo Lorenzo, Pablo Iglesias, and Víctor Pagés (Tuñón 1972, vol. I, p. 177). Borrel had left the organization, and González Morago was in Portugal.

Feeling that the organization of the Spanish Regional Federation needed strengthening because of the increasing governmental hostility toward it, the delegates reorganized the Spanish International into five large federations (north, south, east, west, and center) and gave broader authority to the federations over the local sections. The impetus to centralize the structure of the entire federation probably came from the nonanarchist members of the Federal Council, the *Autoritarios,* men such as Francisco Mora, José Mesa, and Pablo Iglesias who were to organize years later the Spanish Socialist party.

Also, in September, Anselmo Lorenzo attended a world congress of the First International in London. There he met Marx and also witnessed the beginning of the infighting that was to split the world's labor movement into two major groups. This factionalism within the International was to lead to Bakunin's expulsion from the IWA at The Hague congress one year later.

This factionalism also extended to Spain, when, in December 1871, Paul Lafargue fled to Madrid to escape the repression of the Paris Commune. Once in Madrid, Lafargue tried to place the Spanish International under the Marxist banner; to do so, and with the help of Mesa and Iglesias, he turned *La Emancipación* into a Marxist organ. A major goal of Lafargue was the formation of a workers' political party that would enter into an alliance with the republicans. González Morago, a strong *Aliancista,* started publishing *El Condenado* in February 1872 to counter the Marxist orientaion of *La Emancipación.* Embarrassed by the attacks of *La Emancipación* on Bakuninism, the *Aliancistas* agreed to dissolve, at least pro forma, the Spanish Alliance.

Although parliament had declared unconstitutional and therefore illegal the Spanish Regional Federation, the federation organized a congress in the Teatro Novedades of Zaragoza in April 1872. This congress elected a new council, which was mostly made up of Bakuninists—Francisco Tomás, Anselmo Lorenzo, Peregrín Montoro, Francisco Martínez, and Francisco Mora, all of whom were skilled workers. This congress, whose last sessions had to be held in secret, did not heal the growing rift between the *Aliancistas* and the Marxist group controlling *La Emancipación*. On June 3, following the termination of the Zaragoza congress, the *Autoritarios* were expelled from the Madrid Federation. The nine expelled members then formed the New Madrid Federation and petitioned the Federal Council for recognition as a new federation within the Spanish Regional Federation. The council rejected the petition even though the new organization was joined by a number of local federations throughout Spain. The General Council of the IWA in London, however, recognized the New Madrid Federation as a member organization of the IWA.

The Fifth Congress of the IWA was celebrated at The Hague, September 2–7, 1872. Most of the Spanish delegates were Bakuninists: Farga Pellicer, Alerini, Morago, and Marcelau. The New Madrid Federation sent Lafargue and Mesa. The congress supported the Marxist position that the proletariat should organize itself into a political party. It affirmed the linkage between economic and political struggle. It also expelled from the IWA Bakunin and his disciple James Guillaume.

Two weeks later, the anarchist delegates who had taken part in the congress at The Hague met at Saint-Imier, Switzerland, in the company of Bakunin, Guillaume, Fanelli, and Malatesta and decided to reject the decisions taken by that congress. They further declared that they would no longer heed the directives issued by the General Council of the IWA in London. The Saint-Imier congress delcared that "the first duty of the proletariat is the destruction of all political power." Farga Pellicer and González Morago participated in this congress, which purported to form a new International. Both Spaniards then hurried back home in order to call a new national congress of the Spanish International, which, it was hoped, would bring the Spanish Regional Federation into the fold of the Saint-Imier organization.

The Córdoba congress met from December 25, 1872 to January 3, 1873. It clearly rejected the resolutions taken by the IWA congress held at The Hague and adopted those taken by the anarchist Saint-Imier congress. In order to support better the anarchist "antiauthority" stance, the delegates voted to replace the Federal Council by a Commission for Correspondence and Statistics. In the words of Bookchin (1977):

> They tried to create an organization in which guidance could be exercised without coercion and a leadership, such as it was, removed easily when it was necessary or harmful. They also tried to encourage in-

itiative from below and foster revolutionary elan in the sections, federations, indeed, in the factories and villages themselves. On this score, they were eminently successful, for until the outbreak of the Civil War, the Spanish libertarian movement never developed a bureaucracy. (p. 78)

The First Republic was proclaimed by the Cortes on February 11, 1873, after Amadeo of Savoy abdicated the throne of Spain and returned to Italy. The beginning of the republic found its supporters greatly divided. The unitarians favored a centralized republic of the French type. Opposing them, were the federalists, who preferred Pi y Margall's view of a decentralized republic based on strong provincial autonomy. The federalists had split into a parliamentarian group and a militant, revolutionary faction. The first group wanted to obtain a federal republic through peaceful and legal means and tended to side with the unitarians and with liberal constitutional monarchists in the Cortes. The militant federalists, also known as the intransigents or the cantonalists, relied on extraparliamentarian, revolutionary action.

The federalists obtained a working majority in the constituent Cortes, and it appeared that they had sufficient strength to establish a decentralized, cantonal republic modeled after the Swiss example. Pi y Margall, the founder of the federalist doctrine in Spain, became president of the new republic on April 24, 1873. At that time, the federalist cause was supported by thousands of small bourgeois. Everything seemed to indicate the triumph of the federalist dream. But, once in power, Pi y Margall's "socialism" turned into "cooperativism," and, shunning the intransigents, he relied mostly on right-wing or centrist federalists.

Reaction to Pi y Margall's limited reforms soon appeared. The intransigents and their allies, the cantonalists, took over the municipal government of Cartagena on July 12. This act of insurrection induced Pi y Margall to resign on July 18, the presidency then being taken by Salmerón, who was prepared to sacrifice the federal republic for a more centralized state. The cantonalist revolt then spread throughout southern Spain. Between July 19 and July 22, the cantonalists took over the municipal governments of a number of cities in Andalusia and the Levant. Carlist insurrection in the north tied up the government's best troops in that area.

The role of the Spanish Regional Federation during these events was quite limited. Francisco Mora was sent to the Levant and Anselmo Lorenzo headed for Andalusia to form secret groups called Defenders of the International, groups that would lead in the case of successful insurrection or organize underground should the insurrection fail. The federation hoped for a federalist victory, but its apolitical stance limited its participation in the cantonalist insurrection. It joined the latter in forming a Committee of Public Safety in Barcelona and induced uprisings in Alcoy and in Sanlúcar de Barrameda.

However limited the federation's role, the participation of the Spanish International in the cantonalist insurrection invited government repression when, in January 1874, the conservative General Serrano assumed the presidency. The Serrano government promptly dissolved the Spanish International on January 10, 1874. The meeting centers of the Spanish Regional Federation were closed down, many of its leaders were jailed, and the workers' newspapers were outlawed. The right of workers to form associations was expressly forbidden, and troops were dispatched by the government to crush all strikes. The Spanish International survived by going underground. It had to abandon national congresses for secret regional conferences. Persecution turned the International into a smaller but increasingly revolutionary organization.

An Association for the Printing Arts had been formed toward the end of 1871. it successfully conducted a strike during March 1873, and its leaders' courage attracted the attention of Pablo Iglesias, who joined this organization in May 1873. A year later Iglesias assumed the presidency of the association under a mandate to renew its objectives. This was the organization that was destined to form the initial nucleus of the Spanish Socialist party.

The January 10, 1874 government decree dissolving the Spanish International ended the initial phase of development of the Spanish labor movement. At the time, the Spanish Regional Federation included about 130 federations and about 400 sections. Catalonia was its greatest source of strength, with Barcelona representing about one-third of its total membership (Tuñón 1972, vol. I, p. 205). The Andalusian representation was formed mostly by agrarian workers, as well as by workers active in preindustrial crafts. The membership of Asturias and of the Basque area was negligible; Asturian miners had practically no representation in the International. It is fair to conclude that, up to 1874, the dawn of the Spanish labor movement, industrial rather than agricultural workers formed the basis of the Spanish Regional Federation.

THE MARXIST-BAKUNINIST SPLIT IN THE SPANISH LABOR MOVEMENT

In 1875 Alfonso XII became Spain's new monarch, and a conservative government was headed by Antonio Cánovas del Castillo. A new constituent Cortes was elected in 1876 whose task was to draft a new constitution. The latter restricted suffrage to adult males paying at least 25 pesetas yearly land tax or 50 pesetas yearly industrial tax. The new constitution recognized Roman Catholicism as the official state religion and merely tolerated other religions. Cánovas resigned in 1878 and was replaced by General Martínez Campos, a military hero, who remained briefly in power until the elections of 1879 returned Cánovas to the prime ministry. Sagasta, in turn, obtained that ministry in February 1881.

It will be remembered that the Spanish Regional Federation had been outlawed in 1874. The restoration government added to the difficulties of the now underground labor organization. Its Federal Council was directed by an essentially Catalan and *Aliancista* group, which included Farga, García Viñas, Llunas, Soriano, Nácher, Anselmo Lorenzo, and Francisco Tomás. While in 1874 the organization had included 190 regional federations, their number declined to 112 in 1876 and to 73 in 1877. In 1877 Viñas and Morago participated in the last congress of the anarchist International, in Verviers, where Morago defended the thesis of "propaganda by the deed." Indeed, as of 1874, the Spanish Regional Federation had abandoned the strike as its principal weapon and had replaced it by the violence-based "propaganda by the deed." This change in tactics suited very well the Andalusian braceros, already quite familiar with violent activity; it did not, however, please many urban workers, who started abandoning anarchism for a more syndicalist ideology.

The coming to power of Sagasta and his "fusionists" brought a period of more government tolerance; censorship was ended and the very liberal Press Law of 1883 was enacted. Complete freedom of ideas was allowed in higher education, and the government extended de facto authorization to trade union activity. The Sagasta government did not attempt, however, to implement major institutional changes. When the most liberal elements of the prime minister's party pressured him to adopt universal male suffrage, Sagasta decided to resign.

It was the Sagasta government that introduced the system of political party rotation that Bookchin (1977) describes as follows:

A political system of *Turnismo*, or "rotation," was established in which the Liberal party, under the ebullient Práxedes Sagasta, was given the reins of power whenever democratic window-dressing was needed to absorb social unrest or justify the passage of repressive legislation. The Conservative party, led by Antonio Cánovas del Castillo, occupied the ministry under conditions of relative stability. Except for an anticlerical tradition and an interest in secular education, the Liberals were undistinguishable from their Conservative counterparts. What really distinguished the two parties were the agrarian strata whose interests they reflected: the Conservatives spoke for the Andalusian landowners and the Liberals for the Castilian wheat gowers. (p. 112)

At the very same time that the Sagasta government authorized the establishment of workers' organizations, the Spanish Regional Federation expired. Police persecution and internal factionalism had continuously weakened it since 1874. Its end came in 1881. As the Spanish Regional Federation disappeared, a new workers' organization appeared on the horizon that purported to carry on the policies of the First International. The new organization received the name of Workers' Federation of the Spanish Region, a name almost identical to that of the organization it replaced. It was formed at a workers' congress held on September 24, 1881, in the Teatro Circo of Barcelona. This congress was formed by 140 delegates representing 162 organizations. Pablo Iglesias, who had come to attend the meetings as the representative of the Socialists of Madrid, was expelled from the congress.

The new Workers' Federation was to pursue anarchist goals. It declared that private ownership had to be replaced by collective ownership in order for complete human rights and human freedom to be attained. The delegates declared their opposition to parliamentarian politics. Basically, the decentralized form of the old federation was retained.

Although the rhetoric of the delegates embraced anarchism, policies adopted by the leaders reflected moderate, reformist trade unionism. The organization decided to accumulate a strike fund and to limit carefully the use of the strike as a weapon; strikes were to be orderly and nonviolent. The Catalan delegates gave great importance to the avoidance of any confrontation with the Sagasta government. The moderation of the Catalans greatly irritated the Andalusians in the organization, who were more desirous of violent action.

At the second congress of this organization, held in Seville in September 1882, the opportunistic policy of the Catalans prevailed. Even though the majority of the membership was from Andalusia, the Catalans formed most of the organization's leadership. Some of the Andalusian delegates, angered by the reformism of the Catalans, particularly in times of price increases, broke away from the Workers' Federation to form a separate group known as the *Desheredados*, "the disinherited."

The *Desheredados* were supported by the poorest *jornaleros* of Andalusia, particularly the vineyard workers of the Jerez region. Acts of arson and murders had increased in this region, and it appears that the people who were assassinated were either landlords or police informers. In the course of the investigation of the murders of an innkeeper and his wife, the Civil Guard announced that it had discovered documents showing the existence of a secret terrorist society, the *Mano Negra,* or "Black Hand." Spanish historians agree that these documents were falsifications and that the *Mano Negra* was in all probability a police fabrication used to justify the arrest and torture of hundreds of anarchists and other "undesirables." The harsh police persecutions destroyed the Workers' Federation in Andalusia. Fear of arrest induced thousands of workers to abandon the federation, and at its fourth congress in Madrid in 1887, only 16 delegates were present. The existence of the Workers' Federation of the Spanish Region ended in 1889.

The New Federation of Madrid, established in 1872, was mainly represented by the Association of the Printing Arts led by Pablo Iglesias. Jose Mesa had moved to Paris in 1874. Mesa visited Marx and Engels in London and maintained an active correspondence with Iglesias. Iglesias in turn started corresponding with Engels, while Mesa urged his friends in Madrid to organize as Socialists.

The Socialist party was formed on May 2, 1879, following a banquet held in Madrid in which the majority of the attendants were typographers. The new party's organizing committee included Pablo Iglesias, Alejandro Ocina—both of them typographers—Victoriano Calderón, Gonzalo Zubiarre, and Jaime Vera, a medical student. The first meeting of the party took place on July 20 of the same year. Iglesias wrote the party's Manifesto and Program, which declared that the aims of the Spanish Democratic Socialist Workers' party were the eradication of social classes, the transformation of private property into social property, and the obtaining of political power by the working class. In addition, the Socialist party's manifesto revealed some short-run objectives: the right of workers to strike, the shortening of the workday, and political freedom.

Pablo Iglesias was elected secretary of the first Executive Committee of the party, with Inocente Calleja, Alejandro Ocina, Victoriano Calderón, and Gonzalo Zubiarre as committee members.

Similar groups were established in Barcelona and in Guadalajara. By 1882, the Socialist party had established organizations in Madrid, Barcelona, Guadalajara, Valencia, Castellón, Tarragona, Manresa, Villanueva y Geltrú, and Zaragoza. The Madrid group produced the first issue of its organ *El Socialista,* on March 12, 1886.

The Socialist party's demands were, on the whole, quite modest and therefore did not alarm the government. Although in their speeches the party's leaders advocated "Guesdist" rather than true Marxist ideas, in their day-to-day actions they revealed themselves as prudent reformists. These tactics kept out of the party the ebullient and insurrection-minded Andalusian *jornaleros* and attracted skilled workers, most of whom still hoped for the establishment of a bourgeois republic. The violence-minded *Murcianos* and *jornaleros,* who had supported the Workers' Federation, eventually caused its demise. The prudent *Autoritarios* of the Spanish Regional Federation who founded the Spanish Socialist party witnessed its survival.

The Socialist party did not create its own labor organization until 1888. The Unión General de Trabajadores (UGT), or General Union of Workers, was founded in Barcelona on August 12, 1888, with Garcia Quejido as its first president. On August 23, the Socialist party held its own congress in the same city, an indication of the very close relationship between the political party and the labor organization.

The fact that the Socialists were able to adapt themselves much better than the anarchists to the capitalist system of *fin de siecle* is shown by the decisions taken by the second congress of the Socialist party, held in Bilbao in 1890. This congress decided that the party would participate in political elections, presenting its own candidates who would fight for Socialist views and Socialist legislation; the party was not to enter into any alliance with a bourgeois party and would try as far as possible to adhere to the goals of the Second International created in Paris one year earlier. The Spanish Socialist party bound itself to demonstrate every May 1 in support of the labor legislation advocated by the Second International. The Socialist party opposed the general strike because it felt that it was not the proper means to obtain political power; to the extent that the Spanish Socialists were to back a strike, the latter would have to be well organized, orderly, and undertaken for the achievement of clearly established goals.

By 1892, Socialists were already occupying positions in municipal governments.

The determination of the Socialist party not to ally itself with a liberal bourgeois party for electoral purposes was subjected to an important proviso at the party's congress in Madrid in September 1899. A resolution of that congress stated that whenever democratic principles were threatened or misused, the Socialist party could in its discretion cooperate with bourgeois parties in order to safeguard those principles.

Members of the Socialist party's leadership faithfully attended the congresses of the Second International. José Mesa and Pablo Iglesias participated in the congress held in Paris in July 1889, a congress that established the first of May as an international workers' holiday and that advocated a workday of eight hours. Iglesias also represented the Spanish labor movement at the second congress of the Second International, held in Brussels in August 1891. Iglesias represented the Spanish Socialist party, and Quejido the UGT at the third congress meeting in Zürich in September 1893. The fourth congress of the Second International was held in London in August 1896; that congress resolved to expel from its ranks all anarchists in future congresses; Pablo Iglesias, Jaime Vera, and Casimiro Muñoz represented the Socialist party at that congress, and Quejido represented the UGT.

The membership of the UGT, like that of the Socialist party, grew slowly in the 1890s. The UGT counted 65 local unions and about 15,200 members in 1899. Its strongholds were in Madrid, the Basque country, and Asturias. In Madrid, the UGT appealed mostly to typographers, carpenters, bricklayers, and metalworkers. A Socialist Association of Bilbao was established in July 1886 and attracted to it typographers, metallurgical workers, and miners; the young scholar Miguel de Unamuno, contributed to its organ, *La Lucha de Clases.* A similar organization was established in the Asturian town of Gijón in 1891, followed a few months later by another one in Oviedo. Gradually, the UGT and the Socialist party obtained the support of most Asturian miners.

In Catalonia, the reformist and revisionist views of the leadership of the union Las Tres Clases del Vapor and those of José Pamiás, a founder of the Socialist party, inhibited the growth of socialism in that region. Instead of participating in the Paris congress of the Second International in July 1889, the Catalan reformists attended the "possibilist" congress held at the same time and in the same city under the Banner of Paul Brousse's ideology.

With the disappearance of the Workers' Federation of the Spanish Region, anarchists in Spain were left without any supportive organization. The collapse of the Bakuninist International, the appearance of a Socialist party with reformist goals, and the survival of a harsh capitalist system left Spanish anarchists bitter and uncertain about what policy they should follow. An event in Russia eventually presented to some Spanish anarchists an example to follow. On March 1, 1881, a group of young Russian revolutionaries, organized as a terrorist organization known as the People's Will, succeeded in assassinating the czar, Alexander II. This murder was hailed by many European anarchists as a worthwhile act of "propaganda by the deed." Among the supporters of this tactic was Peter Kropotkin, who had become the outstanding spokesman for "anarchist communism." Translations of Kropotkin's works became available in Spain in the 1880s.

Anarchist communism was an ideological pillar of the new Anarchist Organization of the Spanish Region, founded in Valencia in September 1888, structured on the basis of small groups of men who knew each other well, the *tertulias.* These small groups were largely engaged in winning over converts to their cause. Libertarian trade unions, centering their efforts on economic problems, formalized loose relationships with each other in a Pact of Union and Solidarity of the Spanish Region. The pact attracted mostly Catalan unions influenced by both anarchists and militant syndicalists. Besides the Catalan majority, the pact's first congress, held in Madrid, also attracted delegates from Valencia, Alcoy, and Valladolid. The opposition to the pact by anarchocommunists explains the absence at the Madrid congress of delegates from Andalusia. The congress resolved to support any strike undertaken to improve conditions of work or to safeguard the dignity of workers. It advocated the eight-hour work-day and nonparticipation in political elections by workers.

The pact, unfortunately, was entered into at a time when a number of anarchists in Spain decided to intensify a campaign of "propaganda by the deed" through acts of terrorism. The first of such acts occurred in the course of a general strike called by the pact on May 1, 1891, in order to obtain the eight-hour workday. The strike in Barcelona brought clashes between the strikers and the police and the authorities promptly declared a "state of war" in Barcelona. A bomb went off in front of a building, housing the association of Barcelona manufacturers, the first in a series of bombings that was to mark Catalan labor unrest. Some of the bombings were undoubtedly caused by the police to justify the mass ar-rests of workers.

An insurrection in Jerez in January 1892 resulted in the execution of four anarchists. To avenge these executions, a young anarchist, Paulino Pallás, attempted to assassinate in Barcelona General Martínez Campos, then captain-general of Catalonia. Martínez Campos escaped serious in-jury, but Pallas was arrested and executed. On November 7, 1893, some-one threw two bombs into the audience of the Teatro Liceo of Barcelona;· 22 people were killed and many others were wounded. The police reacted by arresting hundreds of workers, who were taken to the Fortress of Montjuich, the military prison. Five anarchists, completely innocent of the terrorist act, were eventually sentenced to death and executed. The real perpetrator, Santiago Salvador, was later arrested and executed. Sal-vador's death was followed by more bombings. The authorities decided to destroy the anarchist movement in Barcelona by creating a "Political Social Brigade" whose task was to engage in counterterrorist measures.

When, on June 7, 1896, a bomb was thrown from a house into Barce-lona's Corpus Christi Day procession, more than 400 people were ar-rested and imprisoned in the Montjuich Fortress where they were bru-tally tortured by the Brigada Social (Social Brigade). Many prisoners died from their tortures and some were executed; those who were eventually acquitted were rearrested and transported to the Spanish colony of Río de Oro under orders from the Cánovas government in Madrid. Cánovas was in turn murdered by an Italian anarchist, Michel Angiolillo.

The Cortes had passed a law of repression against anarchism in Sep-tember 1896. The law ended the Pact of Union and Solidarity of the Span-ish Region but did not end anarchism in Spain. Concurrently with these terrorist episodes, the anarchist press advocated peaceful action. Among some of the anarchist newspapers to do so was *Tierra y Libertad* and the *Revista Blanca*, which contained contributions by nonanarchist intellectuals like Unamuno and Giner. Bookchin (1977) describes anarchists at the end of the nineteenth century as follows:

> As a curious mixture of *pistolerismo* and humanism they were to express the underlying tension that alternately divided the Anarchists and, in moments of crisis, united them in a zealous devotion to freedom and a deep respect for individuality. Perhaps no movement combined such conflicting tendencies in a fashion that served to fuel the enthusiasm and attract the devotion of the most dispossessed elements of Spanish society. (p. 127)

At the end of the 1890s, the Catalans formed a minority in the Socialist party and in the UGT. The establishment of an Opportunist Socialist party, and Socialist opposition to the general strike, weakened the Socialist cause in Catalonia. Socialist strength at that time continued to come from the Basque country, Asturias, and Madrid. The strongest UGT unions were those of typographers, metallurgical workers, and miners. Socialism failed to gain any support by rural workers, and the Catalan textile workers remained loyal to their anarchist-collectivist leadership. The *jornaleros* of Andalusia continued their spontaneous and violent insurrections, but from the end of the 1890s onward they were to embrace the anarchist concept of the general strike. Finally, while the anarchist movement appeared fragmented and weakened by acts of terrorism, the Socialists grew on the basis of a better organized movement under the leadership of Iglesias and Quejido.

THE "TRAGIC WEEK" AND THE DEVELOPMENT OF ANARCHOSYNDICALISM

Spain's population had reached about 18.6 million people by 1900. According to the 1910 census, the total Spanish population slightly exceeded 19.9 million people. Of that population, 66 percent worked in the country's primary sector, while only 15.8 percent derived a livelihood from industry. In the industrial sector, the largest group of workers according to skill were construction workers, representing about 25 percent of all workers in industry; the second most important professional group of workers was constituted by textile workers.

The agrarian structure had not undergone profound changes. The latifundio survived the sales of church lands in the nineteenth century and the high nobility still owned enormous tracts of land.

What the new century introduced were large industrial enterprises, closely linked to a bank or to a group of banks or controlled by foreign interests. A number of new industrial investment banks financed mining activities, manufacturing, and the building of railroad lines. The Banco Español de Crédito, operating on the basis of French and Dutch capital, controlled the country's northern and southern railroad lines, as well as the large insurance company La Unión y el Fénix. The Banco de Bilbao, the Banco de Vizcaya, the Banco Herrero, and other banking establishments financed northern mining activities and promoted the establishment and the fusion of metallurgical firms. The new century brought a wave of industrialization based on the development of metallurgy, cement production, the manufacturing of new chemical products, and the founding of large shipyards.

On the labor front, the manufacturers of Barcelona and the government had dealt a serious blow to the Spanish organized libertarian movement. The Pact of Union and Solidarity had been dissolved in 1896. Intimidated by the government's measures of harsh repression, workers abandoned their trade unions by the thousands. Spanish anarchists correctly concluded that "propaganda by the deed" had failed in Catalonia. Terrorist activities had only brought mass arrests and brutal torture. Anarchists now turned their attention to education as a better way of achieving their goals. Libertarian schools and libertarian pedagogical efforts gave evidence of the new anarchist policy at the turn of the century. Francisco Ferrer's "Modern School," established in Barcelona in September 1901, attracted pupils of both sexes and from all social classes, much to the consternation of the clergy. Ferrer also produced cheap booklets explaining in simple terms a variety of cultural and scientific subjects; these booklets were distributed to both urban and rural workers.

The theory of syndicalism, imported from France, was also becoming very popular among Spanish workers. The basic idea of syndicalism was that revolutionary trade unions rather than a political party could bring about the desired social revolution by means of a general strike. Bookchin (1977) explains syndicalism:

> For one thing, the goal of syndicalism is the elimination of capitalism, not merely the amelioration of the workers' immediate economic problems and labor conditions. Its aim is admittedly revolutionary. Not less important is the syndicalist goal of vesting all economic and social decisions in the hands of the direct producers—the workers in each specific enterprise. The guiding and most important principle of syndicalism is that the management of production occurs at the base of society, not at its summit, and decisions flow from below to above. Hence, syndicalism is anti-authoritarian. The democratic, federalist, and decentralized economic organs of the proletariat replace the political agencies of the state. (p. 133)

Further

> In its emphasis on economic control at the base of society, syndicalism
> in consciously antiparliamentary and antipolitical.... The way to dis-
> solve economic power is to make every worker powerful, thereby
> eliminating power as a social privilege. Syndicalism thus ruptures all the
> ties between the workers and the state. It opposes political action, po-
> litical parties, and any participation in political elections. (p. 135)

In France, the Confédération Générale du Travail, initially established
as a syndicalist organization, had become, under the leadership of Léon
Jouhaux, an essentially reformist trade union federation with a membership made up mostly of urban workers. In France, the term *syndicalisme*
quickly became a synonym for trade unionism; it was a politically neutral term; and it was the concept of "anarchosyndicalism" that took over
its original revolutionary connotation. For the Spanish workers, urban
and rural, syndicalism retained its revolutionary meaning. The poverty-
stricken masses of Andalusia, the discontented *Murcianos* of Barcelona,
the industrial workers whose subsistence wages were further reduced by
inflation—all kept the goal of a social revolution in syndicalist thinking
important and alive.

At the instigation of the bricklayers' union in Madrid, a congress of
trade unions was held in Madrid on October 13, 1900. It was attended
by delegates from labor organizations in Catalonia, Andalusia, the Basque
country, Asturias, and the Levant. It was agreed to form a new labor federation patterned after the organizations established in 1873 and in 1881.
The new organization received the name of Federation of Workers' Societies of the Spanish Region. It purported to continue the work of the
Pact of Union and Solidarity, and the delegates at the constituent congress in Madrid agreed that workers should remain apolitical while fighting for the abolishment of the institution of private ownership of the
means of production. The delegates also supported the idea that the
general strike was the best weapon the workers had to overthrow the capitalist system.

The founding of the Federation of Workers' Societies coincided with
a number of general strikes carried out in Valencia, Seville, and Zaragoza;
strikes spread throughout Andalusia where rural workers demanded the
comunismo libertario.

The new labor federation initiated a major general strike in Barcelona. On December 6, 1901, the metallurgical workers of Barcelona went
on strike in order to obtain an eight-hour workday. The employers refused to negotiate. Even though no strike funds had been accumulated,
the workers refused to return to their jobs for three months. On Febru-

ary 17, 1902, the Barcelona section of the Federation of Workers' Societies called for a general strike throughout the city. The workers of Barcelona responded to the call, and a general strike lasted for one week. By February 24, the strike ended. The authorities responded once again with harshness, and the federation was suppressed. When new strikes started again in 1903, 350 strikers were arrested, and employers left hundreds of workers jobless. Neither the Spanish Socialist party nor the UGT had taken any part in the Barcelona strikes. The UGT tried to justify its inaction by claiming that a general strike invited harsh governmental reaction that adversely affected the process of collective bargaining. The UGT attempted to negotiate with employers at the very same time when Catalan anarchist labor leaders were imprisoned.

These events did not destroy or silence the anarchosyndicalist movement in Spain. Besides the Barcelona group, there were other anarchosyndicalist nuclei in la Coruña, Málaga, Granada, and other Andalusian cities. Madrid counted five anarchosyndicalist trade unions. A strong anarchosyndicalist movement was spreading among the rural masses of southern Spain. A number of newspapers propagated the anarchosyndicalist creed. Francisco Ferrer started publishing in 1902 his *La Huelga General*; Anselmo Lorenzo contributed to *El Libertario*, which appeared in 1903; and, as of August of the same year, *Tierra y Libertad* was printed in Barcelona as a daily. The *Revista Blanca* of Federico Urales presented a more sophisticated version of anarchosyndicalist theory.

The Federation of Workers' Societies was reconstituted in 1904. In August 1907, the federation in Barcelona founded a "pure syndical" organization, Solidaridad Obrera, (Workers' Solidarity), whose task was to pursue immediate economic goals and to engage in collective bargaining. A weekly, *Solidaridad Obrera,* was also published.

The year 1903 was marked by strong strike activity in many parts of Spain. The rural workers of Andalusia cherished the idea of the general strike, and for a few days general strikes were carried out in Córdoba in April, in Bujalance in May, and in Cabra and Villafranca in June. Andalusia was to be subjected to major labor unrest and strike activity until the end of 1905. Striking workers in southern Spain manifested their discontent in often violent ways. Northern miners also struck in 1903 and in 1906. Miners protested wage cuts, the necessity to buy in company-owned stores, the length of the workday, and the fact that employers refused to bargain with their unions.

Labor unrest was to culminate in 1909 with what is generally known as Barcelona's "Tragic Week."

In May 1909, a lockout of a textile factory in Manlleu, carried out by a textile manufacturer in order to force a cut in wages, was promptly imitated by other textile firms. Hundreds of workers were left without jobs, and speakers in Solidaridad Obrera started suggesting in July the launching of a general strike.

At the same time, the conservative Maura government in Madrid called for a mobilization of reservists for active duty in Morocco. The war against the Riff tribesmen was extremely unpopular among the working class; many of the reservists were the breadwinners of poor families, and their anguish induced Pablo Iglesias to make, on July 18, the most radical declaration of his life. On that occasion he stated that "the enemies of the Spanish people are not the Moroccans but the Government. We have to fight the Government using all possible means. . .if required, the workers will go to the general strike with all its consequences, without taking into account the reprisals the Government may take against them" (Tuñon 1972, vol. II, p. 74). Also on July 18, troops started boarding ships for their transport to Morocco.

The Socialist intellectual Fabra Ribas asked for a congress of all labor organizations in Spain to decide on the implementation of a general strike throughout the nation to protest the war in Africa. On July 24, two Barcelona anarchists, José Rodriguez Romero and Miguel Villalobos Morenas, constituted themselves into a Central Strike Committee and were promptly joined by officials of Solidaridad Obrera and by Catalan Socialists. The leader of the bourgeois Radical party, Emiliano Iglesias, who took the place of Alejandro Lerroux y García, then outside Spain, refused to join the committee even though party members who were workers supported a general strike. The committee notified labor organizations in most large Spanish cities that the general strike would start in Barcelona on July 26; for some reason, the national committee of the Socialist party determined that the date of strike for its members would be August 2.

As of July 26, all activity ceased in Barcelona. The authorities declared a "state of war." The general strike extended to other Catalan localities; Sabadell, Mataró, Tarrasa, San Feliú de Llobregat, and Granollers. The Catalan workers, however, had to fight alone against the police and the soldiers. Invited to do so by some of Lerroux's anticlerical radicals, a number of workers started burning down a number of religious establishments. Deprived of any support from outside Catalonia, the Barcelona strike came to an end on July 31. Almost 1,000 people were arrested and among them, Francisco Ferrer. The founder of the Modern School was unjustly accused of being the instigator and leader of the insurrection and was sentenced to die. Ferrer was executed on October 13, in spite of a worldwide protest against the sentence. Thus ended the Tragic Week.

It appears that the Socialist party learned a lesson from the insurrection in Barcelona. On September 22, 1909, the national committee of the Socialist party declared in a manifesto that "the Socialist Party will now fight, either alone, either on the side of any democratic force struggling for the double goal—reestablishment of individual freedoms and the disappearance of the conservative government—as long as its action will be serious and honest and not in contradiction with the aspirations of the knowledgeable proletariat" (Tuñón 1972, vol. II, p. 79).

On November 7, the Socialist party entered into an alliance with the republicans in order to present a joint list of municipal candidates for the December elections and, more important, to achieve in the long run the establishment of a republic. This Socialist-republican entente reflected a realization by the Socialist party leadership that it was not yet strong enough to change by itself the national politicosocial order. For that matter, anarchosyndicalism lacked the same strength in 1909. That Socialists preferred an alliance with republicans over a common front with the anarchists and the syndicalists indicates the deep and bitter gap that divided the Marxist and Bakuninist factions of the Spanish labor movement during the first decade of the twentieth century.

Both factions were not only divided by ideology but also by geography. Anarchosyndicalism continued to center in the east and in the south of the country: Catalonia, Aragón, Levant, and Andalusia. These were the agrarian, largely stagnating, areas of Spain, with the exception of Catalonia. Their poor, despairing, "church-hating" masses constituted the *Murciano* immigrants, who, once in Barcelona, joined the radicals of Lerroux or anarchosyndicalist organizations. These *Murcianos* were quite different from the Gallegans, Leonese, Castilians, and Asturians who migrated to Vizcaya; the latter group was more literate, not as anticlerical, and responded more favorably to Socialist ideas.

What tended to unify the Spanish labor movement was hunger, the workers' feeling that they had been isolated from the rest of society, and the bitterness in the hearts of workers caused by the harsh repression carried out by the Maura government after the Tragic Week. In Catalonia, workers became disenchanted with the Radical party and with politics in general and tended to embrace syndicalism more strongly. In the words of Meaker (1974): "Thus the Tragic Week was the opening gun in the social war that would increasingly dominate Spanish life in the early twentieth century; and it raised before the privileged groups the alarming specter of a proletarian revolution. More and more after 1909, the various social classes retreated into an absorption with private and egoistic concerns" (p. 7).

THE EMERGENCE OF THE CNT AND WORLD WAR I

On the eve of World War I, the Socialist and anarchosyndicalist labor movements in Spain had not yet attracted to their ranks the masses of Spanish rural and urban workers. The great majority of workers in

Spain was still unorganized. Those who pondered about joining either the Socialist or the anarchosyndicalist organizations felt in many instances more attracted to the latter. They liked to hear anarchosyndicalist leaders talk about human dignity, human freedoms, and the imminence of social and economic change in passionate, romantic terms. Socialist leaders presented too great an emphasis on organizational discipline, on prudent action, on the payment of dues. Worse, even, many Socialists advocated revisionist views that put the romantic revolution in a very distant future.

Indeed, Socialist thinking had evolved since the day the Socialist Labor party of Spain had been founded. At that time, the party's philosophy had been established by Pablo Iglesias' "Guesdist" beliefs. Iglesias believed in a historically inescapable triumph of the proletariat over the bourgeoisie; the revolution could be retarded by the economic backwardness of Spain, but in time it would occur. Meanwhile, it was perfectly proper for the Socialist leadership to engage in a daily struggle for limited economic reforms that would strengthen the workers physically and emotionally. This effort had to be undertaken without the help of any bourgeois political faction, just like the seizure of political power by the proletariat had to be obtained without bourgeois help.

Iglesias, just like Guesde, based his model on German social democracy. Indeed, restoration Spain appeared to be closer to Wilhelmine Germany than to more democratic France or Britain or to more autocratic imperial Russia. Spain's government in the 1880s was both authoritarian and permissive, wedded to the intersts of an economic oligarchy and also restrained by a constitution. For Iglesias, the existence of an authoritarian government serving the interests of privileged groups in society made a revolutionary ideology necessary; the fact that revolutionary tactics led only to harsh governmental repression invited prudent reformist measures. This is why the tactics of Iglesias made for a revolutionary rhetoric and for reformist action. What he wanted was to build a Social Democratic party emulating the German model.

The position taken by Iglesias that Socialists should not cooperate with any left-bourgeois party was accepted by the Spanish Socialist leadership, at least until the days of the Tragic Week. Iglesias himself, together with Antonio García Quejido, joined the German delegates in their resolution presented in 1904 at the second congress of the Second International that reaffirmed the ban on any cooperation with a bourgeois party. Following in the same way the German example, the UGT was expected to follow the political leadership of the Spanish Socialist party. In the words of Meaker (1974):

> During the early years of the twentieth century the Socialist Party did not alter its mood or its methods. It remained a proletarian sect, a subculture closed against the world and nearly as cut off from the great mass

of Spanish workers—who remained unorganized—as it was from bourgeois society...it remained moderate in its tactics. The PSOE was, in fact, many things that Spanish workers were not, and it is less than surprising that it grew very slowly. (p. 13)

The noncooperation strategy of Iglesias was set aside not only because of the events of the Tragic Week but also because of the entry into the Socialist party of a number of intellectuals who did not share his views. In 1908, Manuel Núñez de Arenas, a university-trained member of the Madrid nobility, joined the party with the idea of establishing a "New School" designed to educate the workers and to be a center of theoretical studies. Other intellectuals joining the party in that period were Luis Araquistáin, Andrés Ovejero, Julián Besteiro, Rafael Urbano, and Oscar Pérez Solís. Most of these intellectuals were to take issue with the rigidity of *Pablismo*. Some, such as Besteiro, and later on Fernando de los Ríos, accepted the ideology of Iglesias; most found fault with his policy of "revolutionary reformism."

The revisionist banner was carried in the years 1911–12 by Núñez de Arenas, who was followed by a number of other Socialist leaders. These people viewed themselves as a Spanish Fabian Society whose mission it was to guide the Spanish Socialist party along the path of British laborism. They opposed the revolutionary goals of the Socialist-republican alliance, fearing that attempts to overthrow the monarchy would only lead to greater government measures of repression against labor.

The "centrists" loyal to Iglesias, however, emerged victorious by the time of the outbreak of World War I. Iglesias, who had been removed from the editorship of *El Socialista* in 1912, was restored to that position three years later.

Socialists withdrew from Solidaridad Obrera following the events of the Tragic Week. Workers also started abandoning the Radical party, discouraged by the weakness Emiliano Iglesias had shown during the days of insurrection. Anarchists were left free to guide Solidaridad Obrera according to their wishes. In December 1909, delegates representing 27 trade unions belonging to this organization decided to call a national workers' congress to discuss the transformation of Solidaridad Obrera into a national labor organization. This congress met in the Palace of Bellas Artes in Barcelona from October 30 to November 1, 1910. It agreed to form a new national labor confederation bearing the name Confederación Nacional del Trabajo (CNT) the National Confederation of Labor. The first congress of the CNT was held at the same palace, September 8–11, 1911.

The new national confederation was to represent a number of loosely connected regional confederations, each composed of local or district federations, which in turn were made up of the individual labor unions, or *sindicatos.* A National Committee was to coordinate activities, collect statistics, and provide help for prisoners. The anarchists in the CNT wanted, above all, to prevent any bureaucratization or centralization of power within the organization. Administrators were to serve without salary, and funds were to be accumulated only to help prisoners and to finance workers' schools.

The CNT also rejected any involvement with political or religious activities. One of its main goals was to keep alive the workers' revolutionary spirit, and for this end it allowed short and violent strikes.

The spring of 1911 was a period of great political and social unrest. There were demonstrations protesting military action in Morocco; there were demonstrations petitioning for an official exoneration of Francisco Ferrer. There was mutiny aboard the naval ship *Numancia,* which was followed by a general strike in Cádiz. Strikes affected many cities in Spain. On September 11, at the same time the CNT was holding its first congress in Barcelona, a general strike extended throughout Vizcaya.

The national committees of both the UGT and the CNT opted for the general strike to be carried out by all of their organizations. The government promptly suspended all constitutional rights, closed down workers' meeting halls, proceeded to prosecute the UGT judicially, and declared the CNT to be an illegal association. The liberal prime minister Canalejas moved troops to all major cities, and the entire country was placed under martial law. Many labor militants were arrested, prosecuted, and given heavy sentences.

There was no strike activity in Madrid, largely because of efforts by Socialists to avoid it in the capital. No strike developed in Barcelona, but for different reasons. There the police arrested 500 *Cenetistas* before the strike could start, and with the aid of the radicals of Lerroux succeeded in preventing the development of strike activity.

In Vizcaya the strike lasted until September 20. In the Levant, anarchists and extremist republicans proceeded to proclaim the republic in a number of villages, and there were even killings at Cullera, near Valencia, for which five anarchists were later to be given death sentences, eventually commuted to life imprisonment. In Asturias, the miners followed the strike order issued by their UGT union. Meanwhile, the CNT went underground and its press ceased production.

The workers' dissatisfaction with their work conditions was once again revealed by the countrywide railway strike of 1912. The UGT railroad workers union had demanded a 30 percent wage increase, a shortening of the workday, and retirement benefits. The Canalejas government responded by drafting 12,000 workers into the army and by replacing striking workers with soldiers. In spite of these measures, the breakdown of railway services became total. The government finally succeeded in bringing the strike to an end by promising the railroad workers that their demands would be presented to the Cortes in the form of a proposed law. The strike ended on October 5; a month later, Canalejas was murdered in Madrid by an anarchist.

In 1913, the successor of Canalejas, the liberal prime minister Romanones declared an amnesty for all workers who had been imprisoned for their activities in the strike of September 1911. The CNT remained an illegal, underground organization, still active in conducting strikes. Strike activity increased in 1913. A strike by the textile workers of Barcelona, which lasted from July 28 to August 22, resulted in a victory for the workers when the length of their workday was shortened. On this occasion, the textile workers strike was organized by anarchosyndicalists. There were also strikes by officers and seamen of the merchant fleet and by the miners of the British-owned Río Tinto mining enterprise. Many of these strikes were conducted for the explicit purpose of obtaining the employers' recognition of a trade union.

The outbreak of World War I found most Spaniards resolutely opposed to any Spanish participation in the war. The neutrality of Spain was affirmed by Prime Minister Dato on August 25, 1914. Although most Spaniards opposed a Spanish alliance with either group of belligerents, literate Spain divided into two when it came to personal feelings of identification. Spaniards identifying with the "forces of order" tended to sympathize with the Central Powers; these included the conservatives, the landed interests, the bureaucracy, the church, the Carlists, and most of the military. The pro-Allies group included the republicans, the radicals, the reformists, the Socialists, the Basque and Catalan middle class, and most of the intelligentsia.

Those who believed in a hierarchical and authoritarian social order supported the Central Powers; those who hoped for a democratization of Spain sided with the Allies, expecting that an Entente victory would have political and social repercussions in Spain. For Meaker (1974) "The most formidable defender of the Central Powers in Spain was the Catholic Church. . . . The victory of the Allies had to be opposed because it would strengthen liberal and anticlerical tendencies within Spain . . ." (p. 21). The main supporters of the Allies were the left-bourgeois parties and the Socialists.

Initially, the Socialist party had followed the antiwar resolutions of the Second International and had condemned the belligerency of all participants in the war. The party's doctrinaire position soon weakened as German armies penetrated Belgium and France. The Socialist leadership promptly abandoned its pacifist and neutralist positions and embraced the Allied cause as pro-German sentiment grew among Spain's conservatives. The rapid drift toward a position of strong support for the Allies was backed by the republican-Socialist alliance, which identified more with the Western democracies than with the Eastern totalitarian forms of government. Indeed, what this alliance strove for was a bourgeois-democratic republic. On August 30, Iglesias gave public notice of his sympathy for the Allies. Most Socialists followed the position taken by Iglesias, with a few insisting on maintaining doctrinaire neutrality and a strong antiwar position; this latter group was headed by Andrés Saborit. The majority view triumphed at the tenth congress of the Socialist party held in Madrid in October 1915. This congress approved two resolutions advanced by Dr. Jaime Vera and by the academician Julián Besteiro that supported the pro-Allies position followed by Iglesias and permitted continued cooperation between the party and progressive bourgeois groups.

The anarchosyndicalists embraced a very different position regarding the war. Their feeling was that it did not matter to workers which belligerent group would emerge victorious. They demanded Spain's absolute neutrality in the conflict, a view that coincided with that of the strongest conservative groups in Spain. Indeed, pro-German propaganda in Spain and Spain's privileged elites emphasized the maintenance of "absolute neutrality." When Spanish anarchists and anarchosyndicalists learned that the great theoretician of anarchism, Peter Kropotkin, had declared his support for the Allied cause, his disciples in Spain decided to reject him.

NOTES

Bookchin, M. 1977. *The Spanish Anarchists: The Heroic years, 1868–1936.* New York: Free Life Editions.

Droz, J., ed. 1979. *Historia General del Socialismo.* Vol. II. Barcelona: Ediciones Destino.

Meaker, G. H. 1974. *The Revolutionary Left in Spain, 1914–1923.* Stanford, Calif.: Stanford University Press.

Minutes of the General Council's Meetings, 1864. 1962. London.

Payne, S. G., 1973. *A History of Spain and Portugal,* vol. 2. Madison, Wis.: University of Wisconsin Press.

Tuñon de Lara, M. 1972. *El movimiento obrero en la historia de España.* Vols. I and II. Barcelona; Editorial LAIA.

BIBLIOGRAPHY

Lamberet, R. *Mouvements Ouvriers et Socialistes, L'Espagne, 1750–1936.* Paris, 1953.

Lorenzo, A. *El proletariado militante.* Madrid, 1974.

Morato, J. J. *Líderes del movimiento obrero español.* Madrid, 1972.

Nettlau, M. *La Première Internationale en Espagne, 1868–1888."* Dordrecht, Netherlands, 1968.

Termes, J. *Anarquismo y Sindicalismo en España, La Primera Internacional.* Barcelona, 1972.

2

The Political Fragmentation of the Spanish Labor Movement: From World War I to the Beginning of the Spanish Civil War

At the start of the twentieth century, nearly 60 percent of Spanish workers still earned a living in the agrarian sector. This sector, by international standards, continued to be characterized by low crop yields and by the prevalence of traditional crops. The acreage devoted to wheat expanded between 1900 and 1914, and yet wheat continued to be imported during this same period. The output of olive oil showed a slight increase up to 1914, while that of wine stagnated. Only the output and exports of oranges rose significantly before the outbreak of World War I.

The extraction of domestic coal was stimulated by laws that required the public sector and the Spanish navy to consume domestic coal. The output of iron ore experienced a drastic fall in 1914 and never recovered its prewar output levels. The textile industry, on the other hand, was strengthened by war-created demand.

The first years of the twentieth century witnessed the continuation of the formation of large, quasimonopolistic industrial enterprises financed and controlled by large banks. These banks promoted and financed the creation of a number of electric power utilities: the Electra de Madrid in 1910, the Energía Eléctrica de Cataluña in 1911, the Eléctricas Reunidas de Zaragoza in 1911, and the Unión Eléctrica Madrileña in 1912. All of these utilities were established with the help of large banks, patterned after the German *Universalbank*.

At the start of World War I, Spain's economy was still largely agrarian. While small, precapitalist firms supplied the bulk of consumer goods, industrial raw materials and capital goods were produced by quasimonopolistic enterprises operating under the double shield of government protection and bank finance. Spain's economic system was still very far from being an industrial, capitalist system.

THE ECONOMIC IMPACT OF WORLD WAR I

It is difficult to generalize about the economic consequences of the war on the Spanish economy. It brought boom conditions to some sectors, recession to others. It seems that the war favored the urban-industrial zones, which manufactured exportable products, while many agrarian areas suffered increased unemployment. Agrarian recession resulted in a larger flow of migrants to the large cities. The populations of Madrid, Barcelona, and Bilbao increased rapidly because of this rural immigration. Most of the migrants came from the Levant, and most of them remained hungry and unemployed in the cities where they settled.

Although because of price inflation, the value of Spanish exports rose during the war, the monetary value of Spanish imports sharply declined. This foreign trade development had two consequences: On the one hand, Spain's balance of payments suddenly became favorable and the country experienced an inflow of gold; on the other hand, the fall in imports meant greater food scarcities, rising food prices, and deteriorating standards of living for the masses. While the middle and upper-middle classes of Catalonia and the Basque country grew wealthy catering to the demand of the Allied powers, rising costs of living plagued the working class. The price of some basic necessities rose faster than the general price level. As a result, hunger became more widespread and a number of bread riots broke out in many cities.

The liberal government of Count Romanones replaced the conservative government of Eduardo Dato on December 9, 1915. Spain's neutrality in the war was maintained. The government did not enact any restrictions on Spanish exports of foodstuffs, raw materials, and manufactured goods to the belligerent nations, and the living conditions of the Spanish workers continued to deteriorate. A poor harvest in 1915 and wartime restrictions on imports made for continuing increases in the cost of living.

The workers expressed their discontent through strike activity. A number of strikes broke out in 1915, and these were followed in 1916 by general strikes in Barcelona and Valencia.

A proposal was made at the UGT congress held in Madrid in May 1916 recommending the implementaion of a national general strike, in cooperation with the CNT. Even though Julián Besteiro supported the proposal, the congress merely resolved to study the matter over a period of three months and to poll the UGT membership about the desirability of a one-day general strike. At the same time, a congress of the CNT held at Valencia resolved to investigate the possibility of launching a national general strike in cooperation with the UGT.

Representatives of both labor organizations met in July in Zaragoza and agreed to exert joint pressure on the government to induce the latter to take action to curb inflation and unemployment. The parties agreed to threaten the government with a national general strike should the government refuse to initiate proper action. The "Pact of Zaragoza," signed by Julián Besteiro, Francisco Largo Caballero, and Vicente Barrio for the UGT and by Salvador Seguí, Angel Pestaña, and Angel Lacort for the CNT, constituted the first act of cooperation between the two large labor organizations. The government, intimidated by this labor alliance, overreacted by ordering the suspension of constitutional guarantees and the immediate arrest of the signers of the pact. Hundreds of trade union leaders were arrested. In November, representatives of the UGT and the CNT agreed, at the behest of the Socialists, to limit the general strike to one day.

Julián Besteiro had personally informed Count Romanones about the demands of organized labor; labor wanted a lowering of prices, policies designed to increase employment, the release of imprisoned labor officials, and an end to the war in Morocco. Romanones made promises, but his government failed to take any action. A second meeting between labor delegates and Romanones produced identical results. On December 18, 1916, the nation experienced its first successful general strike, which was to serve as a warning to the government.

The inaction of the government induced representatives of both the UGT and the CNT to meet in the socialists' Casa del Pueblo in Madrid on March 5, 1917. Labor leaders participating in this meeting were angry. UGT and CNT delegates found no difficulty in producing a new manifesto calling for a general strike of unlimited duration within a period of three months. The Romanones government, apprehending that the manifesto's purposes threatened the nation's political system, declared the manifesto seditious and its signers were arrested. The arrest of these labor leaders triggered in turn a general strike in Valladolid on March 8; the workers of Vallodolid fully expected that their example would be followed throughout Spain. When this failed to happen, the strike ended in failure a few days later.

On February 1, 1917, the Germans declared unrestricted submarine warfare, and in March the tsarist government was overthrown in Russia. Both events strengthened the pro-Allies voice in Spain. The Socialist party urged the government to take action against any persons and any organizations in Spain that were guilty of facilitating the German submarine blockade. Following the sinking by a German submarine of a Spanish freighter, the *San Fulgencio,* a ship carrying coal from Newcastle to Barcelona, Romanones decided to take steps to break diplomatic relations with Germany. When the Cortes resisted this move, Romanones resigned. The new government of Luis García Prieto decided to follow the established policy of maintaining strict neutrality in the war. This policy infuriated not only the forces supporting the Allies but also the antimonarchical groups, which by now were convinced that the king was a supporter of the Central Powers. Political and economic disappointment started to unite reformists, republicans, radicals, and Socialists.

On May 27, a pro-Allies bourgeois intelligentsia, composed of republican politicians, intellectuals, journalists, and other professionals, gathered in the bullfight ring of Madrid. The philosopher Miguel de Unamuno, more a Socialist than a republican, uttered on that occasion this warning: "It depends on the King whether or not many of us who are not republicans must declare ourselves as such. I, who still have a slender faith in the monarchy... will cease to believe in it if it insists on neutrality at all costs. The King can be useful; but he is not indispensable, much less irreplaceable" (Meaker 1974, p. 55).

The Socialists, although not officially represented at the gathering, shared the same views. The great majority of the Socialists wanted Spain to give at least moral support to the Western democracies; only a small minority around Mariano García Cortés stood for the maintenance of strict neutrality. Unlike the *Cenetistas*, no Socialist talked about an imminent revolution. What the majoritarians in the Socialist party wanted was a victory of the Allied Powers and the restoration of international peace and of the Second International. What the minority Socialists wanted was to keep Spanish soldiers from joining French and British infantrymen in the trenches.

THE REVOLUTIONS OF 1917

Political tension and economic difficulties made 1917 an explosive year. The collapse of the tsarist government, the German submarine blockade, and the entry of the United States into the war appeared to announce apocalyptic changes in the world. The UGT and the CNT, by agreeing to engage jointly in a possible general strike of unlimited duration, seemed to be willing to cast Spain adrift on the sea of revolution.

Curiously, the stability of the Spanish throne was first threatened by a military revolt. Low pay and inflation affected military officers just like it affected the workers. The officers' discontent was reinforced by the fact that awards and promotions were no longer strictly given on the basis of seniority, but were granted by officials close to the king or close to his minister of war, to young officers who served in Morocco and to generals who were favorites of the crown. Infantry and cavalry officers attempted to obtain better pay and pay based on seniority by forming "military trade unions," the *juntas de defensa*. The *juntas* never became antimonarchical and their members never became interested in social problems other than their own. The earliest *juntas* were those of Barcelona, Lérida, Tarragona, and Gerona. The Barcelona *junta* was headed by the liberal Colonel Benito Márquez.

The military *juntas* continued to grow in numbers and in power under the Romanones and the García Prieto governments. The king, who at first believed that the *juntas* would remain loyal and obedient to him, soon realized that this was not the case. Fearing the possibility of a military coup d'état, the minister of war ordered the arrest on May 26 of the 12 leaders of the Barcelona *junta*. After they had been placed in the Montjuich prison, demonstrations of support for the arrested officers broke out in most garrisons of Spain. On June 10, the king ordered the release of the imprisoned officers, an act of questionable legality. The García Prieto government resigned the following day. The military now controlled politics and it compelled the legalization of the military *juntas* and ordered the suspension of the Cortes.

The army had been successful in defying the government, having obtained what it wanted by threatening insurrection. The left-bourgeoisie, the Socialists, and the *Cenetistas* felt that the military had shown them the way and that through joint action they could bring about major political and economical changes. A republican-reformist-Socialist alliance was formed in June. Lerroux represented the republicans, Melquíades Alvarez the reformists, Pablo Iglesias the Socialists; and Francisco Largo Caballero the UGT. The alliance contemplated the formation of a provisional government in which the presidency would be assumed by Melquíades Alvarez and in which Iglesias would become minister of labor. On June 16 the representatives of these various parties signed a document that asserted the need for the overthrow of the existing regime and for the establishment of a new government representing the sovereign will of the Spanish nation.

There was another large group in Spain that desired political change for the sake of national "regeneration." This was the wealthy Catalan bourgeoisie, led by Francisco Cambó, which, with the support of Asturian and Basque industrialists, wanted to take political control out of the hands of the landed oligarchy and of those serving its interests. While hostile to the landed interests, Francisco Cambó's *Lliga Regionalista* remained a very conservative party when dealing with the workers. The Lliga's main objective was the autonomy of Catalonia; it also proposed to form a new provisional national government, and Cambó even offered a seat in it to Pablo Iglesias. On June 15, 1917, the *Lliga* published a manifesto that defined its objectives of regional autonomy. One month later, representatives of nearly all political parties in Catalonia met in the city hall of Barcelona to demand a reconvening of the Cortes in Madrid so that this body, sitting as a constituent assembly, could work out a new political system for the nation. Should the Cortes be unable to meet for this purpose, the politicians in Barcelona decided to form by themselves a constituent assembly that would meet in Barcelona on July 19. What the regionalists wanted was to transform Spain into a federative organization of regions, each region obtaining almost complete autonomy.

Eduardo Dato in Madrid threatened to treat the proposed assembly as a seditious conspiracy, and, having appeased the military, he decided to frustrate the efforts of the Catalan regionalists. The latter met on July 19 in the Palacio de la Ciudadela of Barcelona but were unable to enact any reformist legislation because the civil governor of Barcelona, with the aid of the police, brought a sudden end to the deliberations. Although the assembled politicians were forced out of their meeting hall, they had succeeded in publicly challenging Dato's rigid maintenance of the political and social status quo.

On the same day the assembly in Barcelona was ended by government order, streetcar operators and railroad workers went on strike in Valencia; this strike became a general one by July 20, but seemed to end four days later. It was then that a railway company, the Compañía del Norte, decided to dismiss 36 workers who had participated in the Valencia strike. The National Federation of Railway Workers promptly declared that unless the company reinstated the dismissed workers in their jobs, it would call for a strike of railroad workers, to begin on August 10. The Dato government refused to intervene, in all likelihood expecting that this strike would trigger the outbreak of the threatened general strike at a time when the two large labor organizations were not yet ready to carry out such effort; government officials hoped that a premature general strike would make the task of defeating it much easier for the authorities.

Even though the national committee of the UGT advised against a railroad strike at the time, the federation of railroad workers decided to initiate a strike as of August 13. Because the railroad workers had taken the decision to go on strike, the leadership of the Socialist party and of the UGT felt forced to back the workers. Both Besteiro and Saborit, representing the party, and Largo Caballero and Anguiano, representing the UGT, knew that the railroad workers were acting prematurely and that their action could launch a general strike bound to fail. Nevertheless, they signed a manifesto on August 12 that petitioned for a new provisional government that would conduct elections conducive to the formation of a constituent Cortes and a new constitution.

This manifesto disregarded the advice of the bedridden Pablo Iglesias, who had opposed giving a political or revolutionary objective to the strike. August 1917 marked the effective end of Iglesias as the real leader of the Socialist movement in Spain. Francisco Largo Caballero and Julián

Besteiro, in a mood of great optimism, had decided to ignore the advice of the old, sick leader. Iglesias had advised against a strike whose goal was a political revolution; so did Melquíades Alvarez; both had their recommendations rejected. The strike began at midnight of August 12. During the night of August 14, all of the members of the strike committee—Besteiro, Saborit, Largo Caballero, and Anguiano—were arrested by the police.

Although the strike had begun, not all Spanish railroad workers participated; only the Asturian railroad workers, those of the line Orense-Vigo, and those of some southern railroad companies struck. The Catalan Lliga Regionalista promptly declared that it would not take part and did not support the strike. Most republicans who had agreed to ally themselves with the Socialists now broke their word and did not support the workers' effort. Meanwhile, the government in Madrid declared the country to be in a "state of war."

On August 13, economic life stopped in Madrid, Barcelona, Vizcaya, and Asturias, and there were major work stoppages in Valencia, Zaragoza, Burgos, Vitoria, Sabadell, Tarrasa, and Huelva. In the south, with the exception of the Río Tinto miners, both urban and rural workers ignored the strike. But in Vizcaya there were 100,000 strikers and all mining activity stopped. In Barcelona the strike committee was directed by Pestaña of the CNT in collaboration with other *Cenetistas*. They faced 12,000 soldiers under the command of Captain-General Milans del Bosch, who was determined to destroy the workers' barricades and the workers' efforts.

Throughout Spain workers soon realized that neither the military nor their republican "allies" supported their revolutionary effort. The strike was over in Barcelona and Madrid by August 18 and in most areas of Spain by the twentieth. It lasted longer in Asturias, until August 30, even though General Burguete had ordered his troops to shoot Asturian miners like hunted beasts.

On October 4, a military tribunal sentenced to life imprisonment Besteiro, Largo Caballero, Anguiano, and Saborit; these men were transferred in chains to a military prison in Cartagena. The imprisonment of the leaders of Madrid's strike committee culminated the workers' defeat. The bitterness of the workers was increased when the once revolutionary Catalan Lliga had one of its members participate in the cabinet of the new prime minister, García Prieto, who, on November 3, 1917, replaced Eduardo Dato whose government had been ousted by the military *juntas*. Although the UGT and the CNT survived the failure of the 1917 strike, labor leaders in Spain realized that they had committed the error of directing what should have been a bourgeois-led revolution.

The rural workers and the small landowners of the latifundio areas had shown little interest and had not participated in the strikes of August 1917, which they viewed as ignoring their interests. Also, wartime demand for agricultural commodities had boosted rural employment and rural wages. This rural apathy vanished in the spring of 1918, when the news of the Bolshevik Revolution finally reached southern Spain. Emotions ran high among the small tenants and the small land proprietors whose subsistence holdings adjoined the large estates; on the whole, the landless *braceros* were not affected as strongly by the "Russian fever" as the small landowners, although all showed great interest in the news of land seizures by Russian peasants that were sanctioned by the Bolsheviks. In the words of Meaker (1974):

> The fascination that the November Revolution exerted in the south of Spain was thus closely related to the ever-present hunger for land in the latifundio provinces, and to the popular conviction that there must someday be a redivision of the soil, which, as all knew, belonged only to those who worked it. . . . For them, the Bolshevik victory had a single but very vivid meaning, being essentially the spectacle of an oppressed peasantry breaking its chains, sweeping aside its landlords and seizing the land that belonged to it. (pp. 134, 135)

The news from Russia was first spread by southern anarchist speakers, their example being followed by anarchosyndicalists and a few Socialists. Their message spread rapidly in southern Spain. There was a particularly strong response to the news in the area of Andalusia south of the river Guadalquivir. It was mainly in the province of Córdoba, where, fired by the Russian example, the peasantry resorted to organizational activity, meetings, demonstrations, strikes, and acts of destruction in order to obtain the confiscation, partition, and redistribution of the large estates.

Both Socialists and *Cenetistas* tried to exploit to their advantage the restlessness of the peasantry. Within the Andalusian Regional Confederation of the CNT there was also rivalry between syndicalists and anarchists. This restlessness was expressed in a number of strikes that broke out in May and in June 1918; in October, 34 Cordoban towns experienced a general strike. Agrarian disturbances multiplied in southern Spain between the fall of 1918 and the summer of 1919. In Andalusia and Extremadura, peasants started dividing the great estates among themselves; at the same time, wheat fields, orchards, and vineyards were seriously damaged. In a number of towns a "Bolshevik republic" was proclaimed, and the province of Córdoba experienced three major general strikes before the end of the summer in 1919.

Agrarian disturbances continued to plague southern Spain in 1919 and 1920. Hence this period is known by Spanish historians as the *Tri-*

enio Bolchevista, the three "bolchevist" years. The disturbances peaked in the summer of 1919 but started to lessen when the conservative Maura government dispatched General Emilio Barrera with 20,000 troops to the south to reestablish "law and order."

Peasant unrest during the *Trienio* strengthened the anarchosyndicalist movement not only in Andalusia but also in other areas of peasant revolt, such as Valencia, Alicante, Zaragoza, Murcia, and Estremadura. The central and northern regions, largely under Socialist influence, had remained quieter during this period and provided the UGT with an increasing number of members. In spite of the rapid growth of the UGT, the Socialist party followed a careful and pragmatic policy designed more to win electoral victories than to repeat the disaster of August 1917. In spite of the impact that the Bolshevik Revolution had on the Spanish workers, the Socialists, unlike the syndicalists, minimized their support of a workers' revolution and followed Pablo Iglesias' advice to center on peaceful reforms by means of the slow process of winning seats in the Cortes and in the municipal governments.

1918 was not exclusively a year of revolts by southern peasants. The "Bolshevik fever" also affected Catalan industrial workers, many of them illiterate and impatient *Murcianos* who had migrated to Catalonia during the war years. These migrants from Valencia, Murcia, Almería, and Zaragoza flocked to the Catalonian Regional Confederation, the Confederación Regional del Trabajo (CRT). This labor organization called for a congress that met from June 28 to July 1 in Sans, near Barcelona; 164 delegates met in Sans, representing 73,860 members.

The most important decision passed by the congress was to abandon the craft union as the base unit of the CRT. A new organizational scheme provided for the formation of industrial unions, *sindicatos únicos,* representing major branches of production; the old craft unions were to become simple sections of the new industrial union. These unions were to be grouped in local federations, and the latter were to form regional federations, which, in turn, composed the CNT.

Although the congress reaffirmed the apolitical position of the CRT, it followed on the whole a moderate syndicalist position and avoided anarchist rhetoric. The elected leadership of this organization also represented moderate syndicalists; Salvador Seguí, Salvador Quemades, Camilio Piñón, Salvador Ferrer, and Juan Pey followed a syndicalist ideology. This ideology contrasted with the anarchist orientation of the CNT leadership elected three months later. The provisional National Committee of the CNT was made up of Manuel Buenacasa, Evelio Boal, Vicente Gil, José Ripoll; and Andrés Miguel, all of them strong supporters of libertarian ideology.

Shortly after the end of World War I, on November 11, 1918, the

Spanish Socialist party held its eleventh congress in Madrid, November 24–December 3. The congress adopted a new minimum program that listed both political and economic goals. Among these goals were the abolition of the monarchy, universal suffrage for both sexes at the age of 21, proportional representation in the Cortes, new agrarian legislation, the abolition of church and of indirect taxes, the nationalization of all mines and of all means of transportation, a minimum legal wage, and a work week of 44 hours.

The central organs of the party were reorganized on the basis of a new Executive Committee and of a larger National Committee. Pablo Iglesias, Julián Besteiro, Daniel Anguiano, Francisco Núñez, Manuel Núñez de Arenas, Andrés Saborit, Virginia González, Andrés Ovejero, Indalecio Prieto, and Francisco Largo Caballero were the elected members of the Executive Committee. Largo Caballero became the new secretary-general of the UGT at its thirteenth congress; Pablo Iglesias remained its president. This UGT congress petitioned the National Committee of the CNT for the reestablishment of friendly relations between the two labor organizations in order to obtain eventually a unification of all Spanish labor organizations into a single national body.

FROM THE END OF WORLD WAR I TO THE PRIMO DE RIVERA DICTATORSHIP

Following the armistice of November 1918, a strong European demand for Spanish exports kept economic conditions in Spain favorable until the end of 1920. It was then that shipyards, mines, and steel plants started closing down in response to the contraction of wartime demand. Part of the arable land was no longer cultivated, and urban and rural unemployment started growing. As employers tried to reduce wages, social tensions were bound to rise. Workers, impelled by a dream of a new postwar world, joined the *sindicatos únicos* of the CNT en masse. In Catalonia alone, the membership grew frm 107,096 workers by the end of 1918 to 345,000 one year later (Meaker 1974, p. 149).

1919 witnessed a doubling in the number of strikes over that of the earlier year. Employers resisted more strongly union demands than they had done during the war years. Rising prices, employers' intransigence, and the combative enthusiasm that the Bolshevik Revolution had given to Andalusian and Catalan workers brought in 1919 and 1920 a period of peak labor turbulence. Anarchists and syndicalists played a major role during these years of vigorous strike activity.

Toward the end of 1918, an anarchist congress held at Barcelona had taken the pragmatic position that anarchists should join trade unions in an attempt to infuse them with anarchist ideology. Doctrinal purity was to be sacrificed for the sake of tactical expediency.

At the same time, the Catalan CRT, headed by Salvador Seguí, decided to undertake an intensive campaign throughout Andalusia and the Levant. Syndicalist propagandists were supported by anarchist groups, and their combined efforts succeeded in subjecting Córdoba to a general strike in March 1919. By the end of April, 33 towns of that province were paralyzed by total strikes, strikes that lasted until the end of May in spite of a declaration of a "state of war" by the authorities, the closing down of workers' meeting halls, and the arrest of labor leaders. During the spring and the summer, strike activity, often characterized by violence, extended to the provinces of Jaén, Seville, Cádiz, Málaga, and Huelva.

Not all of these strikes reflected anarchosydicalist influence. True, the Andalusian Regional Federation of the CNT organized a congress in Seville in January of 1919, followed in May by a congress of anarchosyndicalist unions meeting in Castro del Río. The *Ugetistas*, however met in Córdoba in April, and were joined by unions of miners. The Córdoba congress petitioned for an eight-hour workday for agricultural workers, the determination of rural wages by commissions representing both employers and workers, employers' responsibility to take care of workers involuntarily unemployed, and the utilization of lands belonging to the central government, municipal governments, and latifundistas by societies of workers.

A syndicalist show of strength also developed in Barcelona in February. It started on February 5 with a strike against an electric power utility, a Canadian-British enterprise popularly known as La Canadiense that supplied electric power from the Ebro River to homes and factories in Barcelona. Technically, the strike was conducted as an employees' response to an attempt by the management of La Canadiense to reduce wages and to its dismissal of eight workers. Another purpose of the strike was the recognition of the CRT by Catalan employers, a recognition that would contribute to the growth of the CNT. The strike against La Canadiense expanded to all electric utilities in the area. When textile workers joined the strike, about 70 percent of all factories in and around Barcelona had to close. Employees of the city's waterworks then joined in the strike, leaving Barcelona without electricity, water, and gas.

The captain-general of Catalonia, Milans del Bosch, took retaliatory action by drafting into the military all male employees of the water, gas, and electric utilities between the ages of 21 and 31. When the drafted workers refused to follow military orders, 3,000 of them were imprisoned in the Montjuich Fortress.

The Socialists now threatened to have the UGT order its unions to strike in support of the CNT. Count Romanones, back in power since December 1918, tried to diffuse the situation in Barcelona by replacing its civil governor and its chief of police; he then sent to Barcelona José Morote, his personal secretary, to negotiate an agreement between employers and the workers. Morote succeeded in having a strike settlement signed by both parties on March 17, a settlement that represented a strong victory for the workers. Under its terms, all imprisoned workers were to be freed with the exception of those already bound for trial; all of the strikers were to be rehired without penalties and were to receive accrued wages as of the day the strike began; and the employers agreed to an eight-hour workday and to wage increases.

Union leaders and CRT officials urged the masses of workers assembled on March 20 in the bullfight ring to accept the terms of the settlement. They were heckled by anarchists who wanted the strike to continue until a "final victory" over the bourgeoisie would be obtained. The proposal of Salvador Seguí was finally accepted by all. The authorities were given three days to free the rest of the imprisoned workers; if they refused to do so, a general strike would be declared. The military and the authorities refused to free the remaining prisoners, and the CNT, under pressure from militant anarchists, declared a general strike on March 24—an imprudent act because it imposed on the already economically exhausted workers new hardships and the threat of arrest.

The workers nevertheless went on strike, and on March 24 life in Barcelona came to a standstill. Milans del Bosch immediately brought the city under martial law; soldiers, policemen, and a small army of about 8,000 middle-class volunteers—the *Somaten*—were used to cripple the *Cenetista* effort. The entire CNT strike committee was arrested. While the government tried to destroy unionism in Barcelona, it also attempted to appease Spanish workers by ordering, on April 3, the implementation throughout the nation of the eight-hour workday. The tactics of the government succeeded, and the Barcelona strike ended on April 14.

Catalan employers started taking strong action against the recurrence of a similar strike. Militant employees were dismissed or were blacklisted. From April to July 1919, the conservative Maura government, which succeeded the Romanones administration, encouraged a policy of repression against the Catalan *sindicatos*. During this period, the Catalan trade unions were not recognized by the authorities, their leaders were imprisoned, and thousands of CNT militants were taken to the Montjuich Fortress. On July 19, Pablo Sabater, the president of the textile union, was murdered by two men wearing police uniforms.

Unions survived by operating underground. As many of their leaders were jailed or fled the country, union leaderhip tended to pass from moderate syndicalists to a group of younger, anarchist "men of action";

the latter had nothing but contempt for former syndicalist leaders who were accused of having abandoned the purusit of the revolution. The young anarchist militants advocated the use of organized labor to overthrow the bourgeois order. The strengthening of the CNT as a labor organization and the attainment of better living and working conditions for union members were of no interest to them.

Many of the younger anarchist leaders had a very limited knowledge of anarchist theory as formulated by Bakunin or by Kropotkin; they were very much influenced by the myth of the Bolshevik Revolution, by the dramatic impact of the *atentado personal,* and by the possibility of being able to live adventurous, well-paid lives and escape the dullness of everyday life in a factory or shop. Some were inclined to commit violence because of the intransigence and selfishness shown by employers; others chose terrorism to satisfy personal cravings. Many of them were potential criminals who sold themselves as hired gunmen to labor leaders who found no difficulty in identifying murder with Sorel's idea of "direct action." By mid-1919, a good part of the dues paid by union members in Barcelona went toward the financing of the unions' *pistoleros.*

Anarchosyndicalist terror resulted in the development of measures of counterterror on the part of employers and the police. The employers and the military started using their own gunmen to murder CNT officials and union militants. Sabater was probably murdered by the gang following the orders of a former district police chief, Manuel Bravo Portillo, who, after being dismissed from his position in the police force because of his involvement in a German espionage ring, was hired by Milans del Bosch and by the employers. The Employers' Federation also used the services of a "Baron Koenig" who also demanded protection money from various employers. These hired assassins started a war of extermination against the CNT.

During the summer of 1919 it appeared that the efforts of the able civil governor of Barcelona, Julio Amado, had succeeded in reestablishing peaceful relations between the employers and the CNT. Amado succeeded in bringing together for a dialogue representatives of the Barcelona employers and of the CNT. He suggested a provisional agreement between the parties, pending the final solution of labor-management problems by a mixed commission composed of an equal number of employers and of workers. Meanwhile, the trade unions would receive legal recognition, all strikes and lockouts in the Barcelona area would be terminated, and all strikers would return immediately to their jobs. An amnesty for all imprisoned workers was declared, and Barcelona recovered a semblance of tranquility. The arrangement did not please the anarchists, who felt that it strengthened the position of the moderate syndicalists in the trade unions.

On November 12, the members of the mixed commission gave their approval to a proposed labor relations bill that was soon to become law. The bill defined the powers of the mixed commission. It could hear and solve labor disputes of any kind; it could fix minimum wages; and it could propose new labor legislation to the government. The bill further stipulated that all strikes and lockouts would be suspended until the commission could solve the underlying problems.

It appears, however, that already in October the Employers' Federation had resolved to renew its warfare against the unions and to destroy them by means of a gigantic lockout, which would first affect Barcelona alone and later on all of Spain. The lockout was started on November 25 on the basis of the flimsy justification that some workers had not returned to work. The lockout continued until January 26, 1920, idling about 200,000 workers in Barcelona. Employers' terrorism had a new start, employers being encouraged by the appointment of a new civil governor of Barcelona, José Maestre Laborde, Count Salvatierra, a man who had decided to take a position hostile to trade unionism.

The mixed commission disappeared, and gunmen once again dictated management-labor relations in Barcelona. As of the end of 1919, it seemed that the syndicalists and the more moderate anarchosyndicalists had lost prestige among the workers and that the more *exalté* anarchists and anarchosyndicalists had been favored by the employers' reneging their agreement. The extremists in the CNT felt that the collapse of the mixed commission and the renewal of social warfare had to lead, necessarily, to their much desired revolution. They exhorted the workers to ignore the lockouts and to occupy the factories, assuring them that their example would be followed throughout Spain and that the government did not have the needed military power to oppose a workers' insurrection throughout the nation.

On December 10, 1919, the CNT held a congress in the Teatro de la Comedia in Madrid; 437 delegates met, of whom 128 represented Catalan unions. Many of the latter were young extremists who advocated libertarian communism. More moderate delegates from Asturias, conscious of organized labor's defeat two years earlier, proposed a fusion with the UGT; Salvador Seguí supported the Asturian motion, while Angel Pestaña favored the creation of a national, apolitical labor organization that the UGT could join within a prescribed period of time. The formula that was finally adopted allowed all of the workers of Spain to join the CNT within three months; within the same time period the UGT would be given the opportunity to join the CNT.

The CNT congress also resolved that it supported the principles of the First International as approved by Bakunin and that it would temporarily join the Third International—or Communist International—until new policies would be established by a new Universal Workers' Congress.

The congress also declared that the principal goal pursued by the CNT was the establishment of libertarian communism. The ultraleft orientation of this congress was further evidenced by its condemnation of any negotiations with the government or with the Employers' Federation.

1920 was a year of economic contraction and of growing unemployment accompanied by inflation—which contributed to increased strike activity and the number of *atentados*. The year started with a group of soldiers and workers taking over the Carmen barracks in Zaragoza; a captain and a sergeant were killed in the fray that occurred on the night of January 8. Hours later, the Civil Guard took possession of the barracks and executed two days later a corporal and six soldiers as mutineers. In the Cortes, Lerroux complained that "the Soviets are knocking at the doors of military barracks," while the Socialists argued that although the government had allowed the prompt execution of the soldiers in Zaragoza, it had failed to take any punitive action against the rebellious military *juntas de defensa* in 1917.

In January, an attempt to assassinate Salvador Seguí was followed by an attempted murder of Jaime Graupera, the president of the Employers' Federation. The wounding of Graupera infuriated Milans del Bosch, who ordered the closing down of all unions in Barcelona and the suspension of publication of *Solidaridad Obrera*. More than 100 union leaders were arrested.

The newly appointed civil governor, Count Salvatierra, then ordered the dissolution of the CRT. The timing of this order coincided with the end of the long lockout in Barcelona, which had left thousands of workers unemployed and unpaid since November 1919. As the CRT started to operate as an underground organization, its moderate syndicalist leadership was gradually replaced by extremists coming form anarchist "action groups."

The CNT leadership met secretly in Barcelona during the same month, and the majority of those present agreed that *pistolerismo* had to be stopped. Both Seguí and Pestaña warned of the grave dangers that continuing terrorism could have for organized labor. Their warnings, however, had little effect on both employers and the *sindicatos*.

Terrorism actually expanded in 1920 with the founding of the *sindicatos libres*, free trade unions that rejected as a goal any type of social revolution. Grouped into a *Corporación General del Trabajo* (CGT), these unions claimed to be pure trade union organizations that were not controlled or influenced by either employers or the military and that were free of any political or religious inclination. Rivalry with the CRT unions led to new acts of violence; the "free unions," which initially repudiated violence, soon started hiring gunmen to protect their leaders against anarchist terror.

Eduardo Dato, who succeeded Allendesalazar as prime minister, was convinced that the social turbulence in Catalonia in 1920 was simply a repeat performance of the 1917 situation. In 1917, he had allied himself with the military to fight labor; in 1920, he would bring the Catalan employers and the Lliga on his side in a similar fight and he would take a hard position against labor by installing the tough General Martínez Anido as civil governor of Barcelona. Dato's decision to treat labor harshly was evidenced by his choice of Count Gabino Bugallal as minister of the interior, a man who would not shrink from the use of force to destroy the Catalan unions.

Reacting to the obvious implications of a government entente with the Employers' Federation, the Lliga, and the army, the UGT appealed again to the CNT for labor unity. Early in September, an alliance between the UGT and the CNT was signed by the leaders of the two organizations in Madrid.

Pistolerismo went on. On October 11 a metallurgical employer was assassinated, and on the thirtieth, anarchist gunmen killed the president of the Electrical Employers' Association. Martínez Anido decided to prepare a "definitive pacification" of labor, and in order to achieve this goal, he decided to close down all of the unions in Catalonia and to remove from the masses of workers all labor leaders, whether extremist anarchosyndicalists or moderate syndicalists. His plan was carried out on the night of November 20 and during the following days. The CNT leadership was arrested, even Seguí was imprisoned—but the *atentados* went on.

The CNT was not to recuperate from this action, and 1920 was to mark the beginning of its decline. In Catalonia, the *sindicatos libres* offered to many workers an alternative to unions whose funds were exhausted by the claims of the gunmen and whose leaders were in prison.

The strength of Spanish organized labor in 1920 would have been greater had the CNT and the UGT joined forces. Spanish labor unity was impeded by ideological differences between and within the two major labor organizations. A development that set them apart was the establishment of the Third, or Communist, International in Moscow on March 2, 1919. The Comintern appealed for the support of the world's revolutionary workers and gave them a vision of an imminent social revolution desired by all. Its libertarian, antiparliamentarian, and revolutionary ideology was to intensify differences in views within the Spanish labor movement.

Within the Spanish Socialist party, the Center-Right, represented by such men as Iglesias, Besteiro, García Quejido, and Fabra Rivas, believed

that the Spanish proletariat was not strong enough and sufficiently prepared to carry out by itself a social revolution; the latter had to follow
a republican regime and time was needed to organize the Spanish
proletariat. They professed to believe in a revolution, but, like Karl
Kautsky, they felt that this revolution would occur in an undetermined
furture when the required conditions for its success would be present.
Their policy of dogmatic belief in a revolution accompanied by cautious
reformism was supported by such UGT leaders as Manuel Llaneza,
Trifón Gómez, Vicente Barrio, and José María Suárez, who were also opposed to any "spontaneous" workers' action that could lead to a repeti-
tion of the events of August 1917. Farther to the right of this group stood
Oscar Pérez Solís, who advocated nonrevolutionary reformism.

The party's "New Left" and its organ, *Nuestra Palabra*, had accepted
Bolshevism and hoped to convince the entire party to adhere to the Third
International. In this group were Mariano García Cortés, Ramón
Lamoneda, César R. González, Virginia González, and Manuel Núñez de
Arenas. They were supported by the men of the "New School": Eduardo
Torralba Beci, Julio Alvarez del Vayo, Luis Araquistáin, Leopoldo Alas,
Andrés Ovejero, Manuel Pedroso, and Manuel Núñez de Arenas. These
men, who considered themselves to be Spanish democratic "Fabians" in
1918, embraced Leninism and Bolshevism one year later.

Growing unemployment and inflation also induced many rank and
file Socialists to become converts to the Third International. The Socialist
Youth, greatly disappointed by the failure of the 1917 general strike, set
aside *Pablismo* in order to worship Bolshevism. The majority of the party
in 1919 seemed to favor adherence to the Communist International. This
was evidenced at the Socialist party congress in Madrid of December 10–
15, 1919. At that congress, only a compromise arrangement and the desire of most delegates not to bring about a split in the party avoided a
resolution to have the party adhere to the Comintern. The compromise,
offered by the Asturian Isidro Acevedo, pointed out that the party would
remain within the Second International until its next international congress, but if the latter should be unable to join all the Socialist parties of
the world because of differences with the Third International, then the
Spanish Socialist party would adhere to the Third International. The decision to remain within the Second International therefore was very
provisional.

The CNT congress, meeting just a few blocks away in the Teatro de
la Comedia, was dominated by its revolutionary anarchist elements and
resolved to adhere to the Third International and to send Angel Pestaña,
Salvador Quemades, and Eusebio Carbó to Moscow to formalize this act.

The Madrid-based National Committee of the Young Socialist Federation (FJS) decided in February 1920 to transform this organization into

a Communist party. The decision reflected the disappointment and the anger of the FJS leaders due to the failure of the Socialist party to adhere to the Third International. They may also have been influenced by the short and accidental visit in Madrid of Michael Borodin, an agent of the Comintern. The National Committee asked the FJS local committees throughout Spain to have their membership decide on April 15 whether or not they wanted to transform the FJS into a Spanish Communist party. Following the approval of the idea by the great majority of the membership, the Partido Comunista Español (PCE) was founded, its principal goal being the establishment in Spain of a dictatorship of the proletariat. Its young leaders, all of them in their twenties, changed the name of the FJS journal *Renovación* to that of *El Comunista*.

The supporters of the Third International within the Socialist party, the *Terceristas*, were increasing in number and in enthusiasm. The strength of their voice became quite obvious during the 1920 congress of the Socialist party, which convened on June 19 in the Casa del Pueblo in Madrid. Daniel Anguiano and Manuel Núñez de Arenas spoke in favor of the Comintern; Prieto, Llaneza, Pérez Solís, and Besteiro argued in favor of remaining loyal to the Second International. The congress adopted the temporary decision of joining the Communist International; Anguiano and Fernando de los Ríos were to travel to Russia and evaluate from direct observation the Third International. Upon their return and based on their recommendations, a final decision regarding adherence would be taken.

A new Executive Commission was elected. Pablo Iglesias remained the party's president and a member of this commission; the other members were Antonio García Quejido, Daniel Anguiano, Ramón Lamoneda, Antonio Fabra Ribas, Manuel Núñez de Arenas, Andrés Ovejero, Luis Araquistáin, López Baeza, César Rodríguez González, and Fernando de los Ríos. The great majority of these men were *Terceristas*.

Following the PSOE congress, the UGT held its own on June 23. Those who expected that the UGT would follow the international policy of the Socialist party were soon surprised; the UGT decided to remain loyal to the Syndicalist Federation of Amsterdam, an affiliate of the Second International. The cautious UGT leadership convinced the delegates that the Spanish proletariat was not ready for revolution and that hard-won economic gains should not be sacrificed to adventurism. The delegates responded by relegating any revolutionary fervor to rhetoric while actually embracing cautious reformism.

The UGT leadership also advocated the unification of Spain's two largest labor organizations and suggested the formation of a CNT-UGT commission to study how such a fusion could take place. Finally, the congress decided to replace craft unions by industrial unions.

The Communist International held its second congress in Moscow from July 23 to August 7. Its main goal was to define the ideology and the structure of Communist parties that would join it in the future, so as to minimize interparty ideological or structural differences. Lenin desired the formation of strong and homogeneous Communist parties outside the Soviet Union. In order to achieve this objective, "21 Conditions" were voted by the congress that were to be necessary prerequisites for the adherence by new parties to the Communist International. This congress also decided to found an International Communist Trade Union Organization whose first congress would be held in 1921.

On August 26, the national committee of the CNT responded with little enthusiasm to the proposed UGT-CNT fusion, finding it difficult to be implemented at a time when the CNT had joined the Third International while the UGT maintained its loyalty to the Amsterdam International. Nevertheless, as already observed, a UGT-CNT pact was signed a few days later in Madrid.

The Socialist party had not definitely decided whether or not it would adhere to the Third International. Fernando de los Ríos and Daniel Anguiano had returned from Russia with very different conclusions that were to be presented to a new congress of the party held in April 1921. While Anguiano spoke in favor of the Comintern, de los Ríos urged the party not to join the Communist International, among other reasons because the Soviet government denied its people freedom of thought and of expression and because Russian workers were not allowed to change their occupations. Andrés Saborit, Francisco Largo Caballero, and Julián Besteiro also pointed out that if the Socialist party joined the Comintern it would have to accept its "21 Conditions" and these would force the party to expel valuable right-wing members.

The delegates voted against joining the Third International, causing what Pablo Iglesias feared would happen and tried hard to avoid: a party schism. The *Terceristas* decided to abandon the PSOE and to form a new party, the Communist Labor party, or Partido Comunista Obrero (PCO). This party's first national committee included Antonio García Quejido, Manuel Núñez de Arenas, Daniel Anguiano, Facundo Perezagua, and Virginia González. Eduardo Torralba Beci was to be the editor of the party's organ, *La Guerra Social*.

The founding of the PCO meant that there were two Communist parties in Spain at that time, the new Communist Labor party and the Spanish Communist party formed one year earlier. Negotiations aimed at fusion of the two parties failed in May 1921, largely because the young leadership of the PCE insisted on purging the PCO of "nonreliable" individuals and on dictating common ideology and tactics.

There was one more group in Spain that was inspired by Lenin's idea of an elitist core of professionals leading the masses to revolution. These were the Communist-syndicalists.

Communism-syndicalism acquired some influence in the CNT as "pure" syndicalists and anarchosyndicalists lost their positions in the unions in the wave of arrests instigated by Martínez Anido. The Communist-syndicalists, under the leadership of two former bourgeois intellectuals, Joaquín Maurín and Andrés Nin, followed the Leninist position that labor organizations had to be transformed into centralized and disciplined revolutionary forces. They were quite willing to cooperate with other revolutionary movements in order to achieve a Bolshevik-type revolution. The objectives of Maurín and Nin were to move the CNT away from syndicalist or anarchosyndicalist ideologies, and, taking advantage of the popular enthusiasm for the Bolshevik Revolution, establish within the CNT a well-disciplined pro-Bolshevik leadership. The Communist-syndicalists opposed both anarchist individualism and the questionable dedication to revolution of the syndicalists.

Nin had been a journalist who edited the republican journal *Poble Català* and became a great enthusiast of the Bolshevik Revolution; his revolutionary ardor was duplicated by Maurín, an Aragonese schoolteacher who believed in Sorelian collective violence as a necessary means to regenerate society. In 1921, Nin replaced Evelio Boal, who had been arrested, as acting secretary-general of the CNT National Committee.

At a secret meeting of the CNT leadership held in Lérida on April 28, 1921, it was decided that a CNT delegation would be sent to Moscow to represent the Spanish labor organization at the first congress of the Profintern, the Communist International of Labor Unions. The group selected included Nin and Maurín and other Communist-syndicalists, such as Hilario Arlandis and Jesús Ibáñez.

In Moscow, the Spaniards quickly realized that the majority of the Profintern delegates had given their approval to the Russian proposal that the Communist International of Labor Unions should accept political guidance from the Communist International. Acceptance of the proposal would subject the Profintern to the dictates of the Third International. The Spanish Communist-syndicalists, though eager to please their Bolshevik friends, were not quite willing to inform their CNT brethren that they would have to take guidance from the PCE or from the PCO. They therefore suggested that political leadership in any given country should not automatically vest in its Communist party, but should only belong to it if its size was larger than that of the revolutionary labor organization; the congress rejected this idea. In the end, the Spaniards supported the resolution that the Third International alone was to lead the revolutionary labor organizations of the world. The Comintern and its Communist parties were to dominate politically the labor organizations that adhered to the Profintern.

In Catalonia, however, the Communist-syndicalists were not inclined to accept the dictates of the Spanish Communist party. Regional and syndicalist pride prevented them from bowing to the politicians in Madrid. Also, the Catalan Communist-syndicalists were very much concerned by a resurgence of traditional anarchist views among many *Cenetistas.* The repression tactics of Martínez Anido had considerably weakened the *sindicatos únicos,* and *pistolerismo* had come to an end by 1922. The "decapitation" of the Catalan labor movement had tarnished the vision of the Bolshevik Revolution among workers; many ceased dreaming about the dictatorship of the proletariat and reverted to prior, established views.

Anarchist ideology had a revival in the years 1921 to 1923, a revival that cast aside the belief in statist or authoritarian dogmas. Even the anarchosyndicalists started stressing the anarchist ideal of educating the masses and the need to return to old libertarian values. Most *Cenetistas* started favoring the cautious reformism of the syndicalists, and this meant a rejection of the Profintern resolutions. A new journal published in Madrid, *Nueva Senda,* started criticizing the acceptance of Communist leadership by the Nin-Maurín delegation; it pointed out that the CNT was, after all, a libertarian movement based on the ideas of Bakunin, a movement that necessarily rejected authority of any kind. Following this position, an anti-Bolshevik CNT group met secretly in Madrid in August 1921 to reaffirm the anarchist spirit of the labor organization and to reassert its independence of any political party.

While anarchist sentiment within the CNT was growing stronger, the Comintern leadership in Moscow decided to send emissaries to Madrid to attempt a fusion of the two Spanish Communist parties. The first Comintern agent was an Italian professor, Antonio Graziadei. For two weeks in November 1921, Graziadei mediated negotiations for fusion between the PCO and the PCE; Manuel Núñez de Arenas represented the PCO, Gonzalo Sanz the PCE. It was finally decided that until the first congress of the new united party would be held, nine seats in the new Central Committee of the new party would be taken by the PCE and six by the PCO. In exchange for this advantage, the PCE agreed to refrain from demanding the expulsion from the new party of any member of the PCO. The new party's organ was to be a journal edited by the moderate PCE member Rafael Millá, with Juan Andrade of the PCE and Manuel Nuñez de Arenas of the former PCO becoming assistant editors of the newspaper, to be called *La Antorcha.*

Shortly after Graziadei's departure from Spain, the leader of the initial PCE, Ramón Merino Gracia, returned from the Soviet Union. Merino Gracia now advocated the line laid down by the third congress of the Comintern, a political message that could not be accepted by his ultraleftist colleagues in the initial PCE. Merino Gracia now preached caution and moderation, avoidance of "adventurism," and cooperation with other revolutionary groups. Joined by two ex-PCE members and by the PCO representation on the combined party's Central Committee, he promptly established a new majority within that body. When, on December 4, the majority of that committee voted to participate in municipal elections, the ultraleftists in that body decided to oppose that decision and to form a separate Communist entity, the Spanish Communist Group. This dissident group published on January 1, 1922 a manifesto in which the dissidents declared themselves loyal to the Third International but opposed to the "centrist reformism" of the majority of the Spanish Communist party. The members of the Central Committee of that party responded by suspending from office all those who had signed the manifesto.

The Comintern decided to intervene once again and sent to Spain Jules Humbert-Droz, Comintern secretary for the Latin Countries. Humbert-Droz lectured the Spanish Communists about the importance of party discipline; he gave the young dissidents a choice between respecting the party's hierarchy and decisions or expulsion from the party. Most of the young rebels decided to remain in the party. The problem of internal factionalism in the Spanish Communist party appeared to be solved. The party, however, faced other equally important problems.

In the north, the Communists had tried with little success to capture traditionally Socialist miners' and metallurgical workers' unions. Young, inexperienced, violence-prone Communists proved to be no match for the more experienced and cautious Socialist union leadership. UGT and Communist leaders were confronted by determined employers who had resolved to cut wages to compensate for falling profits. The Communists generally took an intransigent position and threatened to strike in order to attract workers to their side. In Vizcaya, the Socialists tried to preserve their unions by negotiating with employers and trying to minimize wage cuts.

The Communists faced a dilemma. The third Comintern congress had prescribed the formation of "united fronts" to be formed by Communist parties and other leftist groups in order to consolidate revolutionary forces at a time of rising capitalist offensive. The idea of a united front implied the cooperation of the Communist party with other leftist parties. In Vizacaya and in Asturias, Communists were battling Socialists in an attempt to establish a Communist trade union movement in the north.

On April 10, 1922, the Spanish Communist party, without the concurrence of the Socialists, claimed to act on behalf of a united front and ordered a strike in the Vizcayan mines. The Socialists, having signed wage reduction agreements with the employers, did not strike. The authorities started arresting Communist leaders.

In Asturias, the Socialist union leadership tried to prevent a strike after the mine owners announced wage cuts; the miners decided, however, to go on strike. Their strike was followed by that of Vizcayan metalworkers. The Communists proposed once more that all Spanish labor organizations should form a united front. The national committees of the UGT and the CNT rejected the proposal.

In 1922, the Spanish labor movement appeared more divided than ever. In the north, a violent rivalry between Communists and Socialists went on; in Catalonia, rivalry separated the anarchosyndicalists and the *sindicatos libres;* elsewhere there was hostility between syndicalists and the Catholic trade union movement, and everywhere there were ill feelings between anarchosyndicalists and Socialists.

There continued to be factionalism within the Spanish Communist party. In the north, young party members had joined the Communist party because they felt it offered the most radical solution to labor problems; they had no interest in politics and considered themselves to be essentially Bolshevik trade union leaders. They did not identify with the "political" majoritarians in the party in Madrid and were accused by the latter of having embraced anarchosyndicalism; their antipolitical stance should have attracted the sympathy of the Madrid ultraleft Communists, but the latter found in the northern "syndicalists" too little interest in political dogma. The result was that there was little rapport between provincial Communist leaders and those in Madrid, and the poor organization of the party and the successful efforts of the police to jail its leaders discouraged many workers from joining it.

In Catalonia, whatever remained of the CNT after the harsh repression of Martínez Anido weighted the possibilities of survival by reexamining past policy. While shots were still traded between members of the *sindicatos únicos* and the *sindicatos libres,* talks were initiated in an attempt to unify the two Catalan labor organizations. The problem of the conflict between the anarchosyndicalist and the Communist-syndicalist ideologies within the CNT had to be solved. As the members' enthusiasm for Soviet leadership declined in 1922, a majority within the CNT felt that the time had come to take the organization out of the Comintern. A CNT leader, Manuel Buenacasa, felt that the CNT should instead adhere to the anarchosyndicalist International, the International Association of Workers, which was to meet in Berlin on June 16 of that year.

The CNT leadership gathered for a conference at Zaragoza on June 11. The great majority decided to submit through a referendum the question of the CNT's separation from the Comintern to the entire membership of the labor organization; the membership would also express its views regarding the desirability of the CNT's adherence to the anarchosyndicalist International. The majority also declared that the CNT was a political organization that should participate in matters affecting national "moral, economic, social, and political problems."

It appeared that in 1922 harsh government repression had discouraged the anarchist militants within the CNT from undertaking further acts of individual terrorism. There were signs that the government of Sánchez Guerra in Madrid was predisposed to tolerate a better behaved CNT; many of its militants were released from jail, and publication of *Solidaridad Obrera* was allowed once more in Barcelona. Angel Pestaña and Salvador Seguí assured their audiences that although the CNT rejected parliamentarism, it was opposed to violence.

Pistoleros, probably under orders from Martínez Anido, nearly ended the life of Pestaña on August 25. Pestaña recovered and once again gave assurances that the CNT would no longer follow the path of terrorism. This was not to be so. Anarchist "action groups" were not only witnessing a revival but now followed a better organized and more centralized direction, very much influenced by a group known as *Los Solidarios,* whose members were to found in 1927 the Federation of Iberian Anarchists, or Federación de Anarquistas Ibéricos (FAI). Leading this group were Francisco Ascaso, Rafael Escartín, Buenaventura Durruti, Juan García Oliver, and Ricardo Sanz. In the spring of 1923, anarchists were commanding again a number of *sindicatos únicos*. Warfare with the *sindicatos libres* had resumed leading to the assassination of Salvador Seguí on March 10, 1923, apparently by gunmen of the *libres* trying to avenge shootings perpetrated by the anarchist *pistoleros*.

Violence also characterized the fifteenth congress of the UGT. The meetings started on November 19, 1922. On the following day, as the guest speakers Léon Jouhaux and J. Oudegeest were about to address the delegates, a number of Communist delegates started protesting; shots were fired, and a security guard, Manuel González Portillo, was killed. The police intervened and arrested a number of Communists in the gathering, among them Núñez de Arenas and Virginia González. The *Ugetista* leadership then obtained a congressional resolution to expel all Communist delegations from the congress; 15 unions opposing this decision were also expelled from the UGT. Besteiro had feared that the congress would have resulted in schism; the murder of González Portillo saved the situation by uniting most member unions around the UGT leadership. A new Executive Commission was elected with Pablo Iglesias as president, Julián Besteiro as vice-president, and Francisco Largo Caballero as secretary; the remaining members were Andrés Saborit, Vicente Barrios, Antonio Fabra Ribas, Lucio Martínez, Manuel Cordero, Francisco Núñez, Trifón Gómez, and Luis Fernández.

The period 1914–23 had brought greater disunion to the Spanish labor movement. Instead of reducing labor factionalism, the excitement caused by World War I and the Bolshevik Revolution only strengthened the dogmatism of the various groups. As long as Socialists, anarchosyndicalists, Communist-syndicalists, and Communists were unable to agree and cooperate, the efforts of the working class to improve its social and economic conditions were doomed to failure. During the early 1920s, many workers in Spain continued to be plagued by lockouts, dismissals, and extended periods of unemployment. The masses of workers continued to suffer from social alienation, and the neofeudal characteristics of extremes of wealth and poverty still characterized Spanish society.

As economic recovery began in Europe, and more slowly in Spain, revolutionary ardor everywhere was weakened. In January 1923 the Second International proclaimed its anti-Communist position and in the autumn of 1922 Mussolini's "black shirts" were, with their "march to Rome," to introduce Fascism in Europe.

In 1923, the Socialist party in Spain counted only 8,215 members (Tuñón 1972, vol. II, p. 349). The party had become purely reformist in tactics, and after the schisms it experienced, no Socialist leader talked any longer about a coming social revolution. The Communists were numerically weak, and ideological differences kept the party factionalized. The anarchosyndicalists, having lost a great part of their trade union membership, discouraged potential followers through their practice of individual terrorism.

By mid-1923, there simply was no evidence that Spanish organized labor threatened a major socioeconomic revolution. There were stikes in Vizcaya but they never amounted to a national calamity.

What bothered the military at that time was the question of "responsibility" for the great defeat in July 1921 at Annual in Morocco; on that occasion, Spanish troops led by General Fernández Silvestre were routed by the Berbers and suffered more than 8,000 casualties. A government commission established to investigate the military blunder was to publish its findings on October 1, 1923. It was this military crisis rather than a fear of a coming workers' revolution that induced a number of generals to plan a coup d'état that was to establish in Spain a new dictatorship under the command of the captain-general of Catalonia, General Primo de Rivera. The coup succeeded on September 13, 1923.

FROM THE PRIMO DE RIVERA DICTATORSHIP TO THAT OF FRANCO

The crown's support of the *pronunciamiento* of General Miguel Primo de Rivera and the establishment of the dictatorship suppressed the publication of the findings of the parliamentary commission regarding the causes of the military defeats in Morocco; rumors that the king had been partly responsible for them were silenced. Primo quickly turned public interest away from possible corruption in the army and unconstitutional use of power by the king and centered it on the "irresponsibility" of a parliamentarian government system. Most Spaniards sympathized with Primo's determination to do away with corrupt politicians and to bring social peace to the country. The dictator did not tolerate opposition parties and tried to build up mass support for his policies by establishing the Patriotic Union, a political organization that was critical of individualism and democracy and advocated obedience to Primo's commands.

Primo's view regarding any organized labor movement was that it would be tolerated as long as it did not constitute a threat to his regime. The Communist party was promptly declared illegal at the end of 1923, and a number of its leaders were arrested. In the following year, the government ordered all CNT meeting halls closed and suspended the publication of *Solidaridad Obrera.*

The Socialist leadership refused to stage with the CNT a large anti-Primo demonstration in Madrid. Although angered by the suppression of parliamentarian political life, the Socialists refrained from taking any overt acts of hostility against the new government. The Primo government in turn allowed the Casas del Pueblo to remain open.

The UGT tried to collaborate with the new regime. Manuel Llaneza, head of the Asturian miners, received, at the end of September, an invitation to come to Madrid for personal talks with Primo de Rivera. Without consulting anyone within the UGT or the PSOE, Llaneza took the train for Madrid on October 1, and, upon his arrival in the capital, he was escorted directly to a meeting with Primo. Only after the meeting did Llaneza consult with his colleagues in the UGT and in the PSOE. Most of them appeared to agree to some sort of an entente among the dictatorship, the Socialists, and their trade unions; only Indalecio Prieto and Fernando de los Ríos opposed any type of collaboration with the government.

On November 23, the civil governor of Madrid, the Duke of Tetuán, visited the Casa del Pueblo in Madrid and praised the services it rendered. The meeting probably confirmed an informal pact of toleration between the army and the Socialists. On January 9, 1924, however, the national committee of the Socialist party resolved that no Socialist should participate in Primo's government unless the office was the result of free elections. On this basis, the Socialists agreed not to be part of the newly formed Consultative National Assembly.

On May 1, 1924, the government prohibited all workers' demonstrations. In September, a royal decree reorganized the Council of State and Primo invited the *Ugetistas* to participate in it; when the latter elected Largo Caballero for the position and he accepted to sit in the council as a paid functionary, Prieto gave up his seat in the Executive Committee of the PSOE to dramatize his opposition to the party's cooperation with the dictatorial government. Largo Caballero, on the other hand, used his position in the government to strengthen the PSOE and the UGT during the 1920s. When the dictatorship came to an end in 1930, Largo Caballero, to survive politically, quickly adopted a different political position.

The quiescence of the UGT and of the *sindicatos libres* allowed these labor organizations to function freely during the dictatorship. When, in 1926, the government established "parity committees" made up of representatives of government, the employers, and labor to settle wage disputes, UGT leaders sat on these committees and became, in effect, government bureaucrats.

In 1928, the Primo de Rivera government appointed the members of a Consultative National Assembly; the *Ugetistas* Largo Caballero, Núñez Tomás, Lucio Martínez, Santiago Pérez, Fernando de los Ríos, and Llaneza received appointments as labor representatives. All declined to serve in the assembly, and their decision was supported by extraordinary congresses of the Socialist party and of the UGT. The latter proposed, however, that it would send delegates to the assembly if their selection was left to the free choice of the labor organization.

Pablo Iglesias had died on December 9, 1925. The presidencies of the Socialist party and of the UGT were given to Julián Besteiro. Besteiro advocated peaceful coexistence with the dictatorship. He presented this view at the twelfth congress of the Socialist party, which met in the Casa del Pueblo in Madrid from June 29 to July 4, 1928. The majority of the delegates supported Besteiro's position, while a minority, led by Indalecio Prieto and Teodomiro Menéndez, urged the party to oppose the Primo regime. A new Executive Committee was elected composed of Besteiro, Largo Caballero, Andrés Saborit, Lucio Martínez, Wenceslao Carrillo, Fernando de los Ríos, Trifón Gómez, Andrés Ovejero, Manuel Cordero, Anastasio de Gracia, and Aníbal Sánchez.

In September of the same year, the UGT held its sixteenth congress, which elected to its Executive Committee practically all of the same men who served on the Executive Committee of the Socialist party.

Immediately after Primo's *pronunciamiento,* the CNT declared a general strike, which, without Socialist support and proper preparation, was doomed to failure. On December 30, the CRT held a plenum at Granollers and another one at Sabadell on May 2, 1924. On both occasions, this Catalan labor organization affirmed its dedication to anarchist principles. When a Barcelona police official was assassinated a few days after the Sabadell meeting, Primo's government ordered the arrest of all the CNT committee members and of all the members of anarchist groups the police could locate. The CNT was driven underground; in order to avoid arrest, many of its members joined the legal *sindicatos libres.* At the same time, anarchist "action groups" continued their desperate acts of terrorism, which generally ended in failure.

Illegality and arrests were not the only factors that weakened the CNT in the 1920s; perhaps of greater importance was the internal factionalism that tended to separate the moderate followers of Seguí and Pestaña from the revolution-impatient "pure" anarchists. The latter, at a secret conference held at Valencia on July 24 and 25, 1927, organized the Iberian Anarchist Federation (FAI), an organization established primarily to keep the CNT faithful to anarchist principles. The FAI was organized on the basis of small, secret "affinity groups," groups of no more than a dozen persons who knew each other well and were to act largely on the basis of group initiative. Groups were linked by a Local Federation, and these federations constituted in turn District and Regional Federations. A Peninsular Committee acted as an administrative center.

Under the influence of men such as García Oliver, Durruti, and the Ascaso brothers, the Peninsular Committee quickly took the role of a Bolshevik-type Central Committee; its directives were, however, interpreted by the "affinity groups" in a discretionary fashion and the latter remained very autonomous in their activities. Many of these groups were formed by young people who were more interested in dramatic acts of violence against the established order than in the inner politics of the CNT.

The leadership of the FAI, however, was very much concerned with ousting the moderates from the CNT national committee. These militant anarchists were dedicated to the destruction of the state, regardless of its form, whether monarchical, dictatorial, or republican. This view necessarily clashed with that of the moderates who controlled the leading CNT committees. The moderates viewed the revolutionary movement as consisting of two stages. Initially, a bourgeois republic should be formed in which the CNT would play an accommodating role as a legal labor organization; in an uncertain future, the bourgeois republic would be followed by a libertarian society. Although neither faction clung consistently and inflexibly to these views over time, their differences were to cause a split in Spanish anarchosyndicalism.

In the 1920s, Spain, under the rule of General Primo de Rivera, had experienced improved standards of living and rising profits. Primo's rule, in Payne's (1973) words "was probably the most gentle and liberal 'dictatorship' of twentieth-century Europe, unstained by a single political execution" (p. 624).

As of 1928, several social groups, most of them belonging to the political Right, started showing open hostility to the Primo regime. Primo's rejection of regionalism, with his dissolution of Catalonia's regional government, the *Mancomunitat*, turned the Catalan bourgeoisie against him. The wealthy opposed the tax reform program proposed by Primo's finance minister, José Calvo Sotelo. The large landowners apprehended that the dictator would embrace agrarian reform. Intellectuals and students wanted a return to constitutional government, and military officers resented Primo's attempt to alter their seniority-based promotion system. The general, feeling that the officer corps no longer supported him, resigned on January 29, 1929, and left for Paris, where he died a few months later.

As noted, Indalecio Prieto and Fernando de los Ríos favored a Socialist-republican alliance. Both men participated in a conspiratorial meeting of republican leaders that was held in San Sebastián on August 17, 1930. There, both Socialists had agreed to participate in the provisional government of a republic and to cooperate with the reformist bourgeoisie. On October 20, the Executive Committee of the Socialist party confirmed the Prieto-de los Ríos decision and named Prieto, de los Ríos, and Largo Caballero as potential ministers in a republican government. Not all Socialist leaders voted to support the participation of Socialists in a bourgeois, republican government. Voting against the majority decision were Besteiro, Saborit, Trifón Gómez, Anastasio de Gracia, Aníbal Sánchez, and Lucio Martínez.

Spontaneous strikes occurred at that time in Bilbao, Murcia, Logroño, Málaga, and Seville. The CNT organized strikes in Barcelona, Madrid, Alicante, and elsewhere.

The San Sebastián conspirators had fixed December 15, 1930 as the date for an all-out uprising against the monarchy. The CNT had agreed to support this revolutionary effort but the Communists decided not to cooperate with the San Sebastián conspiracy. General strikes were launched in a number of Spanish cities and in the northern mining areas on December 15; in a number of localities strikes continued until the nineteenth. These strikes failed to force the collapse of the monarchy; the objective of the San Sebastián conspiracy had not been reached. One of the reasons for this failure was that no strikes occurred in Madrid because Largo Caballero never gave an order to the workers to strike.

The government of General Damasco Berenguer, which had succeeded that of Primo de Rivera, was replaced on February 19, 1931 by the government of Admiral Aznar. This government called for municipal elections to test the strength of the monarchy. The resulting Socialist-republican electoral victory induced Alfonso XIII to leave Spain in order to avoid a possible civil war. The abdication of the king marked the birth of the Second Republic on April 14, 1931.

The Socialist party held an extraordinary congress in July, three months after the proclamation of the republic. This congress agreed on a minimum program that was to be presented to the constituent assembly, which was to open its sessions days later. The Socialists demanded the nationalization of railroads, banks, mines, and forests, social security, agrarian reform, a divorce law and a neutral position on the part of the state in regard to religion, a progressive income tax, secular education, and government support of regionalist movements.

The party's thirteenth congress was held in Madrid, October 6–13, 1932. Its main debate centered on the question of Socialist participation in the republican government. This government had three Socialist ministers. Indalecio Prieto spoke in favor of such participation and claimed that it was necessary in order to safeguard the leftist orientation of the government. His views were shared by Besteiro and Largo Caballero. A majority of the delegates agreed with Prieto. A new Executive Committee was elected and the party's presidency was given to Largo Caballero. The committee included Remigio Cabello, Enrique de Francisco, Juan Simeón Vidarte, Pascual Tomás, Fernando de los Ríos, Indalecio Prieto, Manuel Cordero, Anastasio de Gracia, Wenceslao Carrillo, and Antonio Fabra Ribas.

The UGT held it seventeenth congress starting on October 14. Besteiro was elected president, and a new Executive Committee was formed by "conservative" and reformist Socialists.

Both the Socialist party and the UGT had experienced enormous growth because of their cooperation with the government of the republic. The party counted 16,878 members in June 1930, 25,000 in June 1931, and more than 75,000 in October 1932. The UGT's membership rose from 287,333 in December 1930 to more than 1 million in June 1932 (Tuñón 1972, vol. III, p. 115). This spectacular growth was also due to the UGT's efforts to attract to its ranks the poor *braceros* of southern Spain. In April 1930, the UGT founded a separate labor organization, the Federación Nacional de Trabajadores de la Tierra (FNTT), or the National Federation of Land Workers, which started with a membership of 27,000 that reached 451,000 by June 1933.

The massive influx of poor, land-hungry, impatient rural workers into the FNTT strengthened the left-wing orientation of the rural labor organization, and this orientation was to gain strength in the Socialist party.

The CNT viewed with alarm the creation of the FNTT and its success in areas of CNT strength. Other developments intensified the hostility that the *Cenetistas* felt for the UGT. The government of the republic had passed a law that made it illegal for a labor organization to strike before it had presented its grievances to a mixed jury composed by an equal number of representatives of employers and of labor; the latter was to propose a settlement between the parties, the settlement not being mandatory on either party. If the members of the jury could not arrive at a decision because of a tie vote, a government representative could then vote to break the tie. Largo Caballero, as minister of labor, appointed Socialists as government representatives sitting in these mixed juries; this allowed the *Ugetistas* to gain a majority vote in the juries and gave them a major role in settling labor-management disputes. The anarchosyndicalists correctly perceived that the way in which this law was implemented strengthened UGT influence over the masses of workers at the expense of the CNT. The law also angered the *Cenetistas,* who preferred to deal directly with the employer.

The conflict between the CNT and the UGT became a three-way confrontation in Seville. Although the Communist party had very little influence on Spanish labor, it had succeeded in obtaining control of a number of unions in Seville; in the Andalusian capital, employers, Communists, *Ugetistas,* and *Cenetistas* started using *pistolero* terrorism against each other. In Catalonia, the Communists formed a new organization, the Bloc Obrer y Camperol (BOC) or Worker-Peasant Bloc, which advocated cooperation between the working class and leftist-bourgeois groups. Others, grouping around Trotskyist ideas, formed the Izquierda Comunista (Left-Communists), which outnumbered the Spanish Communist party in Catalonia and probably in the entirety of Spain. In 1936, these two organizations were to merge to form the Partido Obrero de Unificación Marxista, (POUM), the Workers' Party of Marxist Unification.

During 1931–33, the Socialists faced a number of problems besides those presented by anarchists and Communists. The platform of the republican-Socialist coalition had four principal goals: the separation of church and state and the curtailment of the church's privileges, the recognition of regional autonomies, social and economic reforms, and military reforms. The strong anticlerical position of the republican-Left, as well as that of many Socialists, turned masses of tradition-minded Spaniards against the republic from its inception. When Manuel Azaña, the leader of the republican-Left, decided to reduce the size of the army and to retire about half the officer corps at full pay, the republic lost the support of many officers. The fact that Azaña became prime minister in October 1931 did not enhance his prestige among army officers.

The problem of Catalan regionalism appeared to be solved when the government in Madrid enacted in September 1932 the Catalan Statute, which provided for a Catalan government, the *Generalitat,* with its own regional parliament, prime minister, and president. Peace was not to come to Catalonia in the years 1931–33 because of the turmoil generated by the FAI revolutionaries.

What disappointed the Socialists was government action, or rather inaction, in the areas of economic and social reform. A major issue was agrarian reform. The Socialists wanted an extensive reform, the expropriation of most landholdings except for small holdings, and the establishment of collective farms. The republican-Left appeared to be more interested in church-state relations than in a meaningful agrarian reform program. The agrarian reform law that was finally enacted in September 1932 represented a very conservative, complex, and poorly financed program that could not satisfy the land-hungry peasants. The Socialists, who had agreed to participate in the government in order to facilitate the establishment of a Socialist republic, were disappointed. The slow pace of agrarian reform, rising unemployment, and increased strike activity were signs that the bourgeois republic was not the panacea hoped for by the working class. By 1933, the government had not achieved the social and economic reforms wanted by the Socialists; disillusioned, the three Socialist ministers left the government. Disenchantment with the republic was also widespread within the Socialist party, resulting in the replacement of moderate, reformist Socialist leaders by "revolutionaries."

Revolutionary anarchists, mostly members of the FAI, were also to gain greater control of the CNT during these years. On June 10, 1931, the CNT held a congress in the Teatro del Conservatorio in Madrid. This congress was attended by 418 delegates representing 511 unions and 535,565 members (Tuñón 1972, vol. III, p. 135). The delegates quickly grouped themselves into possibilists and reformists. From the start there was little agreement between them. Nevertheless, a minimum program was adopted by the congress that demanded the right to strike, secular schools, and agrarian reform. The *Cenetistas* demanded the expropriation without compensation of all latifundios and the award of the use of parts of such estates to unions of rural workers. Beyond this, extremists and reformists could not agree. The extremists supported immediate revolution, pointing out that the collapse of the dictatorship and of the monarchy were signs that the revolution could be successfully carried out without further delay; the moderates argued that anarchosyndicalism was influencing only a small minority of the working class and that the views of the extremists were those of a minority within a minority.

Many CNT rank and file members, however, shared the revolutionary enthusiasm of the *Faistas*. Their insurrectionary mood was reflected in a number of strikes that developed in July. The first incident was a strike by telephone operators belonging to a CNT union. The strike stopped or restricted telephone communications in a number of key cities; it also resulted in fights between armed workers and government security forces. The strike was declared illegal by the Ministry of Labor. The UGT did not hesitate to provide the telephone company with scab workers. The outcome of the strike was a CNT defeat; the telephone company hired back only those strikers who would acquire membership in the UGT. In Seville, the telephone workers' strike was followed on July

20 by a general strike that lasted nine days. The government imposed martial law on the city and used artillery fire to demolish completely the CNT headquarters.

These events polarized the CNT leadership even more. The extremists claimed that the July strikes and their outcome indicated that the present government was no better than that of the monarchy. The moderates claimed that violence had only created a needless hostility between the government of the republic and the CNT. In August, 30 moderate CNT leaders signed a statement that denounced the policy of violence of the extremists. Angel Pestaña was one of the *Treintistas* who signed the statement. The document stated that the signatories "did not entrust the revolution to more or less audacious minorities, but wanted it to be a sweeping movement of the masses, of the working-class, which would take it to its final liberation . . ."(Tuñón 1972, vol. III, p. 136). The *Treintistas* did not name explicitly the FAI in the statement, but they warned the CNT membership that the tactics of those having a simplistic understanding of the revolution would lead to the establishment of "republican Fascism."

Many Catalan workers, however, shared a great enthusiasm for the action-prone FAI. The FAI had no difficulty in gaining control of the Barcelona CNT unions and of the editorship of *Solidaridad Obrera*. In October, Pestaña was expelled from his own union. The CNT was now controlled by the *Faistas*.

The FAI tactic of violent insurrection was implemented in January 1932. In the towns of the mining area of the Alto Llobregat in Catalonia, miners seized the town halls and proclaimed the establishment of libertarian communism. The government in Madrid dispatched troops to stop the insurrection. When sympathy strikes developed in Barcelona and in other cities, thousands of workers were arrested and jailed. One hundred and four *Cenetistas* were deported to Spanish West Africa, among them, the *Faistas* Durruti and Francisco Ascaso.

The strikes and the insurrections strengthened the reputation of the FAI among the workers and facilitated the ouster of CNT possibilists from their positions in the CNT. The antagonism between moderates and extremists had to lead to a split within the CNT. It finally occurred during the meeting of a regional plenum held at Sabadell in April 1932. A number of federations and of unions representing 70,000 members left the CNT to form their own organization, the Sindicatos de Oposición, the Opposition Unions. Pestaña and other moderates were voted out of the CNT's National Committee and were replaced by militant anarchists, such as Durruti, Ascaso, and Federica Montseny.

In January 1933, this leadership plunged the CNT into further insurrectionary activities. On January 8, anarchist militants attacked military barracks in Barcelona, and acts of insurrection were carried out in various towns of Catalonia, in some villages of the Levant, and in Andalusia. The authorities responded through mass arrests; most of the members of the FAI's Peninsular Committee were arrested and jailed. The arrests, however, did not dispel the dream shared by many urban and rural workers that *comunismo libertario* was about to be established or had been established in many parts of Spain.

This dream led to the tragedy of Casas Viejas, a small village near Jerez de la Frontera. In that village, an old man known as Seisdedos (Six Fingers) believed that the anarchist utopia had finally arrived and that the time had come for him, his family, and friends to take over the village. The local Civil Guard responded by shooting and killing Seisdedos and his group. Prisoners taken from this group were executed and some members of the group perished in a burning barn or were shot as they tried to escape. The news about this incident caused much disenchantment with the government of Manuel Azaña and was undoubtedly an important factor that led to the victory of the political Right at the elections of November 1933.

The CNT continued to launch a massive wave of strikes during the spring of 1933. The CNT leadership also started a major campaign to persuade its membership and workers in general to abstain from voting at the November elections. The militant anarchists reasoned that a victory of the political Right would be followed by a Fascist dictatorship, which, in turn, would bring about a popular revolution. This prediction was to be partly supported by future events.

During the few weeks that followed the establishment of the Second Republic, the Spanish Communist party counted at most 1,500 members. It celebrated its fourth congress at Seville, May 17–20, 1932. José Bullejos, the party's leader, after a sharp attack on the "socialfascists" and the "anarchoreformists," urged the establishment of workers' soviets. His report was followed by that of Manuel Adame, who advocated the maintenance of an ideological struggle with the anarchists of the FAI and a greater effort to induce them to join the Communist party.

The Spanish Communists did not abandon the concept of the United Front as prescribed by the Comintern authorities. On March 16, 1933, the party called on the UGT, the CNT, and the FAI to form a "common front" to oppose a Fascist dictatorship—a plea that they rejected. The Communist party then formed an "Antifascist Front" with the help of small political groups, such as the Federal party and the Left Radical Socialist party, the latter being directed by Eduardo Ortega y Gasset.

The Spanish Communists were aware that one of their main weaknesses was the lack of a labor organization they could direct or influence. In November 1931, they had called for a National Conference of Labor

Unification; the UGT refused to participate in it, and the CNT responded to the invitation to participate with cold silence. One hundred and eighteen delegates, representing more than 133,000 union members, attended the conference in Madrid, which was held from June 30 to July 2. The delegates established the Confederación General del Trabajo Unitaria (CGTU), the Unitarian General Confederation of Labor. Instead of becoming a Communist-controlled labor organization, the CGTU joined the UGT in November 1935.

As mentioned above, the influence of the Spanish Communist party on the Catalan labor movement was weakened by the formation of the BOC and of the Izquierda Comunista.

The Communists were not the only ones facing difficulties in obtaining a strong trade union base. The Catholic labor movement was also doing poorly; it probably counted 60,000 members in 1932. It identified politically with right-wing political groups, such as Acción Popular and CEDA, which did not appeal to the masses of the Spanish poor.

The elections of November 19, 1933 resulted in victory for the center and right-wing parties. The Right was represented by the Confederación Española de Derechas Autonomas (CEDA), led by José María Gil Robles. The CEDA, with 110 seats, became the largest party in the Cortes. The radicals of Alejandro Lerroux obtained 100 seats. The number of Socialist deputies was reduced by half, and the outcome of the elections wiped out any Left-republican representation. The once anticlerical Lerroux became prime minister and lost little time in bypassing or ignoring the reformist legislation passed by the constituent Cortes. Although clerical salaries had been abolished, Lerroux had them restored; on the other hand, the implementation of the agrarian reform program came to a stop. Lerroux was soon replaced by another radical, Ricardo Samper.

CNT and FAI leaders decided to wage a new campaign of insurrection. The uprising began on December 8, 1933. In Barcelona, the government promptly arrested CNT and FAI leaders and closed down their unions. Fighting was also short-lived in Zaragoza. In many villages of Aragón and of the Rioja the peasants proclaimed the establishment of *comunismo libertario* and announced that land would be redistributed. Similar events took place in other parts of Spain, such as in Villanueva de la Serena in the province of Badajoz, and in Bujalance, near Córdoba. These insurrections, however, were quickly controlled by the army and the Civil and Assault Guards. By December 13 they had ended.

The influence of the large influx of rural militants into the Socialist ranks tended to radicalize the Socialist party. The party's move toward the left was best expressed by a program it adopted in January 1934. This program was not per se socialist. There were no demands for the nationalizations of banks, railroads, and key industries. What the program demanded were a reform of the tax system, the transformation of the armed forces into a national militia, and the banning of certain members of the clergy from Spain. More important, the program demanded that the Socialist party pursue revolutionary activity. The Socialist party, therefore, no longer considered itself a party of government support.

During February, Spanish Socialists were shocked by the news of the brutal repression of Vienna's Socialists by Chancellor Dollfuss. Awareness of Fascist brutality increased when Hitler's "Night of the Long Knives" of June 30 became known in Spain. These events induced the Spanish Socialists to enter into "workers' alliances" with small political and labor groups in Catalonia. During February 1934, *alianzas obreras* were formed by the Socialist party, the UGT, the BOC, the Unió Socialista, the Partit Catalá Proletari, and other groups. In March, the Asturian federations of the UGT and of the CNT also entered into an *alianza obrera*. In June, the Communist party proposed the formation of a "common front" with the Socialist party; the latter in turn suggested that the Communists should participate in an *alianza obrera*. The Communist party accepted this suggestion on September 12 and agreed to suspend further criticism of the Socialist party. The CNT retained its hostility toward the Socialist party, but at a June plenum of its regional federations, it was agreed that at a local level, CNT organizations could enter into agreements with the UGT. This policy ratified the March agreement between the Asturian federations of the CNT and the UGT.

The CEDA wanted participation in the government. The president of the republic, Alcalá Zamora, had until then attempted to keep CEDA out of the government because of that party's questionable commitment to republican institutions. By October 1934, Zamora could no longer refuse participation in the government to the party that had the largest parliamentarian representation. A new government was formed at the beginning of October under the leadership of Lerroux that included a number of CEDA ministers. The CEDA's participation in government constituted a threat to the republic for various social and political groups in Spain. An attempted insurrection in Catalonia, led by the *Esquerra* movement of Luis Companys and weakly backed by the CNT, promptly ended in disaster. The October 1934 miners' insurrection in Asturias was far more serious.

On October 5, Socialist, CNT, and Communist miners started attacking the barracks of the Civil and Assault Guards in a number of towns along the Aller and Nalon rivers. They occupied towns as they marched toward the provincial capital of Oviedo. They succeeded in occupying most of Oviedo as well as the industrial city of La Felguera. Unfortunately, the alliance of the various organizations to which the miners belonged did not operate as well as it should have. When the anarchist miners of Gijón and Avilés demanded arms from their Socialist and Communist allies so that they could defend these seaports, their requests were ignored. Gijón and Avilés became the landing points for the troops the government brought in from Morocco. The government repression was brutal. Bookchin (1977) describes it: "The repression of the miners was marked by wanton carnage in battle; later, by the torturing and horrible mutilation of captured miners, many of whom were shot in batches without trial or owing to the slightest whim or provocation. Estimates of these executions numbered in the thousands..."(p. 272).

In May 1935, Gil Robles succeeded in having a new cabinet formed composed mostly of CEDA ministers or ministers belonging to the conservative and CEDA-controlled Agrarian party. The government policy became ultrareactionary. The agrarian reform program came to a standstill; army officers suspected of being sympathetic with the Left or with the republic were retired; tribunals were packed with right-wing, antilabor personnel; and General Francisco Franco y Bahamonde was appointed chief of staff of Spain's armed forces. Most Spaniards felt that Gil Robles was about to become Spain's Dollfuss. Meanwhile the economy continued to deteriorate and unemployment increased.

The rapid abandonment of republican reforms by the CEDA government persuaded Alcalá Zamora that a political change was necessary. A minor cabinet difficulty allowed him to appoint a new prime minister. To the great surprise of the political Right, Zamora appointed as prime minister Manuel Portela Valladares, a Gil Robles opponent. Portela closed the Cortes for one month and scheduled national elections for February 6, 1936.

All the political groups left of center feared the consequences of a CEDA victory in February. These fears induced the Left to start forming electoral coalitions in order to prevent what could amount to a Dollfuss-type experience in Spain. The liberals united in an Izquierda Republicana (Left-republicans) led by Azaña. The Socialist party favored an alliance with these Left-republicans. In January 1936, a Popular Front with a strictly middle-class program was formed by the Socialist party, the UGT, the Left-republicans, the Socialist Youth, the Syndicalist party headed by Pestaña, the Communist party, Nin's Left-Communists, and Maurín's BOC. The alliance was limited to political collaboration in view of the coming national elections. It did not demand any nationalization or any workers' control of industry. Meanwhile, anarchists and syndicalists within the CNT initiated a policy of rapprochement that would lead in March to the return of the Sindicatos de Oposición to the CNT fold. As election day approached, neither the CNT, nor the FAI leadership urged their members not to vote; both organizations stressed the dangers of a Fascist victory, and in spite of the way anarchists had been treated by Socialists during the October 1934 uprising, the CNT and the FAI advocated cooperation with the UGT.

The Popular Front won the February elections by the narrow margin of 700,000 votes; their victory was undoubtedly due to anarchosyndicalist support. Anarchists voted in order to avoid the "greater evil." As Bookchin (1977) observed: "Having taken to the vote, they began to take to politics. This tendency, which the FAI had originally been created to block, was reinforced by the increasing bureaucratization of the CNT" (p. 285).

The Popular Front victory was not to introduce social peace during the following months. The UGT and the CNT conducted strikes in support of an immediate amnesty for imprisoned leftist workers, which was conceded by Azaña; peasants were seizing large amounts of privately owned land without waiting for agrarian reform; political street violence between *pistoleros* of the right-wing Falange and workers plagued a number of Spanish cities; and CNT-inspired general strikes plagued the economy.

The Popular Front government tried to solve all these problems but without great success. The government arrested both anarchist leaders and Falangists, including the Falange leader José Antonio Primo de Rivera, the son of the dictator. It censored *Solidaridad Obrera* and closed down the CNT headquarters. All to no avail. Political assassinations and violence were practiced by the paramilitary forces of both the Falange and the Socialist Youth.

Dissension and violence developed even within the Socialist party. While Indalecio Prieto urged moderation and ministerial collaboration with the Left-republicans, Largo Caballero, once a minister of Labor, denounced any Socialist participation in the government. In 1926, Largo Caballero had willingly cooperated with the Primo de Rivera government; ten years later he had become the "Spanish Lenin," revered by the Socialist Youth and the prophet of the Spanish revolution.

Most of Largo Caballero's decisions in 1936 were to hurt the Socialist party. Believing that he would increase the number of his followers, he allowed a fusion between the Socialist Youth and the Communist Youth; the Communists used this union to their advantage. His support of a union between the UGT and the CNT failed.

Largo Caballero's plan was to allow the Popular Front government to collapse in disgrace and to have an all-Socialist government take its place. Manuel Azaña, aware of Largo Caballero's scheme, was determined to prevent its realization. When, in May, Azaña replaced Alcalá Zamora as the president of the republic, he chose his friend Casares Quiroga as prime minister in the hope that the republican government would survive.

The Socialist party was divided between the Prieto and the Largo

Caballero factions; the republicans had to respond to attacks from both the Right and the Left. The CNT held a congress in May at Zaragoza during which the delegates tried to define the postrevolutionary, libertarian society.

Meanwhile, a number of army generals and right-wing politicians were plotting to overthrow the republican government. The head of the conspiracy was General José Sanjurjo, who lived in Portugal and who was represented in Madrid by Colonel Valentín Galarza. Other military plotters were Generals Mola, Gonzalo Queipo de Llano, Villegas, Fanjul, and Goded. The leading civilian conspirator was José Calvo Sotelo, once a finance minister under Miguel Primo de Rivera and then a monarchist deputy enamored of Fascist ideologies. These men determined the date, July 17, of the uprising following the assassination of José Calvo Sotelo in retaliation for the murder of a socialist lieutenant of the Assault Guard by members of the Falange.

The government of Casares Quiroga, even though under notice of the conspiracy, appeared to ignore it and refused to deliver arms to leftist parties led by Largo Caballero. On July 17, 1936, elite units of the Spanish army in Morocco rebelled against the government in Madrid. The Spanish civil war had begun.

NOTES

Bookchin, M. 1977. *The Spanish Anarchists: The Heroic Years, 1868–1936.* New York: Free Life Editions.

Meaker, G. H. 1974. *The Revolutionary Left in Spain, 1914–1923.* Stanford, Calif.: Stanford University Press.

Payne, S. G. 1973. *A History of Spain and Portugal.* Vol. 2. Madison: University of Wisconsin Press.

Tuñón de Lara, M. 1972. *El movimiento obrero en la historia de España."* Vols. II and III. Barcelona: Editorial LAIA.

BIBLIOGRAPHY

Barcells, A. *El Sindicalismo en Barcelona, 1916–1923."* Barcelona, 1968.

Brademas, J. *Anarcosindicalismo y Revolución en España, 1930–1937.* Barcelona, 1974.

Brenan, G. *The Spanish Labyrinth.* Cambridge, 1943.

Bruguera, F. G. *Histoire Contemporaine d'Espagne*. Paris, 1953.

Comin Colomer, E. *Historia del Anarquismo Español*, 2 vols. Barcelona, 1956.

Diaz del Moral, J. *Historia de las agitaciones campesinas andaluzas*. Madrid, 1929.

Lorenzo, C. M. *Los Anarquistas Españoles y el Poder, 1868–1969*. Paris, 1969.

Malefakis, E. *Reforma agraria y revolución campesina en la España del Siglo XX, Orígenes de la Guerra Civil*. Ann Arbor, 1970.

3

The Spanish Labor Movement Since 1936

THE SPANISH LABOR MOVEMENT DURING THE CIVIL WAR

The history of Spanish trade unionism during the Spanish civil war is the history of that war itself since the republic's defense forces were largely constituted by members of the various labor organizations. For nearly four years, two different Spains were at war with each other. What were to be known as General Franco's Nationalists represented the interests of the army, the aristocracy, the landowners, the upper bourgeoisie, and the church; the Loyalists, fighting to preserve the republic, were mostly urban and rural workers and the low middle class.

The uprising against the republic started in Melilla, in Spanish Morocco, on the night of July 16–17, 1936. It began with the assassination of the local military commander, General Romerales, and with the arrest by the rebel forces of all those who were known trade union members, members of left-wing political parties, or members of Masonic lodges. The killing of military officers loyal to the government of the republic and the imprisonment or execution of trade unionists and of leftist politicians were to become the trademark of Nationalist insurgency. The uprising against the republic soon followed in Tetuán and Ceuta; and, as in Melilla, anyone resisting the "national movement" was shot.

In Madrid, the prime minister, Casares Quiroga, at first seemed to attach little importance to the events in Spanish Morocco and refused to arm the workers. While Radio Madrid assured the citizens of the capital that no one had revolted on the mainland, insurgency was taking place in Andalusia. The provincial governors, however, followed the example of Casares Quiroga and ignored the pleas of labor organizations to arm their members.

In a number of southern towns, the local garrisons on July 18 rose against the national government with the aid of the Falange and of the Civil Guard. The insurgency was opposed by Socialist, anarchist, and Communist workers, led in some cases by military officers who had remained loyal to the central government with the occasional support of the Assault Guard.

In Madrid, the Socialist press demanded arms for the workers. Casares still refused to do so, fearing perhaps that if he armed the unions they would pursue their own revolution. Not knowing how to cope with the military rebellion, he decided to submit his resignation to President Azaña on July 18. Azaña replaced Casares with Martínez Barrio, hoping that he could come to an agreement with the rebels. Martínez Barrio tried to do so but failed. His request for a peaceful settlement was turned down by Generals Mola and Cabanellas of the Nationalist conspiracy. Martínez Barrio was then replaced by José Giral, who quickly ordered the distribution of arms to the workers. On July 19, 65,000 rifles were distributed to the UGT and to the CNT; of these, only 5,000 had bolts. The remaining 60,000 bolts were located in the Montaña barracks, on the outskirts of Madrid.

In Barcelona, the uprising was scheduled for July 19 and was to take place under the command of General Fernández Burriel. General Goded was to fly to Barcelona from Palma de Majorca and become the leader of the insurgency in Barcelona. On the eighteenth, Luis Companys, president of the *Generalitat,* had refused to give arms to the workers; the CNT, however, had succeeded in raiding a number of arms depots and the Civil and Assault Guards remained loyal to the national government. The insurgency failed, and General Goded was imprisoned.

On the same day, workers in Madrid assaulted the Montaña barracks with their 5,000 rifles; in spite of many casualties, they succeeded in taking over the barracks and obtained the rifle parts they needed.

Elsewhere, in many towns and cities of Spain, insurgent military officers declared a "state of war," often proclaimed under the pretense of "saving the republic"; they shot officers who refused to take part in the conspiracy, and, in order to confuse the people, had their troops march through the streets holding up an arm with a clenched fist. In Burgos, General Dávila told the people that the uprising had been necessary in order to "save the republic."

By the end of July, the insurgents controlled about one-third of Spain but had failed to take the two principal cities, Madrid and Barcelona. In Madrid, the UGT had become responsible for the supply of food and of essential services. In spite of recent enmity, there was cooperation between the UGT and the CNT. The Communists asserted in *Mundo Obrero* that they were pursuing a nonrevolutionary policy and that they would fight together with the Left-bourgeoisie to maintain the republic. At the same time, they acquired virtual control of the united Socialist-Communist Youth, led by Santiago Carrillo.

Barcelona was ruled by both an Anti-Fascist Militias' Committee and by the *Generalitat*. The committee was controlled by the CNT and the FAI and was in charge of keeping production going, of the food supply, and of the city's defense. Barcelona, to a much larger degree than Madrid, had become an anarchist city. Hotels, banks, and factories had been expropriated and were run by workers' committees; churches were damaged or burned. Church schools were closed. The *Generalitat* took over the administration of functions that properly belonged to the national government: the right to issue money, the control of customs and border guards, and the administration of railroads and docks. On July 31, Luis Companys, president of the *Generalitat*, declared himself president of Catalonia. Three members of the Socialist-Communist party of Catalonia, the PSUC, were invited to join the government of the *Generalitat*. The PSUC refused, largely because of anarchist opposition. The government of Luis Companys was then formed on the basis of nine *Esquerra* representatives, a representative of the *Rabassaires*, and one of the more conservative Catalan Action party.

In Barcelona, the UGT and the CNT membership was expanding rapidly; so was the anti-Stalinist POUM. In the *pueblos* of Catalonia and Aragón, representatives of POUM, PSUC-UGT, and CNT-FAI formed Popular Front committees that took charge of the social and economic life in the villages.

When Germany and Italy started supplying the Nationalists with weapons, airplanes, and ships, it became imperative for the Popular Front government to be led by someone who could unite the various leftist factions and increase the military strength of the republic. President Azaña's choice was Francisco Largo Caballero, who, at the beginning of September, replaced Giral as prime minister. Largo Caballero's cabinet included six Socialists, four republicans, two Communists, one representative of the Catalan republicans, and one of the Basque Nationalists.

The danger of war was to encourage greater cooperation among the various Spanish labor groups. Ideological differences gave way to *realpolitik*, when, on October 23, German airplanes bombed Madrid and about 25,000 men under the command of the insurgent General Mola approached Madrid's western and southern suburbs. On November 4, the anarchists decided to participate in Largo Caballero's government and four new CNT ministers entered the prime minister's cabinet. On November 14, the anarchist Buenaventura Durruti arrived in Madrid with 3,000 men and was assigned the defense of the University City, which the Nationalist General Varela was about to attack. Durruti was killed one week later.

The Nationalists were unable to take Madrid.

The defense of Madrid revealed that the Communists had shown the best example of discipline, efficiency; and courage. It was a Communist woman, Dolores Ibarruri, better known as "La Pasionaria," who, on the front lines as well as through speeches on the radio, encouraged the *madrileños* and prevented panic.

On July 18, 1936, the Spanish Communist party counted at the most 30,000 members. By mid-1937, its membership had risen to 1 million (Jackson 1965, p. 360). Because the Communists stood as the defenders of middle-class democracy, they started attracting to their ranks young intellectuals, civil servants, army officers, and members of the low middle class. The delivery of Russian military equipment to the Loyalist government increased their prestige. A number of high-ranking Loyalist military commanders, such as General Miaja, head of the Madrid defense junta, became members of the Communist party.

It is not the purpose of this book to give a detailed account of the development of the Spanish civil war and of the many events that tended to weaken the government of the republic, which, as of November 6, 1936, had been moved to Valencia. This government never received the quantity of military aid from the Soviet Union that the Nationalist forces obtained from Italy and Germany. The Fascist supporters of General Franco were geographically much closer to Spain than Russia and were probably more interested in the outcome of the civil war than the Soviet government.

Another factor that limited the effectiveness of the government was the continuing disagreement between the leftist political groups. Republicans and Communists disagreed on military tactics to be followed. In April 1937, Largo Caballero wanted the Loyalist forces to initiate an offensive in Estremadura to isolate Nationalist forces in the northwest from their supply sources in Andalusia; his plan was opposed not only by his Russian advisers but also by members of his cabinet. In Barcelona, anarchists and the POUM opposed the Communists and the PSUC, and the prime minister's Communist cabinet members criticized him for failing to take action against the POUM. Many ranking Socialists left their party, feeling that Largo Caballero was unable to cope with the Nationalist threat; among them was Santiago Carrillo, who joined the Communist party. Under increasing criticism by both Socialists and Communists, Largo Caballero decided to resign in May 1937.

Juan Negrín, a moderate Socialist and a former physiology professor at the University of Madrid, formed a new government on May 17, 1937. Indalecio Prieto became defense minister, and José Giral was minister for foreign affairs. This government continued to be unable to resist Nationalist territorial gains. The republic's offensive at Brunete in the summer of 1937 and at Teruel in December turned into Nationalist victories. The Nationalists were favored by both superior military equipment and by the endless political rivalries that divided their opponents. Indeed, the Communists were trying to achieve political and military unity under their control in those parts of Spain still under republican rule. They succeeded in having most of the leaders of the POUM arrested, and they assassinated Andrés Nin in their own prison in Alacalá de Henares, near Madrid. They proposed the fusion of the Socialist with the Communist party; but the former refused to do so.

Meanwhile, Nationalist forces continued their advance, reaching the Mediterranean coast at Viñaroz in April 1938. General Franco was to wait another eight months before launching a major assault on Catalonia. The assault started on December 23; the troops of the insurgent General Yagüe entered Barcelona on January 22, 1939. About half a million Spaniards retreated from Catalonia into France between that date and February 10 (Jackson 1965, p. 465). Franco's troops entered Madrid on March 27, and by April 1, the Nationalist leader had truly become the "Chief of the Spanish State."

THE SPANISH LABOR MOVEMENT UNDER FRANCO'S RULE

Spain's independent labor organizations were declared illegal by the Nationalist government on April 24, 1938. Ramón Serrano Suñer, General Franco's brother-in-law, drafted a Trade Union Unity Act that became law in 1940; it established "a single system of syndicates" and declared that "the Syndical Organization of FET y de las JONS is the only one recognized by the State..." (Lieberman 1982, p. 327). Serrano Suñer, a sympathizer of the German National Socialist movement and a political adviser of Franco, had also formulated the 60 articles of the Fuero del Trabajo, the Labor Charter of 1938. This charter reflected to a large extent the Nazi *Fuehrerprinzip:* workers were deprived of the right to strike but the state took the responsibility of taking care of their interests; the workers were to remain "loyal and obedient" to their employer, who kept complete control over the firm; the employer was in turn responsible to the state for the proper performance of the enterprise.

The Fuero del Trabajo established a single labor organization, and membership in that organization was mandatory for both employers and employees. This organization, the Organización Sindical (OS), was to follow the principle of "Unity, Totality, Hierarchy." The implementation of this principle was detailed in a Basic Law of December 6, 1940, the Ley de Bases de la Organización Sindical. The OS was to include 24 *sindicatos* defined by the type of production involved. The Basic Law placed in the Syndical Organization "all Spanish producers as members of a great national and syndical community, conceiving Spain as a gigantic syndicate of producers, syndication being the political form of the entire economy of Spain" (Lieberman 1982, p. 327). Article 1 stated that "Spaniards, collaborating in production, constitute the national syndicalist community as a militant unity under the discipline of the Movement." The preamble of the law also established "the subordination of the Syndical Organization to the Party, since only the latter can give it discipline, the unity and the spirit needed by the national economy to serve national policy" (Lieberman 1982, p. 327).

Franco's corporatist state thus forced both employers and employees into identical syndicates whose main purpose was to serve the interests of the state and whose administrators were government officials who did not necessarily identify with the interests of either employers or employees. The administrators of the OS were the militants of Franco Spain's only political party, the Falange Tradicionalista Española y de las Juntas Ofensivas Nacional-Sindicalistas (FET y de las JONS). Years later, the name of the party was changed to the Movimiento Nacional. The control of workers by militants of the Falange gave Spain during the early years of World War II the appearance of a Fascist state. The control would be lessened as soon as the "Caudillo" realized that victory was slipping away from the Axis Powers.

The ideology of the FET y de las JONS had mixed origins from the start. The party itself was the result of a fusion of various political groups. In the early 1930s, the founder of the Juntas Ofensivas Nacional-Sindicalistas, Ramiro Ledesma Ramos, developed a revolutionary vision based on opposition to the capitalist system and on a strong desire to "regenerate" the country by eliminating the traditional social and economic nineteenth-century elites. Ledesma Ramos admired the revolutionary zeal of the anarchists, although he had goals that differed from those of the CNT.

In October 1933, the charismatic son of General Miguel Primo de Rivera, José Antonio Primo de Rivera, denounced both liberalism and Marxism in a speech he gave at the Teatro de la Comedia in Madrid. José Antonio proposed, as so many other Spanish "regenerationists" had done before, to save Spain from an overmaterialistic republic that ignored the spiritual needs of the Spanish worker (Amsden 1972, p. 33). He succeeded in building a new party, the Falange Española, which attracted mostly right-wing university students and persons identifying with his father.

On February 11, 1934, the group of Ledesma Ramos fused with that of José Antonio Primo de Rivera, and the Falange Española de las JONS was thus constituted. Although this party established Falangist unions, very few workers joined them. Before the civil war, Falangists were mostly occupied fighting left-wing students in university cities. Following the outbreak of the war, José Antonio tried to negotiate an agreement with the insurgent generals in order to assure to the Falange an important political role following the Nationalist victory.

To help in the establishment of Nationalist rule, the Falange was used as a paramilitay force in charge of "pacifying" areas conquered by the insurgent forces. In order to control the hostility of the people against the insurgent power, the Falangists used terrorist action against anyone suspected of sympathizing with the Popular Front government; hundreds of people were shot daily by José Antonio's "blue shirts" in order to purge the Spanish population of the hated "reds" (Amsden 1972, p. 36). Joining the Falange was a way of surviving for many people, and it is not amazing that as the years of war passed, the party's membership increased at a rapid pace.

General Franco started to fear that it would be difficult to control a party of such size; an obvious solution was for him to become the head of the party. On April 17, 1937, he issued a decree under which the Carlist Comunión Tradicional was united with the Falange. The new organization became the Falange Española Tradicionalista y de las JONS (FET y de las JONS). Manuel Hedilla, who had succeeded José Antonio Primo de Rivera after the latter was executed by the republicans on November 20, 1936, was promptly jailed for refusing to accept an inferior position in the party assigned to him by Franco.

The role that the Falange played after the end of the civil war was a limited one. It was given the responsibility of administering the new *sindicatos*; it also participated in the Labor Ministry and in the civil service. After the defeat of the Axis Powers, the "Caudillo" quickly declared Spain to be a monarchy, a monarchy without a monarch. The powers of the Falange were gradually reduced, and the Fascist salute was abolished. By the mid-1950s, the Falange was only in charge of the Syndical Organization.

In his effort to make his regime more acceptable to the victorious Allies Franco introduced in 1947 the concept of the *jurado de empresa*, literally translated, the "factory jury." The government's regulations that allowed the actual formation of these factory juries were enacted six years later. The decree of 1947 stated that the *jurado de empresa* would be the true representative of the workers in a firm when dealing with its management, the Syndical Organization, or the state. Each firm or factory with 50 or more workers had to have a *jurado de empresa*. This "jury" was to be constituted by a president and ten delegates chosen from the body of administrative and nonadministrative workers of the firm by means of an election. The *jurados* were to operate within the legal trade unions but their members were not required to be Falangists. This was to allow in later years workers who were members of clandestine political parties or labor organizations to infiltrate the *jurado*. This possibility became of great importance to workers when the government, in an effort to show the Western powers that it was pursuing a policy of economic liberalization, enacted in 1958 the Law on Collective Contracts. This law replaced wage orders, until then issued by the Ministry of Labor, by collective bargaining between workers and employers over wages and conditions of work.

The government's policy of "liberalizing" and "democratizing" the Spanish economy in the 1960s in order to give at least the appearance that Spain was slowly following Westen European economic policy brought some structural changes to the Syndical Organization. A syndical congress was to serve as a center of open debate by both appointed and elected officials in matters relating to the policy of the OS. The congresses were to meet at regular intervals; they did not democratize the various *sindicatos*. The third syndical congress of 1964 created separate councils of workers and councils of employers at both the provincial and national levels. These bodies had only advisory capacities.

More important for the workers were the implications of the Law on Collective Contracts of 1958. Under its terms, the representatives of the workers in the bargaining process were to be selected on the basis of free and open workers' elections. Elected representatives had to have membership in the official *sindicato* but could also hold more or less secret membership in one of the underground independent labor organizations. This was to give a marked advantage to the illegal and clandestine Spanish Communist party, whose leaders continued to be active in Franco's Spain. Communist workers, by infiltrating the *jurado de empresa*, were free to pursue their interests in all legality. Because most of the collective bargaining agreements in the 1960s were reached at the plant level, the bargaining process appeared to be entirely the work of members of the Organización Sindical.

Another type of collective bargaining, completely independent of the OS, also developed in Spain during the 1960s. This type of bargaining was related to the rise of the Comisiones Obreras (CCOO), Workers' Commissions.

Following the end of the civil war, the CNT and the FAI attempted to go on opposing the Nationalist government through terrorism; bloody clashes between the anarchists and the police terminated these activities by the end of the 1940s. The surviving anarchists joined UGT leaders in their exile in Toulouse, in southern France. This leadership, living in relative isolation, rapidly lost effective influence over workers in Spain.

The Communist party, although an illegal organization in Franco's Spain, continued to be active in the country. In May 1958, Communists attempted to carry out their first public demonstration in opposition to the Franco regime; during the "Day of National Reconciliation," they organized brief work stoppages in a number of factories and appealed to the public to boycott public transportation. These signs of protest were not successful. Neither were the Communists' later calls for general strikes. A more successful tactic, however, was Communist participation in the new Comisiones Obreras.

In 1960, the UGT and CNT leaders living in France decided to join forces in order to manifest the presence of their organizations in Spain. Both groups established a new clandestine labor organization in Spain under the name of Alianza Sindical, the Syndical Alliance. It was, however, soon supplanted by a new organization formed by Socialist and anarchist militants living in Spain, the Alianza Sindical Obrera (ASO), the Workers' Syndical Alliance. The ASO was not successful, probably because it had been created at a time when the new Workers' Commissions were already under the control of Communist and Catholic groups.

The most prominent Catholic labor group at that time was the Hermanos Obreros de Accción Católica (HOAC) the Catholic Action Worker Brotherhoods. The HOAC was, in principle, dedicated to give spiritual assistance to workers and was thus favored by the church. Out of this group, however, developed militant workers' organizations, such as the Juventudes Obreras Católicas (JOC), or Catholic Workers' Youth; Catholic Workers' Vanguard; and Unión Sindical Obrera (USO), the Workers' Syndicalist Union, which was strongly anti-Communist. Catholic militant workers did not hesitate, however, to participate with Communists in the Workers' Commissions.

It was in Asturias and in the Basque provinces that workers first organized independently of the government's Syndical Organization. The first independent Workers' Commission was probably organized by the miners of La Camocha coal mine, located near Gijón, in 1958. This organization, established spontaneously by miners to fight for the retention of their coal allocations and of a daily wage of 100 pesetas, included both Socialist and Communist workers, as well as the priest and the mayor of the district of La Camocha. This commission ceased to exist in the same year it had been created. It served, however, as a prototype for other miners' commissions created in the early 1960s.

Miners struck in Asturias in 1962 and in 1963, and the strikes extended to the Basque country, Catalonia, and Madrid. These strikes were organized by the Comisiones Obreras, generally known in Spain as the CCOO. Workers elected to these commissions trustworthy colleagues who were willing to assume the risk of acting on behalf of a group of workers without legality. The establishment of these temporary and illegal commissions involved serious dangers for participating workers. Existing laws gave the government wide powers to indict and prosecute members for treason, rebellion, sedition, and crimes endangering the security of the state. Employers had the right to dismiss such workers (Almendros et al. 1978, p. 43).

During a formative period, which extended from the late 1950s to about 1964, the Workers' Commissions did not represent any specific political or economic ideology; the workers who participated in them were Communists, members of various Catholic oganizations, independents, leftist Falangists, Christian Democrats, and others.

The enactment of the Law on Collective Contracts of 1958 acted as a stimulant to the formation of Workers' Commissions. Employers started negotiating with the latter on a plant or firm basis. In 1962, a CCOO acting at a provincial level was organized in Vizcaya; its members were received as trade union representatives by employers and government officials until they were suddenly arrested and indicted in the spring of 1963. At the same time, commission members were nominated as delegates to the *jurados de empresa* in the legal syndical elections of 1963. In 1964, a second provincewide CCOO was created in Madrid. At the beginning of 1965, the Coordinadora Local of Barcelona was founded to coordinate the activities of various Workers' Commissions.

By the mid-1960s, CCOO representatives were not only active in the legal factory juries and in the process of collective bargaining but also organized demonstrations that demanded greater civil liberties, workers' freedom to organize independently of government agencies, and the release of political prisoners. The government's toleration of these activities must be explained in terms of the economic boom that then favored the national economy; rapid economic growth allowed the Franco regime to ignore for the time being the antigovernment stand of the CCOO. By 1967, the CCOO had become the most effective anti-Franco force in Spain. More than 100,000 workers joined the CCOO in antigovernment demonstrations in Madrid in January and October of that year. The first National Assembly of the CCOO was held in June 1967.

The increasing defiance of the government by the CCOO and the greater visibility of their members as collective bargaining negotiators within the hierarchy of the OS induced the government to act to prevent the CCOO from acquiring de facto legality. A court holding of 1967 declared the CCOO to be illegal and a decree-law of November 27, 1967 ordered the suspension of all collective bargaining for a year (Almendros et al. 1978, p. 47). Government repression began in 1968 and assumed various forms. Employers started dismissing workers known to be active in the CCOO; CCOO leaders were arrested, and most of them received harsh punishment; finally, workers who had obtained positions in the official trade union system and who were suspected of belonging to clandestine organizations were summarily dismissed from the OS. More than 1,000 workers were tried before the Tribunal of Public Order on charges of illegal association.

The government's repression was made more severe by the fact that the government maintained the suspension of collective bargaining at the end of 1968 and allowed maximum wage and salary increases of only 5.9 percent. The government's action against unlawfully constituted labor organizations was intensified in 1969, when a "state of exception" was proclaimed by the authorities for the entire Spanish territory. The CCOO were then faced with both external and internal problems.

The mounting threat of arrest and imprisonment of CCOO members brought the question of whether or not the commissions should operate clandestinely as underground organizations; the CCOO leadership chose to continue to operate in the open in order to show the government that the commissions had the support of large numbers of workers and had become a de facto institution in the contemporary labor market. The CCOO were determined to continue negotiations with employers regarding wages and conditions of work, even though such activities were in violation of the law. The audacity of the CCOO workers during these times of harsh government repression paralleled the workers' courage during the years of the civil war, when, poorly armed, they doggedly confronted a better equipped foe. Their determination to go on bargaining and striking in 1969, at a time when the Tribunal of Public Order was handing out long prison sentences, is indeed remarkable.

The CCOO policies had two immediate consequences: In many cases, and in spite of employers' protests, the authorities decided to tolerate or ignore CCOO activities; these activities also increased the prestige that the Spanish Communist party enjoyed among the workers and increased the party's influence in the CCOOs.

The period from 1970 to the death of General Franco in November 1975 witnessed increased harshness in confrontations between workers and the security forces; workers were shot in Granada in 1970 and in Barcelona in 1971. Also, general strikes were declared for the first time since the end of the civil war. The first general strikes occurred in El Ferrol and in Vigo in 1972, and a large number of workers were arrested or dismissed by their employers. In June, the top leadership of the CCOO was arrested in Pozuelo de Alarcón, near Madrid, and became part of the noted "trial 1001." There was a general strike in Pamplona in 1973 and another one in the Bajo Llobregat in Catalonia in the following year.

The death of Franco in November 1975 opened up a new chapter in the history of the Spanish labor movement.

SPAIN'S POST-FRANCO LABOR ORGANIZATIONS

It has been observed that during the latter part of Franco's rule the CCOO established themselves as a true independent labor organization in Spain. Let us look at the ideological and structural evolutions of what Spanish workers called the "new labor movement" in the early 1960s. These evolutions can be seen in terms of three main stages.

The first stage, an intitial period during which the commissions showed no stable structure and had no coordinating agencies, and during which their demands were purely economic in nature, covers the years 1958 to 1964. The first commissions were characterized by the democratic nature of their elections; CCOO representatives were elected and recalled by assemblies of workers; in the words of the CCOO leader Marcelino Camacho, "The CCOO were born in the Assemblies, which are the basic part of the movement . . ." (Camacho 1976, p. 74). In this period, the main objectives of the commissions were higher wages and better conditions of work. No sociopolitical demands were made before the outbreak of the miners' strikes in Asturias in the early 1960s; it was then that the commissions started to demand the free right of assembly, the right of workers to strike, and the right to form political parties. These demands were to be given greater emphasis in the subsequent period.

The first commissions were formed spontaneously to respond to workers' needs. Until the early 1960s, commissions were formed on a temporary basis to negotiate with management; once the labor-management problem was solved, the commission was dissolved. It was only in the 1960s that more permanent commissions were established.

These commissions were formed by workers representing various political and syndical views; Communists, members of Catholic groups, Socialists, and independents were elected to the commissions. Many of their representatives were official factory jury members who gave the commissions some appearance of legality. All of the members of the commissions were united in their opposition to the official Organización Sindical, which was perceived as a pure government agency that did not truly represent the interests of wage earners.

The period 1964–76 constituted a second stage. During these years, the democratic characteristic of the CCOO was maintained; workers of different political and religious ideologies continued to constitute commissions whose economic goals were to benefit nonmembers as well as members of the CCOO. These now demanded political freedoms, and they declared themselves ready to cooperate with any democratic political and syndical group willing to fight for such freedoms. The CCOO also made it clear that they opposed the capitalist system.

The last stage covers the period since 1976. It was during this time that the CCOO became a major national labor organization in Spain. This organization proclaimed that its long-term goal was the suppression of the capitalist system and its replacement by a new order based on workers' self-management. It declared itself independent of governmental influence and of employers' associations and independent of any political or economic group. It rejected the Leninist thesis that a labor organization should serve as a "transmission belt" for a political party. It demanded free education, decent housing for workers, workers' participation in managerial decisions, syndical and political freedoms, and a Socialist society.

As noted, the first commissions were established on a temporary and spontaneous basis. Until 1963 there was no agency that coordinated the activities of the various commissions. There was no directing, permanent committee above the enterprise level. It was during the period 1963–65 that the Workers' Commissions were established on a more stable and permanent basis at the firm level, and the new commissions' structure facilitated in turn the creation of organizational forms at a higher level. The first coordinating commission at a provincial level was established in Vizcaya in 1963. It was followed in 1964 by the organization in Madrid of a provincial coordinating agency, by a Coordinadora Local for Barcelona in 1965, and by a National Workers' Commission of Catalonia in 1966.

As of 1964, the first provincial commissions cooperated in order to define common national policies. These contacts prepared the celebration of the first National Assembly of the CCOO, which took place in Madrid in June 1967.

The government repression of 1968 and 1969 forced the CCOO leadership again to choose between continuing their activities in the open or to turn the CCOO into a clandestine, underground organization. In order to establish the CCOO as a mass labor movement, the decision was taken to operate openly. The leaders wanted to impress Spanish workers with the fact that the CCOO represented the interests of all Spanish workers.

Between 1971 and 1975, a Coordinadora General acted as the highest directive organ of the CCOO. In 1976, it proposed to other major Spanish labor organizations that a single, united, and independent Spanish labor organization should be founded. The UGT, the USO, and the CNT did not support the idea. The CCOO then held a General Assembly at Barcelona in July that approved the transformation of the CCOO into a national labor organization called the Confederación Sindical de Comisiones Obreras" (Syndical Confederation of Workers' Commissions), still known as CCOO. This decision led to a schism; some groups left the new national organization to form their own independent federations: the Confederation of the National Workers' Commissions of Catalonia, the CSUT, and the SU.

The highest level of authority in the new national organization was its Confederal Congress. This congress elected the 200 members of the

Confederal Council, the members of the secretariat, the secretaries-general for nationalities and for regions, and the secretaries-general of the various member federations. Farther down the hierarchical ladder were the industrial unions and the Workers' Commissions at the enterprise, local, and provincial levels.

The growth of the organization was quite spectacular. Eighty thousand membership cards had been distributed in October 1976; this figure rose to 200,000 in November, with most members residing in Catalonia and in Madrid. The membership rose to 500,000 in June 1977 and to 1.4 million in October of that year (Almendros et al. 1978, pp. 66, 67).

The Unión Sindical Obrera (USO) was the first independent labor organization operating in post-civil war Spain. It was established in 1960 by a group of workers opposing the way the Franco regime dealt with labor problems. The USO was to be a mass labor movement whose main goal was the attainment of a Socialist society based on workers' self-management (USO 1977, p. 17). In 1961 USO leaders drafted the organization's Founding Charter, which was approved in secret by its National Committee in 1965. Article 1 of the charter defined the USO as a "free and sovereign labor organization, created and directed by the workers of the fields, of industry and of the services, in order to develop a mass labor movement, instrument of defense and of collective improvement of the workers." It also declared its incompatibility with the capitalist system and with any type of totalitarian regime (Guinea 1978, p. 196).

The organization was initially founded by members of Catholic groups, such as the Movimiento Apostólico, the HOAC, and the JOC. The USO founding members proclaimed, however, that the new organization would accept in its ranks any and all workers regardless of their religious or political preferences. The USO was to be a Socialist organization, indifferent to religious creed.

The USO leadership also proclaimed its desire to bring all clandestine labor groups operating in the country into a single Gran Central Sindical Democrática de Trabajadores, the Great Democratic Syndical Central of Workers. Following this policy, it joined in 1962 the Alianza Sindical Obrera (ASO), which had been established by representatives of the CNT, the UGT, and the Solidaritat d'Obrers Catalans Cristians (SOCC). It also participated in the first established Workers' Commissions.

USO militants took part in the strikes that developed in 1962 in the north and in the area around Barcelona. In 1966, in order to protest the ever closer ties between labor organizations and political groups, the USO withdrew from the ASO. In that same year, the Catalan Federation of the UGT decided to join the USO for similar reasons. The USO's opposition to undue influence exercised by political parties on labor organizations was also to produce a gradual separation of the USO from the CCOO, a separation that became final in 1969.

A First Assembly of Delegates of the Syndical Sections of the USO took place in Barcelona in October 1976. The delegates declared insufficient the minimum legal wage of 300 pesetas per day, manifested their discontent with the economic policies of the government, and demanded more healthful conditions of work.

The First Confederal Congress of the USO met in Madrid in April of the following year. Among its resolutions were the rejection of the capitalist system and the determination to strive for a unitarian labor organization in Spain. This interest in forming a single national labor confederation had already been manifested by the USO when, in July 1976, it had actively promoted the creation of the Coordinadora de Organizaciones Sindicales (COS), an agency whose task was to coordinate the policies of the CCOO, the UGT, and the USO. On the other hand, proposals for a fusion between the two large Socialist labor organizations in the early 1970s, the USO and the UGT, were rejected by an Extraordinary Congress of the USO meeting in Madrid in October 1977.

Before the legalization of labor organizations in 1976, the USO counted only about 18,000 members, 10,000 of whom resided in Madrid. The legalization of independent trade unions brought an impressive expansion of the USO's membership. By October 1977, membership cards had been distributed to 355,000 persons. In April 1978, membership had risen to 556,060 persons. The members were most numerous in the province of Valencia; Catalonia, Andalusia, and Madrid followed by membership size in that order.

At the base of the USO's structure was the *sección sindical*, an enterprise-based union. For a given locality and for a given industry, a group of such unions constituted a local federation defined by type of production. These Federaciones Locales del Ramo were in turn grouped into regional and national federations. Coordinating the activities of various federations at the local, regional, and national levels were interprofessional *uniones*.

The hierarchy within the USO was made up at the top by a Confederal Congress, a Confederal Council, a Confederal Secretariat, and an Executive Commission.

When, in October 1976, the CCOO leadership decided that their organization would become a national labor organization distinct from others operating in Spain, about 900 CCOO members met on November 7 in Coslada, near Madrid, to discuss their opposition to CCOO policy. That group, nearly splitting in two, organized two new labor organizations. A group headed by José Miguel Ibarrola created the Sindicato Unitario (SU), the Unitarian Syndicate. The second group, led by

Jerónimo Lorente, organized the Confederación de Sindicatos Unitarios de Trabajadores (CSUT), the Workers' Confederation of Unitarian Syndicates.

The constituent congress of the SU was held in Madrid on May 1, 1977. The new organization was described as a "class" organization formed to engage in the class struggle in order to help the working class to gain political power. Its founding charter denoted it as unitarian, democratic, and independent, based on decisions arrived at by free assemblies of members, and internationalist. It advocated the unity of the labor movement and the SU's complete independence of government, employers' associations, and any political party. In fact, most of the members of its secretariat were affiliated with the Maoist-Trotskyite party, Organización Revolucionaria de Trabajadores (ORT).

The SU strongly condemned existing unemployment and supported regional autonomy. By the beginning of 1978, the SU counted about 500,000 members. It was strongest in Madrid and in the Basque area.

The CSUT was established in March 1977 in Vallecas, a suburb of Madrid. It claimed to be a unitarian organization, open to any worker regardless of political or religious beliefs and without consideration for age or sex. It declared itself democratic and independent of government and any political or economic groups. It criticized the CCOO for being dominated by the Spanish Communist party at a time when nine out of the ten members of its Confederal Secretariat were members of the Marxist-Leninist Partido del Trabajo de España (PTE). Its bylaws, reflecting this political orientation, declared that the emancipation of the working class could only be achieved after the abolition of private ownership of the means of production.

Its organizational structure was similar to that of the SU except that its unions were established along both craft and industry lines.

In February 1978 this organization counted about 460,000 members, most of them located in León, Extremadura, Galicia, and Madrid, in that order.

Following the military victory of General Franco, UGT and Socialist leaders fled either to France or Mexico. Mexico became a haven for many Spaniards who feared living in Nationalist Spain. In August 1942, a meeting of 150 delegates of industrial federations of the UGT took place in that country. An Executive Commission was elected and charged with the task of reorganizing what was left of the UGT; Rafael Mira became its new secretary-general. It was also resolved at that meeting that a special committee should work out an agreement of cooperation with the CNT. The CNT leadership in exile was willing to cooperate with its UGT counterpart; the most important manifestation of such joint effort was a memorandum that both organizations submitted to the United Nations in 1945, a document that denounced the dictatorial regime in Spain.

Once the German military forces had been expelled from France, exiled Spanish leaders in that country, most of them living in Toulouse, attempted to maintain the viability of the PSOE and the UGT in France. The exiled Spanish Socialists in that country held a congress in September 1944 and elected as their president Enrique de Santiago, with Trifón Gómez as vice-president and Rodolfo Llopis as secretary-general. The *Ugetistas* held their first congress outside of Spain in November of that year; the congress ratified the agreement of cooperation with the CNT entered into in Mexico; it also resolved that "the UGT, in the course of its activities in France, considers itself represented in political matters by the (PSOE) party, and will support it in favor of a reestablishment of republican legality in our country" (Almendros et al. 1978, p. 123). This congress elected as President Trifón Gómez; Enrique de Francisco, Rodolfo Llopis, and Pascual Tomás were members of its Executive Committee.

Some UGT leaders, such as Francisco Largo Caballero, opposed the delegation of the organization's political responsibilities to the PSOE. A schism occurred that split for some months the UGT into an "authentic" and a "dissident" UGT.

Neither the exiled UGT leadership nor that of the PSOE was to have any significant influence over the course of events in Spain for many years. In Spain, the police stopped any attempt to reconstitute UGT unions. A large part of the UGT membership was in jail. The harshness of Franco's repression of clandestine labor activity caused in turn a growing estrangement between UGT militants in Spain and the leadership in France. While the exiled leaders in Toulouse insisted that UGT militants in Spain should not cooperate with Communists, militants in Spain were ready to collaborate with any group that opposed the Franco regime. Ensuing disagreements between the "exterior" and the "interior" UGT leaders became major obstacles to the reorganization of the UGT as an active, clandestine labor organization during the years of the Franco dictatorship. When, in 1953, the Socialist leader Tomás Centeno was arrested in Spain, the Spanish police was able to identify many Socialist and UGT militants operating in the country. Most had to leave Spain in order to avoid arrest; this new movement out of the country of many UGT militants further prevented efforts to reorganize UGT groups in Spain.

In the 1950s, a new generation of workers in Spain had practically no knowledge about the role the UGT had played in pre–civil war days. It may be said that the UGT lost any meaningful existence in Spain between 1939 and 1960.

It was only in 1961 that the UGT, together with the CNT and the Basque STV, formed the Alianza Sindical in an effort to respond to the rising Communist and Catholic influences among Spanish workers. The lack of cooperation between UGT militants in Spain and the "historic" leadership in France led to the founding of the rival ASO in 1962. The ASO ceased to exist in 1965, when Catalan *Ugetistas* chose to leave the UGT and entered the new Socialist labor organization, the USO.

UGT policies further weakened the perception of its existence by Spanish workers. Claiming that the Workers' Commissions were dominated by the Communists, the UGT leadership prohibited its members from participating in the CCOO. The UGT also refused to take part in the legal syndical elections within the apparatus of the government's "vertical unions." Instead, the UGT leaders urged the formation of "factory committees" composed of workers who had no official positions in the legal OS. These policy positions strongly limited the interest Spanish workers in the 1960s could have in the UGT.

Realizing the need to revitalize the organization in Spain, the UGT leadership in France decided in 1971 to return to Spain in an attempt to give new life to a moribund UGT. These leaders finally recognized that unless UGT activities in Spain expanded rapidly, the labor organization would be replaced forever by the new labor associations, such as the CCOO and the USO. Their attempt to give the UGT a stronger foothold in Spain was supportd by the PSOE in 1975 and in 1976. A thirtieth congress of the UGT, the first in Spain since 1932, could be held in Madrid in April 1976. On July 23 of the same year, the UGT joined the CCOO and the USO in establishing the coordinating agency COS. After 40 years of clandestine existence, the UGT received legality in May 1977.

On July 30 and 31, 1977, the UGT held an Extraordinary Congress in the Palacio de Congresos in Barcelona. The purpose of this congress was to debate what policies the organization should pursue in post-Franco Spain. Two thousand delegates, representing 2 million members, attended this congress. The UGT had achieved a remarkable recovery since 1971.

The base of the UGT's structure is presently formed by the *sección sindical de empresa,* a union composed of all UGT members working in the same enterprise. All UGT members in the same locality join a *sindicato local;* groups of these *sindicatos* form a provincial or regional federation based either on industry or on "nationality." All local unions are also grouped into a *unión local;* all of the *uniones* of a given province, region, or nationality form also *uniones provinciales, uniones de región,* and *uniones de nacionalidad.*

The highest level of authority is vested in a congress made up by the delegates of the *uniones.* Regular congresses are held every two years. Between these congresses, policy is directed by a Confederal Committee composed of the secretary-general, the members of the Executive Commission, and the head officials of the various federations and *uniones.* The Executive Commission is the permanent directing body of the UGT. As of 1977, its secretary-general was Nicolás Redondo.

The history of the anarchosyndicalist Confederación Nacional del Trabajo during the civil war discloses the generous contribution of manpower made by the CNT to the forces of the Popular Front government. During the war, the popularity of the CNT rose among Spaniards. The size of its membership, which had reached 1 million persons before the outbreak of the war, increased beyond that figure after 1936. In turn, the civil war brought death to thousands of CNT members. Additional thousands were imprisoned or executed following the Nationalist victory.

The exiled CNT leadership tried to reorganize the confederation within Spain, hoping that guerrilla warfare and the eventual help of the victorious Allies would bring about the overthrow of the Franco regime. Between 1939 and 1945, clandestine regional and national committees were formed in Spain to lead armed resistance against the Nationalist government. The Spanish police, however, was able to discover the identity of the members of ten successive national committees during this period of time; once arrested, the CNT militants were given either death sentences or long periods of imprisonment by the Spanish courts. It is remarkable that, in spite of the arrests of key militants, the CNT continued to be an active underground resistance organization in Spain until the end of World War II. It has been reported that the organization still counted 200,000 Catalan members in 1944 and that until 1951, 30,000 issues of *Solidaridad Obrera* were distributed in Catalonia (Almendros et al. 1978, p. 158).

On November 6, 1945, the members of the tenth clandestine national committee were arrested by the police. As of then, the CNT practically vanished as an opposition movement in Spain. Deprived of their cadres, exhausted by guerrilla action, disappointed by the failure of the Allies to take action to force the fall of the Franco government, CNT militants in Spain, in and out of jails, gave up their clandestine opposition. Guerrilla warfare ceased in 1951.

The few who were still interested in the survival of the CNT disagreed with the exiled leaders; in spite of the rapidly vanishing membership, some nuclear groups of the CNT joined similar UGT and STV groups in 1961 to form the Alianza Sindical, a new organization formed to obtain legislation that would allow political freedom, the right of assembly, and the right of workers to strike.

The Alianza Sindical Obrera was founded two years later by UGT and CNT militants who attached greater importance to syndical activity by employees in their place of work than to armed resistance against the Nationalist regime. They disagreed with the exiled leadership, which still advocated acts of rebellion and acts of sabotage.

The rebirth of the CNT in Spain had to wait until the end of 1975. It was only in December of that year that an assembly of anarchosyndicalists met in Madrid to discuss the revival of the long dormant organization. A second assembly was held on February 29, 1976, in Barcelona; at that meeting it was agreed that dissension between "exterior" and "interior" leaders had to cease and that "historic" and new leaders would have to cooperate in rebuilding the CNT in the country. The confederation recovered legality in May 1977 and was soon able to show that it continued the traditions of the CNT of the 1930s.

The continuity in ideology was clearly expressed by *Solidaridad Obrera* in May 1976. It stated the following points:

> a) Freedom: Convinced that man is only fully such when he is free, we strive for his maximum freedom in a just and coordinated society in which factors such as repression, economic discrimination and authoritarianism will have disappeared. Since man is the basis of society, only if he is free and cognizant will the community of which he is part be also free and cognizant.
>
> b) Self-management: Self-management, which claims the equal participation of each citizen in whatever concerns it, is the practice of freedom in cooperation which eliminates, by its own function, privileges and hierarchy.
>
> c) Direct action: Direct action, which does not imply violence nor imposition, consists in avoiding intermediaries. This means that the CNT, for the solution of all problems, claims the direct participation of all concerned persons. In this way, the freedom of each man is respected and absorbing and abusive bureaucracy becomes unnecessary.
>
> d) Federalism: Through the federal practice, which moves from the bottom up, and which allows the participation of all without the underrating or the isolation of anyone, one can organize society at all levels.... (Almendros et al. 1978, p. 166)

The base of the CNT's structure is the *sindicato*, composed of a number of sections formed either along craft or industrial lines. The policies and activities of the *sindicato* are determined by an assembly of all its members. The assembly may delegate for a given period of time some of its powers to a *junta*. The *sindicatos* of a given locality or area, *comarca*, are grouped into local or area federations reflecting industrial activity. These federations in turn form regional confederations, each of which sends a delegate to the National Committee.

The highest administrative body is the National Congress. Most of the CNT's directives, however, are provided by *plenos,* meetings at local and regional levels. A number of support organizations are part of the CNT administrative system; these include federated organizations such as the

Association of Retired Persons, Free Women, and the Iberian Federation of Libertarian Youth.

By May 1978, the CNT reported a membership of 300,000 members (*El Pais*, 1978). The distribution of this membership among Spanish regions was quite similar to that prevailing in the pre–civil war period. In 1978, Catalonia contained 70 percent of the CNT's membership.

Details of many other independent labor organizations that were legalized after the end of Franco's rule will not be presented here. In brief, these organizations can be classified as reflecting nationalities or regions, organizations based on a professional membership, and organizations with certain political or apolitical preferences.

Among those based on nationalities or regions were the Solidaridad de Trabajadores Vascos (ELA-STV), a Basque Socialist organization; another purely Basque association was the Langile Abertzaleen Batzordeak (LAB), a regionalist and anticapitalist organization, especially strong in the southern areas of the Basque region. In Catalonia, the Solidaritat d'Obrers Catalans Cristians (SOCC) was influenced by Catholic groups, while the Sindicato Libre de Catalunya (SLC) looked at the strike as a weapon of last resort and took an anti-Marxist stance. Other regional organizations were the Sindicato Obreiro Galego (SOG), the Sindicato Obrero Canario (SOC), and the Confederación Canaria de Trabajadores (CCT).

Some of the labor organizations based on professional activities were the Sindicato Libre de la Marina Mercante, the Sindicato Libre e Independiente de los Cuerpos de la Administración de la Justicia, and the Federación Español de Cuadros y Confederación General de Cuadros. There were also a number of independent agrarian labor organizations.

Finally, a number of independent labor organizations with their own political views, ranging from one extreme to the other of the political spectrum, appeared on the scene in the late 1970s. Among them were the Confederación Democrática de Trabajadores, the Confederación de Trabajadores Independientes, the Confederación Española de Sindicatos Independientes, the Comisiones Obreras Anticapitalistas, and the Confederación de Trabajadores Sindicalistas.

CONCLUSION

As will be observed in the following chapters, the German Federal Republic emerged out of World War II with a strongly unified free labor movement. When Spain returned to a system of political democracy in 1975, Spanish labor organizations were fragmented along ethnic, regional, professional, and ideological lines. A major reason for the differences in labor organization between the two countries relates to the timing and the speed of the countries' transformation from an essentially traditional, preindustrial social state to that characteristic of a modern industrial society.

In the preindustrial society, individuals are taught from early childhood to accept without question the time-hallowed matrix of social institutions; alien customs are perceived as hostile and dangerous. Traditional life requires conformity with inherited and established customs, views, attitudes, and values. The preindustrial, tradition-ruled society is generally static, closed, and quiescent. In such a society, means of transportation and communications are deficient quantitatively and qualitatively. Geographic, social, and economic mobilities are very low. The identification of people with "their" society is limited to a village or to a group of villages, perhaps even to a particualr region within the nation, but rarely extends to the nation as a whole or to a given social class within that nation. In the static, immobile, unchanging traditional society people identify strongly with a given group, the group being necessarily geographically and socially limited.

Whereas traditional society gives emphasis to conformity, modern industrial society gives value to adaptability to change, individualism, and initiative. In the industrial society, marked by constant technological, social, economic, and political change, the individual must constantly learn and adapt to new ways of thinking and to new behavior patterns. In this society, people trade a sense of security derived from the ability to feel part of a given community for a higher material standard of living in the impersonal modern society. Modern industrialization commands a price often expressed in terms of higher rates of delinquency, crime, divorce, mental illness, and suicide. The less adaptable the individual is to change, the higher the price that individual will have to pay for the social process called "modernization."

Germany experienced a true Industrial Revolution during the second half of the nineteenth century. This revolution moved masses of people from the countryside to the growing industrial cities. In the urban setting, traditional attitudes and values tended to weaken. Localist and regionalist feelings were soon forgotten in the factories.

Such a revolution occurred in Spain nearly 100 years later. The Industrial Revolution took a firm foothold in Spain only in the 1960s. This explains why, in the late 1970s, Spain, when compared to Germany, still exhibited many of the characteristics of traditionalism. It is important to understand that until the coming of the Spanish "economic miracle" in the 1960s, most Spanish people still lived in a traditionalist, unchanging, static world in which individuals identified with a *pueblo,* a town, or a region rather than with the nation as a whole or with a given social class within it. The Castilian viewed Spaniards of other regions as "second-class" Spaniards, while the Catalan tended to perceive the Castilian as an arrogant social parasite.

The localism and regionalism of Spaniards in 1960 were probably as strong as they were when Fanelli first came to Spain. Different topography, different climates, different forms of land tenure, and different social and economic traditions made for great differences in the perception of desirable social and economic change among Spaniards. There were more than "two Spains"; there were many Spains. There was a northern Spain composed of small, independent, conservative farmers and of equality-minded miners and industrial workers; there was the Spain of the central *Meseta* inhabited by poor and small farmers living side by side with rich aristocratic or bourgeois landlords. Both rich and poor felt, however, that they were the "true Spaniards," the defenders of the central government in Madrid. The wealthy Castilians remained loyal to Catholic conservatism, while the lower bourgeoisie flirted with moderate liberalism; the peasantry was politically indifferent, while the relative few skilled urban workers became interested in anarchist and Socialist ideologies. In southern Spain, society was divided into two classes hostile to each other; the landed magnates lived in a world of luxury constantly threatened by the masses of hungry landless laborers. These conditions were also found in the western region of Extremadura, where the rural proletariat faced a seasonal and uncertain source of earnings.

In that preindustrial Spain, the rural workers were bound to their low-paid rural activity because a sufficiently large secondary or tertiary economic sector where they could find a new livelihood simply did not exist. The masses of Spanish workers remained tied to unchanging forms of economic activity and to unchanging ways of thinking.

It is only natural that when industrialization came in the 1960s, and democracy in the 1970s, Spanish workers would not be able to organize on the basis of a single, centralized labor organization, which in many ways would have required Spaniards, until then dominated by localist or regionalist traditional culture patterns, to perceive in a similar way economic problems and their solution. The long repression of regionalist feelings under the Franco government resulted in an explosion of regionalist sentiment after Franco's death.

In the 1980s, at a time when a favorite debate in Spain is whether there exists one, unified country or only a loose federation of Spanish regions, the Spanish trade union movement naturally fragmented into a large number of organizations reflecting the great cultural and regional diversity so many Spaniards are proud of to this day. In the still neotraditional Spain, too many Spaniards still see their *pueblo*, their *patria chica* as being more meaningful to them than the *patria grande*—a type of social identification that is also reflected in the diversity of labor organizations in which they seek membership.

NOTES

Almendros, F., et al. 1978. *El Sindicalismo de Clase en España, 1939–1977.* Barcelona: Ediciones Península.

Amsden, J. 1972. *Collective Bargaining and Class Conflict in Spain.* London: Weidenfeld & Nicholson.

Camacho, M. 1976. *Charlas en la prisión.* Barcelona: Editorial LAIA.

El Pais, 13-V-78.

Guinea, J. L. 1978. *Los movimientos obreros y sindicales en España, de 1833 a 1978.* Madrid: Ibérico Europeo de Ediciones.

Jackson, G. 1965. *The Spanish Republic and the Civil War, 1931–1939.* Princeton, N.J.: Princeton University Press.

Lieberman, S. 1982. *The Contemporary Spanish Economy: A Historical Perspective.* London: Allen & Unwin.

USO. 1977. *Libertad, Autonomía, Unidad.* Madrid: Ediciones Túcar.

BIBLIOGRAPHY

Abad de Santillan, D. *Historia del movimiento obrero español.* Madrid, 1967.

Garcia-Nieto, J. and A. Busquets. *La Nueva Ley Sindical.* Madrid, 1972.

Garcia Venero, M. *Historia de las Internacionales en España.* 3 vols. Madrid, 1956.

Gomez Casas, J. *Historia del Anarcosindicalismo Español.* Madrid, 1968.

Marti, C. *Orígenes del Anarquismo en Barcelona.* Barcelona, 1959.

Padilla, A. *El Movimiento Socialista Español.* Barcelona, 1977.

Payne, S. G. *The Spanish Revolution.* New York, 1970.

Ratcliff, D. F. *Prelude to Franco.* New York, 1957.

Rosal, A. Del. *Historia de la UGT en España, 1901–1939.* Madrid, 1977.

Thomas, H. *La Guerra Civil Española.* Barcelona, 1976.

4
The Evolution of the German Labor Movement: From 1848 to 1914

THE INTELLECTUAL ROOTS OF THE GERMAN LABOR MOVEMENT

The political entities that constituted pre-1871 Germany depended largely on agrarian economies. Even though their aggregate population had risen from about 24.5 million in 1800 to more than 35 million in 1850, two-thirds of the German population still made a living in the agricultural sector at the time of the Revolution of 1848. In that year, Prussia had 850,000 craftsmen working in small traditional workshops and 550,000 factory workers. In the late 1840s, most of these factories operated with a labor force varying between 30 and 100 workers; in 1846, the Krupp enterprise employed a labor force of 130 persons (DGB 1973, p.9).

Compared to the British and the French experiences, industrialization and the development of a labor movement came relatively late for both Spain and Germany. During the 1840s, craftsmen and rural workers in both countries did not identify with a nation or with a social class. The Spanish *jornaleros* and the German *Tageloehner* accepted tradition-determined standards of living and were generally too ignorant to be interested in political or social reform. August Bebel, the German socialist, wrote about the lack of class consciousness of German workers as late as the 1860s (Grebing 1980, p.67).

Germany experienced the Industrial Revolution much earlier than Spain. Whereas, starting in the 1870s, Germany's industrialization effort transformed Wilhelmine Germany into a foremost industrial power by 1914, Spain had to wait until the 1960s to acquire a modern, capitalist, industrial economy. Even though Spain failed to industrialize significantly in the nineteenth century, a national labor movement was organized by a few workers in Barcelona and Madrid in the 1860s. As noted, this movement became pluralistic in ideology and fragmented in structure. Born with the Revolution of 1848, the German labor movement was to evolve in a completely different fashion. It soon achieved a unity that prevails to this day.

There was no German labor movement before 1848. One reason for this tardiness was the strict laws passed by the German states that prohibited the formation of workers' associations and invoked severe press censorship. An equally important reason may have been the lack of interest on the part of German workers to increase their political and economic strength by means of clandestine organizations.

German workers had to be taught new, foreign ideas before they realized that they could join forces in an attempt to improve their social and economic conditions. These new ideas were not disseminated by workers living in Germany. Rather, they were propagated by members of two distinct social groups.

Members of associations of university students, the *Burschenschaften*, wrote and talked about a new unified, democratic, and possibly republican Germany that would guarantee freedom and equality to all of its citizens. The students convinced skilled German journeymen living in England, France and Switzerland of the necessity of a revolution in the homeland that would not only unify the German fatherland politically but would also bring about desired social changes. The members of these associations of German expatriate journeymen craftsmen, the *Auslandsvereine*, readily accepted the vision of one unified and democratic Germany.

The goal of German unification became of paramount importance to the German workers' associations formed in Paris in the 1830s. The *Deutscher Volksverein* (German Popular Association), founded in 1832, started sending revolutionary tracts to Germany; the *Bund der Geaechteten* (League of the Outlaws) and the *Bund der Gerechten* (League of the Just) were established in 1834 and in 1836. The League of the Outlaws published the review *The Outlaw* for which Theodor Schuster, a former instructor at the University of Göttingen, wrote articles on the ideas of the French utopians and advocated the establishment of government-financed national workshops. The League of the Outlaws was supplanted by the League of the Just, whose influence extended into England, Switzerland, and even Germany.

A clandestine association of German workers was also formed in Switzerland under the name of Young Germany and was led by the Mazzini-inspired German student Ernst Schueler. Other groups of expatriate skilled German workers were influenced by the *Burschenschaftler* Karl

Schapper, whose radical social demands appeared in the journal *Nord-licht (Northern Light)*.

The membership of the associations in Paris and London probably never exceeded 100 in the late 1830s. The Swiss organizations counted perhaps 400 members. These groups, composed of expatriate or touring skilled workers, students, and intellectuals sympathetic to the workers, embraced both nationalistic and internationalistic ideologies that emphasized the importance of social equality and the need for democratic institutions in the homeland. This is why the *Auslandsvereine* showed a great deal of hostility toward communism, which was considered despotic. These associations were instrumental in spreading Christian-Socialist ideas throughout Germany in the 1830s and in the 1840s. They translated, for export to Germany, the books of the French liberal Robert Lamennais, *Words of a Believer* and *The Book of the People*. In the words of Jacques Droz (1976), the *Auslandsvereine* excelled in teaching the German masses "demotheocracy" (p. 424).

A number of German thinkers and writers who lived or had lived abroad showed great concern for the existing social conditions in Germany before the Revolution of 1848. A critic we are most familiar with is Karl Marx. Marx, however, was mainly concerned with the exploitation of the industrial worker by the modern capitalist.

The destitution and the misery of the German workers in the period of the *Vormaerz* were not connected with the beginnings of industrialization in Germany; rather, they were caused by lack of industrialization at a time of rapid population growth. Emigration could not solve the problem of high unemployment. The rapid disappearance of guild restrictions made the labor supply curve more elastic and the competition for jobs fiercer. As the struggle for survival became harder, Silesian textile workers finally rose in insurrection in 1844, burning the homes of merchants and middlemen and destroying machinery and public records.

Most of the German workers simply started listening to the ideas of men who had observed more advanced economic systems abroad. These men had been very much influenced by the French and English utopian socialists, for example, Saint-Simon, Fourier, Cabet, Lamennais, and Owen. These were the men who gave the German workers the concept of class identity.

The Hegelian philosopher and professor at the University of Berlin, Eduard Gans, had visited France before and after the 1830 revolution. In his lectures, which were attended by Karl Marx, he advocated the complete liberation of all people through a better organization of production and a more equitable distribution of wealth. Gans believed that the state should assume the responsibility of providing the necessities of the poorest and most numerous social class. Carrying this idea further, Georg Buechner, who had lived in Strasbourg during the early 1830s and who belonged to the *Burschenschaft* of Giessen, argued that the problem of German unification and the social problems were inseparable; any revolutionary effort required the support of the masses, and thus attention had to be paid to the material interests of the working class. His clandestine newspaper, the *Hessische Landsbote (Hessian Rural Messenger)*, advocated "peace to the cottages, war to the palaces."

Another man who contributed to the slow infiltration of socialist ideas in Germany was a young mining engineer who, on several occasions, had visited Great Britain, Franz von Baader. Baader argued before Marx did that society progresses through the accumulation of capital possessed by the few; while the Industrial Revolution increases the wealth of industrial entrepreneurs, it impoverishes the masses of workers. Baader, who became a professor of philosophy at the University of Munich, claimed that only the church could protect the interests of the proletariat and obtain from the government the right of workers to form associations.

Rather than to rely on the church, Franz Josef Ritter von Buss, a deputy of the diet of Baden, demanded in 1837 an ample program of social legislation designed to protect workers in an industrializing society.

Foreign socialist ideas were perhaps best communicated to the German masses by the 1842 book of Lorenz von Stein, *Socialism and Communism in Contemporary France*. Although Stein was an undercover agent for the Prussian government charged with the task of identifying the members of the *Auslandsvereine* of Paris, he urged government and economic elites in Germany to show more concern for the conditions of the workers. He argued in his book that the proletariat formed a new class in Germany, a class created by the separation of capital and labor, the workers being forced into a neofeudal condition of dependency on the owners of capital. To achieve greater social justice, the proletariat had to resort to violence. Stein, neither a Socialist nor a Communist, urged government to take needed social action to prevent what could otherwise end as a violent revolution.

For the Catholic priest who was to become bishop of Mainz, Wilhelm Emmanuel Freiherr von Ketteler, the social problem in Germany was of paramount importance. Ketteler, quite aware of the low standards of living of German workers, called on all German Catholics to effectuate a voluntary redistribution of wealth in conformity with their religious beliefs. For Ketteler, as well as for the Protestant Johann Heinrich Wichern, only the church, not the government, could bring about an improvement of social conditions.

This view was not shared by Wilhelm Weitling. Weitling, a touring journeyman tailor, published in 1838 his first book in Paris, *Humanity as It Is and as It Should Be*, a book that was very well received by German expatriates in France, England, and Switzerland. Weitling was influenced both by the utopian vision of Fourier and by the Christianity of Lamennais; he rejected reformism and counted on the proletariat to produce a revolution that would introduce a totally new society. In this ideal society, people would live in "associations of families," and goods and means of production would be owned collectively. This communal type of living was presented as the authentic Christian society. Weitling's utopia retained many similarities to the world of peasants and craftsmen in which he grew up as a child. Weitling appeared more interested in preserving the values and the ways of the small crafts–based town than in coping with the social problems brought by modern industrialization.

Forced to move to Geneva, Weitling became the editor of two publications that were to implant socialist ideas in the future German labor movement: *Der Hilferuf der deutschen Jugend* (*Cry for Help of the German Youth*) and *Die neue Generation* (*New Generation*). In 1842, he published his principal work, *Guarantees of Harmony and Freedom*, in which he invited the working class to initiate revolutionary action; he rejected social reformism and political democracy and advocated the establishment of a dictatorship that would organize the new Communist society.

In his book *The Evangelium of the Poor Sinner*, Weitling presented Christ as the first revolutionary proletarian engaged in a battle against the Pharisees and the rich. Weitling's call for revolution gave him for a long time Marx's admiration; Marx felt that Weitling was by far superior to most German political economists.

Weitling had numerous disciples in and outside Germany. He also had numerous critics. Wilhelm Marr, author of the book *The Young Germany in Switzerland*, which appeared in 1846, wrote about Weitling's communism: "Communism is a social theology. It has its sacred books, its prophets, its Messiahs and its heaven" (Droz 1976; p. 428). The German critics of Weitling preferred the atheistic humanism of Ludwig Feuerbach, and Weitling's influence started to decline in the mid-1840s.

An important causal factor in the rise of a German labor movement in the late 1840s was the Silesian textile workers' insurrection in 1844. The insurrection was a protest against heavy feudalistic impositions and a harsh putting-out system. The workers burned the houses of merchants and destroyed some machinery. The government's repression was severe.

Wilhelm Wolff, a young professor from Breslau, denounced the poor living conditions of the Silesian cottage workers and the government's refusal to assist them. Members of the German liberal middle class, influenced by Hegelian philosophy, started asserting that the state was responsible for the promotion of social justice. The industrialist Gustav Mevissen felt that drastic action should be taken by government to fight destitution and hunger. In the 1840s, a number of German intellectuals cautioned the government to assist the working class and to make a better distinction between the poor and the criminals. August Theodor Woeniger, Alexander Scheer, Friedrich Sass, Heinrich Wilhelm Bensen, Robert von Mohl, and Anton Freimund von Arnim pointed to the dangerous implications of a widening economic gap between the capitalists and the proletariat. H. B. Oppenheim, a law professor at the University of Heidelberg, maintained in 1847 in his *Philosophy of Law and Society* that freedom could not exist as long as capitalist gains resulted in the impoverishment of the proletariat.

Social problems were widely discussed in the *Bildungsvereine*, the educational associations, whose number rose rapidly after 1844. In the *Bildungsvereine* of Hamburg, the carpenter Martens and the journalist Schirges propagated the ideas of Weitling. In that of Berlin, skilled workers and members of the liberal bourgeoisie discussed German unification, communism, and Christian ideology. Many of the middle-class discussants had been greatly influenced by the atheist philosophy of Feuerbach. The contacts made in the *Bildungsvereine* between members of the liberal bourgeoisie and the workers were to facilitate the formation of an alliance between these two groups during the revolutions of 1848 and 1849.

Moses Hess was the first writer in Germany to develop a theory of social revolution caused by the misery of the proletariat. In his *Sacred History of Mankind*, published in 1837, Hess predicted the unavoidable coming of a revolution that would reinstate social and economic equality and introduce "God's kingdom." Hess preceded Marx in explaining how in the capitalist society the worker is deprived of the entire fruit of his labor by the employer.

Many books have been written giving detailed accounts of Marxist theories. Let us simply note here that Karl Marx became interested in political economy following his acquaintance with Friedrich Engels in 1842. The problem of human alienation was of paramount importance for Marx. He explained this problem in terms of the characteristics of capitalist production. The worker, forced to sell his labor to survive, receives a compensation from the capitalist whose value is much lower than the value created by the worker. Human labor in the capitalist system becomes a mere commodity bought by the entrepreneur in the market at the lowest possible price; labor is a factor of production bought and sold just like any other productive input. The worker has no role in the planning and supervision of the production process, and can be separated from the latter at the command of the capitalist. Alienation is thus a purely social phenomenon and can only be eliminated through a radical transformation of the social system. This transformation requires the abolition of the institution of private ownership. The transformation will be brought about by the class struggle that ends with the establishment of a Communist society.

THE FORMATION OF THE GERMAN
SOCIAL DEMOCRATIC PARTY

Very few German workers were influenced by the writings of the social critics. Rather, their interest in a proletarian political movement and in the formation of trade unions was largely the result of the efforts of workers' associations, the *Arbeitervereine*, which proliferated in 1848. In spite of police repression in the 1850s, these organizations were to provide the cadres of the political parties formed in the 1860s by Ferdinand Lassalle and by Wilhelm Liebknecht and August Bebel. It was the elite of the *Arbeitervereine* membership that was to demand in 1863 the formation of a workers' independent party. It was that elite which, in 1875, brought to an end the petty quarrels between various labor leaders and succeeded in unifying German social democracy.

The insurrections of 1848 were directed by the low bourgeoisie—lawyers, physicians, professors, and merchants, with the support of the craftsmen. These revolutionaries attempted to establish a bourgeois republic, not a "red" republic. They were, however, interested in social problems, and in the singing and gymnastics clubs, as well as in organizations belonging to the *Lichterfreunde* (Friends of Light) or to the *Deutsch-Katholizismus* (German Catholicism). Members of the liberal middle class contacted members of the workers' elite. They spoke about rationalism, religion, and socialist thought. Socialist ideas were often propagated by churchmen; in the *Liebfrauenkirche* of Bremen, its pastor, Rudolf Dulon, presented socialism as a modern form of the Scriptures; he organized throughout northern Germany a network of organizations that studied social problems. In Hesse, a friend of Buechner and of Weitling, August Becker, established a club in Giessen whose members were concerned with the problems of the peasantry.

The education of the working class was also promoted by two other groups. One was Stephen Born's *Verbruederung* (Fraternity). The other group listened to Karl Marx in Cologne and read his *Neue Rheinische Zeitung (New Rhenish Newspaper)*.

Most workers in 1848 had little interest in any social movement and showed little consciousness of a class feeling. Even skilled craftsmen believed that their difficulties were due to the disappearance of the feudal corporate society. A workers' congress meeting in Frankfurt on the Main in September 1848 declared that the "French principle" of freedom of employment and unrestricted competition were the main causes of workers' problems. March 1848 was marked by violent and ill-prepared strikes, by the destruction of machinery by workers, and by their petitions to have employers dismiss foreign and female workers, which were seen as constituting unfair competition.

In Berlin, however, 1848 witnessed the awakening of class consciousness in the workers; workers' clubs were formed that advocated socialist ideas. A young printer from Posen, who had established himself in Berlin in 1840, Stephan Born, was to found the first workers' political organization in Germany. Shortly after the outbreak of revolution in Berlin, Born became the leader of the local *Arbeitervereine*; he called for a General German Workers' Congress to meet in Berlin on August 23, 1848. This congress lasted until September 3 and established the Allgemeine deutsche Arbeiter-Verbruederung, generally known as the Verbruederung. This organization soon counted 170 local branches; its central committee, headed by Born, was in Leipzig. The first trade unions in Germany, those of the printers and of the cigar makers, adhered to the Fraternity.

Although initially a disciple of Marx and Engels, Born soon abandoned Marxist theory for reformist policies. He wrote about Marxist revolutionary theories: "They were suddenly forgotten by me, all the Communist thoughts which had no bearing at all on what was demanded by the present... what concern of mine were the distant centuries, when each hour brought pressing tasks and plenty of work?" (Grebing 1980, p. 44).

Born advocated an alliance between the bourgeoisie and the workers. He stated: "In Germany, we have a double obligation; on the one hand to support the bourgeoisie in its fight against the aristocracy and the forces of divine right, and on the other, to also support the worker, the craftsman, in order to obtain for the people new political rights..." (Droz 1976, p. 465). Born's program was modest by design; he did not want to alienate the low bourgeoisie. The Fraternity demanded a parliamentarian and democratic state based on universal suffrage, the right of workers to organize and to form producers' and consumers' cooperatives, better labor legislation, social security measures to protect the workers in case of sickness, disability, and old age, and free education.

The supporters of these demands were journeymen craftsmen and skilled factory workers who did not identify with the masses of unskilled workers and who were not yet conscious of being part of a Marxist-type proletariat. These were not men who perceived a class conflict between themselves and the bourgeoisie. Although they referred to themselves as "workers," *Arbeiter*, they nevertheless felt socially closer to the low bourgeoisie than to the much despised *Tageloehner*. They demanded that unskilled workers address them as *Herr*. In this they clearly differed from the early Spanish labor leaders, who felt from the beginning that an un-surmountable gap separated them and all other workers from the other social groups in Spain. The beginnings of the German labor movement did not fit at all the Marxist model, a point recognized by Grebing when she wrote (1980) that "the dualism of social revolution and social reform, of proletarian consciousness and bourgeois-inspired pride of status, had its origins in 1848; it was later to be reflected in increasingly acrimoni-ous arguments between different camps within the social-democratic la-bor movement..." (p. 46).

The Fraternity was banned by federal law in 1854. The law, however, allowed the existence of nonpolitical and religious workers' associations. This permitted the Catholic Journeymen's Association of Adolf Kolping, once a shoemaker journeyman, later a priest, to establish branches throughout Germany. By 1855, this organization counted 104 *Vereine* with an aggregate membership of 12,000. These organizations offered the workers religious teaching and continuous professional training. Social problems were, however, discussed at the general meeting of the *Vereine* in Mainz in October 1848.

For Marx, the cooperation between workers and the bourgeoisie was to be temporary. In Germany, Marx published his "17 Demands of the Communist Party" in an effort to adapt the principles of the *Communist Manifesto* to German conditions. He called for a democratic republic and included in his "17 Demands" a number of socialist claims: the nation-alization of feudal estates, mines, and means of transportation and the replacement of private banks by a public bank. Marx believed that the German workers still lacked an adequate class consciousness to engage successfully in revolutionary action; this is why he advocated in the *Neue Rheinische Zeitung* a provisional alliance between the workers and the progressive elements of the middle class in the fight against feudalism and the absolutist monarchy. In June 1848, Marx wrote:

> The proletariat must advance with the great democratic army at the ex-treme of its left wing, but trying always not to break contact with the main body of the army. It must be most impetuous during the attack and its fighting spirit should encourage the army, should lead to the assault on the Bastille. Because the Bastille has not yet been taken, because ab-solutism has not yet been destroyed. While the Bastille shall stand, the democrats must remain united. The proletariat, as hard as this may seem, must reject everything that could separate it from its allies. (Droz 1976, p. 469)

Marx had hoped that the *Arbeiterverein* of Cologne would lead a Ger-man revolution, a revolution that would bring social reform. Hoping to exploit the dislike of Rhinelanders for the Prussians, Marx also contributed articles to middle-class papers such as the *Neue Koelnische Zeitung* and the *Waechter.*

Marx soon came to believe, however, that the bourgeoisie could not be trusted and that it was too willing to compromise with the forces of conservatism. In the *Neue Rheinische Zeitung* he started writing again about the inevitability of the class struggle. His attempts to educate the German proletariat were temporarily ended when the authorities shut down the newspaper on March 19, 1849.

The revolutions of 1848 and of 1849 ended with the victory of the conservative groups in Germany. Harsh repression against the workers followed in 1850. Marx had to leave Germany; after a brief stay in Paris, he went on to London. Marxian influence on the workers during the two years of revolution was probably negligible; for only a few workers were able to understand his writings. Only in the 1860s did Marxist thought significantly penetrate the workers' minds in Germany.

In London, Marx did not give up his interest in the German proletariat. Having reorganized in that city the League of the Communists, Marx dispatched to Germany Heinrich Bauer, who created a number of branches of the league there. Marx and Engels also started the publication of a new review in Hamburg named after the Cologne newspaper, the *Neue Rheinische Zeitung.* Marx affirmed in it that there existed an irreconcilable conflict between the bourgeoisie and the proletariat. Meanwhile, branches of the league spread throughout Germany. Its representatives taught Marxist theory in gymnastics and rifle clubs.

The league and its teachings of Marxism received a hard blow when a German League member was arrested in May 1851, thus enabling the police to identify a large number of German members of the league. Massive arrests followed, which, in effect, terminated the existence of the league in Germany and put an end for the rest of the decade Marx's revolutionary activities in the German states.

The 1850s were not propitious to workers. Although Germany experienced a wave of industrialization during this period, the workers' misery reached an all-time high; the massive migration of rural workers to the cities retarded the development of class consciousness among workers in general, and work conditions remained poor. In spite of the hardships, skilled craftsmen tried to maintain their organizations in the guise of mutual aid societies.

Toward the end of the decade, both the conservative and the liberal bourgeois parties tried to create their own *Arbeitervereine* in order to widen their electoral base. In Prussia, Hermann Schulze-Delitzsch, a lawyer who had been dismissed from the Prussian civil service, tried to organize craftsmen and small merchants on a cooperative basis. His idea was that the cooperatives should function without any aid from the government. Credit cooperatives were to ease the financial problems of the members of producers' and consumers' cooperatives. Schulze-Delitzsch rejected the Marx-Engels class struggle argument and claimed that hardworking, frugal craftsmen and small traders could become part of an independent middle class. He recommended the same "self-help" measures to factory workers, showing little understanding of the economic conditions of the proletariat. His success in the 1850s must be attributed to the fact that many craftsmen and small merchants still identified with the bourgeoisie and still looked to the liberals for political guidance.

At the start of the 1860s, the workers most interested in a labor movement were the specialized craftsmen, who felt threatened by the development of factory production. In many German cities, workers' associations were formed that were generally hostile to bourgeois influence on the labor movement. In Leipzig, a Tradesmen's Educational Association, the *Gewerblicher Bildungsverein*, was founded. A small group in this organization formed *Vorwaerts* (Forward), a separate association that gave priority to the discussion of political problems. At the end of 1862, two of its members, the shoemaker Julius Vahlteich and the journeyman cigar maker Friedrich Wilhelm Fritzsche, asked Ferdinand Lassalle to draft a program for a "workers' party" that would be independent of both the liberal bourgeoisie and the Junker aristocracy.

Lassalle had been a member of the League of the Communists. Like Marx, he had studied law and philosophy in Berlin and, like Marx, he had become interested in "neo-Hegelianism." He practiced law in Düsseldorf, met Marx in 1848, and from 1854 on, lived in Berlin where he devoted himself to philosophical studies. He devoted the last two years of his short life to the German labor movement.

On March 1, 1863, Lassalle published his "Open Letter to the Central Committee for the Convention of a General German Workers' Congress in Leipzig." In that letter he advocated the formation of a workers' party that would be totally independent of both the government and the liberal bourgeoisie. That party was to seek universal suffrage and the eventual domination of the state by legal means. The state would then extend its help to producers' cooperatives, which would be able to compete successfully with capitalist firms.

This program was approved by the central committee of a workers' congress in Leipzig in March 1863. Among the delegates at this congress were militants of the 1848 revolution, members of the League of the Communists, and labor leaders such as Wilhelm Liebknecht from Berlin, Gustav Lewy from Düsseldorf, Hugo Hillmann from Elberfeld, and Moses Hess from Cologne. Lassalle's program was also adopted by a number of *Arbeitervereine* in Hamburg and in various cities of the Rhineland. The program meant a definite rupture between labor and the liberal bourgeoisie, which Lassalle attacked in his *Herr Bastiat von Schulze-Delitzsch.*

The Leipzig workers' congress established the first German Socialist party on May 23, 1863, the *Allgemeiner deutscher Arbeiterverein* (ADAV) or the General Association of German Workers. Lassalle became its president.

As of May 1863, Lassalle also started a correspondence with Prince Otto von Bismarck. It was Lassalle's hope that the Prussian government would eventually become the welfare government that would found a new, united Germany under a popular monarchy. Lassalle never committed himself to a political system of parliamentarian democracy. Given the authoritarian way he directed ADAV—its secretary, Julius Vahlteich, resigned from the party in protest against Lassalle's dictatorial rule—one can surmise that Lassalle was not adverse to a dictatorship that would fulfill his social goals.

At the time of Lassalle's death, on August 31, 1864, ADAV counted about 4,000 members, most of them residing either in Hamburg or in the Rhineland. The party published two newspapers, the *Volksfreund (Friend of the People)*, in Frankfurt, and the *Nordstern (North Star)*, in Hamburg.

Lassalle gave the German labor movement an alternative to the revolutionary socialism of Marx and Engels; he claimed that a strong national government could help the working class through reformist legislation. Because of Lassalle's sympathy for the Hohenzollern government, Marx and Engels took an increasingly hostile position toward him, even though they had to recognize that he was the only German labor leader who insisted on a divorce between labor and the liberal bourgeoisie. On the other hand, Lassalle drew support from the bishop of Mainz, W. E. von Ketteler; in his book, *The Workers and Christianity*, published in 1865, Ketteler adopted Lassalle's concept of the "iron law of wages" and his ideas about producers' cooperatives and rejected the tactics of Schulze-Delitzsch.

Because of his belief in the "iron law of wages," Lassalle attached little importance to trade union activity as a means of improving the standards of living of the workers. In his mind, the main goal of the ADAV was political rather than social. He was mostly concerned with the revolutionary potential of workers and showed little interest in an alliance of workers with either the peasantry or the low bourgeoisie.

Lassalle impressed the great mass of German workers at a time when Marx and Engels were only known by a few in Germany. Unfortunately, Lassalle's successors tried to carry on the authoritarian ways of the founder of the ADAV, which produced a lot of resentment in a number of *Arbeitervereine.*

Many workers' associations had refused to follow Lassalle. These associations established in Frankfurt in June 1863 a Federation of German Workers' Associations, the *Verband deutscher Arbeitervereine* (VDAV). The leaders of this federation were mostly members of the liberal bourgeois parties. Having been disappointed by the personality cult of Lassalle in the ADAV, Wilhelm Liebknecht left that organization and joined the VDAV. Liebknecht had been a student of theology, philosophy, and philology and had participated in the Revolution of 1848; forced into exile, he spent a few years in Switzerland, then lived in London where he became familiar with the theories of Marx and Engels. He returned to Berlin in 1862, where he criticized the policies of Bismarck in the middle-class newspaper *Oberrheinischer Kurier*.

Ordered to leave Berlin in 1865, Liebknecht went to Leipzig, where he became acquainted with the master turner August Bebel, a leader of the local *Bildungsverein*. Both men disliked the pro-Prussian inclinations of Lassalle. Liebknecht taught Bebel Marxist theory, and Bebel became a convert to scientific socialism. Both men also felt that the German workers were not yet ready to form an independent political party and accused Lassalle of having divided the democratic forces in Germany. Sharing a belief in the formation of a German federal republic, they decided to ally themselves with democratic, bourgeois groups in southern Germany that opposed Bismarck. They were therefore to collaborate with Leopold Sonnemann, editor of the *Frankfurter Zeitung*, a man who rejected the concept of the class struggle but who shared with Liebknecht and Bebel the vision of a non-Prussian, democratic greater Germany.

The Popular German party, or *Deutsche Volkspartei*, was founded in Darmstadt in September 1865. Its platform called for German unification, but not under Prussian rule, for universal suffrage, and for very limited social legislation. The new party's organ was the *Deutsches Wochenblatt (German Weekly)*. In order to mobilize all the democratic forces against Bismarck, Liebknecht and Bebel agreed to limit their social demands in order not to alienate the bourgeoisie. Bebel became president of the federation in October 1869.

Both the ADAV and the VDAV were gaining rapid support among the workers; while the former expanded in Frankfurt, Berlin, Hamburg, and the Rhineland, the federation made significant advances in Saxony, Thuringia, and Württemberg.

Following the establishment of the First International in London in 1864, a number of clandestine sections of this organization were founded in Germany by Johann Philipp Becker. The organ of these sections was a paper printed in Geneva, the *Vorbote (Forerunner)*. Marx was highly interested in the establishment of the International in Germany and corresponded with its militants in Germany, such as the Hannover physician Ludwig Kugelmann, Paul Stumpf, founder of the Mainz section, Karl

Klein of Solingen, and Sigfried Meyer, who published the first German edition of the *Communist Manifesto*.

At the VDAV congress that met in Nürnberg in September 1868, Bebel and Liebknecht declared that their organization would follow the program of the First International. They may have feared the implications of an accord between Marx and the then leader of the ADAV, Johan Baptist von Schweitzer. The Bebel-Liebknecht decision meant a rupture between the VDAV and the bourgeois democrats. Liebknecht realized that he had to sacrifice his bourgeois supporters in order to strive for a unified German proletarian organization; the VDAV had to become a revolutionary workers' organization, the foundation of a proletarian party Marx would approve of.

Liebknecht also became active in forming international trade unions, *Internationale Gewerkschaften*, organizations that would conform with the policies of the International.

The congress of the federation, meeting in Eisenach in August 1869, established the Social Democratic Workers' party, or the *Sozialdemokratische Arbeiterpartei* (SDAP). The party's program was inspired by the bylaws of the First International and by Marx's belief in a joint political and economic struggle. The president of the SDAP was Wilhelm Bracke, a former member of the ADAV who had left that organization, disappointed by the personality cults it supported. The SDAP's organ, the *Volksstaat*, was printed in Leipzig and reflected the ideas of Bebel and of Liebknecht.

The Franco-Prussian War was initially perceived by the SDAP leadership as a war forced upon Germany that impelled the country to defend itself; the SDAP therefore urged German workers to fulfill their military duty. The Lassalleans Hasselmann and Hasenclever took an even stronger position and claimed that the war not only constituted a French attack against Germany but also a French attack on socialism. The SDAP sections of Saxony were alone in advising their members to oppose the war.

In the Reichstag, Bebel and Liebknecht abstained from voting on war credits. The General Council of the International published, on July 23, 1870, a memorandum written by Marx and Engels stating that Germany had to defend itself, therefore justifying the German war effort. The position taken by Marx and Engels probably reflected their view that Napoleon III represented a threat to all social freedoms and therefore had to be defeated; with Napoleon's end, Marxist views would acquire a stronger foothold in Europe and those of Proudhon would rapidly vanish in France.

After the French defeat at Sedan and the establishment of a French republic, German socialist views changed. On September 5, 1870, the SDAP published a manifesto in which it called for immediate peace and condemned the German annexation of Alsace and Lorraine. A few days later the International issued a proclamation to the effect that it was the duty of Socialists to fight against the German annexation. On November 26, Bebel and Liebknecht explained in the Reichstag why they felt compelled to vote against further war credits. Bismarck had the two men arrested and indicted for high treason.

As of that time, it became clear that the policies of the Prussian government and those of the German democratic forces followed distinct directions. The Lassalleans had to recognize that their dream of a "popular Prussian government" had vanished; in the new imperial and neofeudal Germany of the Hohenzollern the working class was to be a pariah class.

For most Germans, the SDAP stand against the annexation of Alsace and Lorraine rendered the party unpatriotic. Bismarck branded it as *vaterlandslos und Reichsfeind*, apatride and enemy of the empire. Bebel and Liebknecht were sentenced to two years in jail. These events tended to turn the SDAP leaders into stronger Marxists.

The beginning of Bismarck's Reich, the so-called *Gruenderjahre*, the "founding years," were plagued by numerous strikes caused by the long workday, the poor living conditions, and the high cost of living the workers had to endure. The strikes were harshly repressed, but the popularity of the Socialists rose. Whereas the Socialists had obtained only 3.3 percent of the popular vote in the elections of 1871, they obtained 6.5 percent of that vote three years later, receiving 36 percent of the total vote in Saxony and 40 percent in Hamburg (Droz 1976, p. 497).

The international trade unions started to advocate the unification of the Lassallean and the Eisenach labor parties. In February 1875, negotiations for this unification were started in Gotha. The Lassalleans were represented by Hasenclever and by Hasselmann; the Eisenach group included Liebknecht and Vahlteich. An agreement was reached that provided for the dissolution of the ADAV and for the establishment of a new political party, the *Sozialistische Arbeiterpartei Deutschlands*, the German Socialist Workers' party.

The aim of this party was to establish a socialist society in Germany, by "all the available legal means." The negotiating parties in Gotha were probably not aware of the contradiction contained in their program, a contradiction well perceived by Karl Marx. On the one hand, they purported to embrace Marxist theory and they had to recognize that in the hierarchical empire of Bismarck, class struggle had intensified; this intensified class struggle had to lead to revolution in the Marxist explanation of social development. On the other hand, they pledged to pursue their goals by "legal means" only. The contradiction was denounced by Karl Marx in his *Critique of the Gotha Programme*.

The Gotha program was, however, to facilitate the unification of the German labor movement. Until then, the movement had gone in various directions. At the VDAV congress held at Nürnberg in 1868, most delegates resolved to support the policies of the First International and the theories of Karl Marx. Marx believed that trade unions played an important role in the emancipation struggle of the proletariat. According to Marx, trade unions not only endeavored to improve the working and living conditions of their members but they also acted as "schools for socialism."

Following the VDAV congress of 1868, Johan Baptist von Schweitzer, the leader of the Lassallean party, ignored Lassalle's view of trade unions and called for a General Congress of German Workers to be held in Berlin in September of the same year. This congress started its meetings on the twenty-seventh and resolved that 12 central associations of trade unions should be formed; a General Association of German Workers was to coordinate and direct their activities.

The congress expelled a group of workers led by Max Hirsch, who entertained different views. This group met near Berlin and, with the participation of a factory owner, Franz Duncker, established a new organization of trade unions. The leaders of the Hirsch-Duncker unions rejected the Marxist belief in the class struggle and advocated class cooperation. The unions were patterned after the British model, and their members were not allowed to join the Social Democrats. These unions never played a significant role in German trade union history.

Shortly after the VDAV congress of 1868, Bebel published his ideas about the organizational structure a trade union movement should take. Local unions were to be grouped into central associations that would have the authority to call and end strikes.

Three distinct directions were thus taken by the German labor movement at the close of the 1860s. The Hirsch-Duncker unions accepted the existing social and economic systems. The other unions were either connected with the Lassallean or with the Eisenach faction of German socialism. As early as 1870, Theodor York had advocated the unification of these two trade union groups. In order to implement this idea, a trade union congress was held at Erfurt in 1872; this congress supported the idea of establishing a single trade union federation whose organ would be a newspaper titled *Die Union*. Police intervention prevented the implementation of the project.

The congress at Gotha renewed interest in a unification of trade union organizations. At the close of that congress, a conference of trade union leaders who belonged to both Socialist factions decided to unify their activities and to keep their unions out of politics. Their trade unions were to be theoretically independent of any political party; union members, however, were required to join the German Socialist Workers' party.

In 1877; the Socialist labor movement counted 26 central associations representing about 49,000 members (DGB 1973, p. 19).

The Socialists and their ideas were criticized in the 1870s by a number of church-connected writers. Bishop Ketteler had died in 1877. In the same year, a young priest, Franz Hitze, published his first book, *The Social Problem and Efforts for Its Solution with Particular Regard to the Various Social Parties in Germany.* A few years later, Hitze published *Capital and Labor and the Reorganization of Society.* In his books, Hitze attacked capitalism, wrote about the impoverishment of the masses under this form of social organization; and predicted its necessary breakdown. He argued that modern, mechanized production had to lead to socialism. Socialism could take one of two forms: "state socialism," that is, dictatorial socialism, which Hitze rejected; or the form he supported, "conservative socialism of the classes." Hitze did not propose a return to a medieval system in which society was organized in corporations and guilds. Nevertheless, what he did propose was a class-structured society, each class having its own political and economic functions. For Hitze, capitalism should be replaced by a new society composed of seven classes: large and small landowners and cultivators, large and small industrialists, large and small businessmen, and the working class.

Hitze's views were disputed by another Catholic theoretician, Georg Freiherr von Hertling. Hertling believed that social systems had to reflect both Christian and "natural" rights and values. He argued for a "correct" liberalism that would oppose any intervention by government in society unless that intervention was necessary to uphold "natural" rights. This view would be espoused about 60 years later by Walter Eucken and Franz Boehm of the University of Freiburg. Hitze was already interested in the "welfare state"; Hertling defended the "natual rights" state.

The Catholic social critics were often inspired by Marx and Lassalle but attacked the Socialists for having rejected religion and the social role of the church. They claimed that the Socialists' goals were inconsistent with "Christian goals" and warned that a believing Catholic could not be a member of a Socialist organization. These Catholic critics thus opposed both capitalism and socialism, a religious liberalism, and dictatorial state rule. Above all, they condemned social democracy for being based on erroneous and amoral principles.

Protestants, too, condemned German social democracy. To reduce Socialist influence on workers, Adolf Stoecker, a Protestant court clergyman, founded in January 1878 the 'Christian Workers' party. This party advocated reliance on Christian beliefs and love and loyalty to the crown and the fatherland. It rejected social democracy for being non-Christian and unpatriotic (Grebing 1980, p. 84).

As of 1882, Protestant *Arbeitervereine* were founded whose aggregate membership probably numbered 40,000 by 1890.

Among the critics of socialism were also the "pulpit socialists," who advocated reform within the basic structure of the existing society. Among them were Gustav Schmoller, who advocated "state socialism" based on Prussian traditions, and Lujo Brentano, who proposed that German society should follow the British liberal pattern.

THE TRADE UNION MOVEMENT AND BISMARCK

The Gotha negotiations led to a discussion by trade union leaders on whether or not a centralized trade union federation should be established. A trade union congress to debate and decide this question was planned for the spring of 1878.

Bismarck had been observing the growth in Socialist representation in the Reichstag with great concern; the Socialist press had also expanded; and the chancellor felt that it was spreading unrest and discontent among the workers. Bismarck knew that he shared his dislike for German social democracy with the industrialists; the latter had established in 1878 an Association for the Furthering of the Common Economic Interests in Rhineland-Westphalia, which proclaimed that "the fight against Social Democracy is the duty of every citizen and in particular of the industrialists" and requested that all employers should prohibit their workmen from becoming members of Social Democratic organizations (Guttsman 1981, p. 58).

Two successive attempts on the life of Emperor William I by men who were falsely associated with the Socialist party gave Bismarck the opportunity to introduce the anti-Socialist legislation he wanted. The so-called Anti-Socialist Law was passed by a majority of the delegates to the Reichstag on October 21, 1878. It was to be systematically renewed until after the elections of 1890. The major provision of this law read as follows:

> Associations which through Social Democratic, Socialist and Communist efforts aim at the overthrow of the present order of State and society are prohibited. The same applies to associations in which Social Democratic, Socialist or Communist efforts directed towards the overthrow of the existing order of State and society result in a manner threatening to public peace, particularly to the harmony between the classes of the population. (DGB 1973, p. 20)

Under this law, all Socialist organizations and demonstrations were prohibited. The law extended beyond the activities of the SAPD to cover activities of trade unions and of individuals deemed to be supportive of social democracy or socialism. The police received the power to expel from their home districts people under suspicion of engaging in the proscribed activities. By the end of November 1878, 67 Social Democrats had been forced to leave Berlin within three days; by 1890, more than 800 people had been ordered to leave their home cities. During the 12 years in which the *Sozialistengesetz* was enforced, German courts sentenced Social Democrats to more than 600 years of imprisonment. Only Social Democratic delegates in the Reichstag and in other parliamentary bodies were protected from arrest. Police harassment extended to gymnastics and glee clubs; 246 of these clubs were closed by police order between 1878 and 1886 (Guttsman 1981, p. 61).

The Anti-Socialist Law was also utilized by the authorities to cripple the labor movement. Within a few seeks after the enactment of the law, 62 local trade unions and 17 union associations were closed by orders of the authorities. It quickly became evident to the workers that the law had been enacted to support the interests of the employers. As described by John Moses (1982):

> Even where the constitution of a union emphasized its purpose as being only the material improvement and intellectual elevation of its members with all available legal means, it could still be dissolved. This was because the shortening of working hours, the increase in wages, the abolition of overtime and female and child labour were interpreted as dangerous to the common good within the meaning of the act. But beyond this extraordinarily elastic application of the law, many police officials simply nominated as grounds for the liquidation of a union the political views of the executive members or the appearance of a known Social Democrat to address a union meeting. Additional grounds would be the obligation on members to subscribe to the union newspaper, the existence of Marxist literature in the union library . . . . (p. 67)

The liberal Hirsch-Duncker unions were not touched by the police; and a few other unions succeeded in avoiding police persecution by changing their constitution and taking on the appearance of a pure mutual help association. After 1881, many trade unions were set up as craft unions with no interests beyond the economic improvement of their members.

Bismarck's famous social security legislation was enacted by the government in order to diminish the appeal of social democracy for the workers and to further a feeling of loyalty of the proletariat to the Prusso-German state. Workers continued to register with the craft unions. By 1885, the number of these unions had risen to 1,021, with a total membership of about 58,000. The growth of the craft unions was accompanied by a rising number of strikes in the period 1883–85. This increase in strike activity induced the imperial government to pass a new law on April 11, 1886, which gave increased powers to the police to suppress strikes, especially when these strikes were interpreted by the police as being influenced by the Social Democrats. In spite of this new legislation, the membership of the craft unions continued to increase, one reason for which was the inadequacy of wages.

The craft unions started grouping themselves into centralized federations, which, although not officially connected with the banned SAPD, still supported Socialist rather than liberal or religious ideology. These union organizations soon became known as the "free" unions, "free" of any bias favoring a religious denomination or the bourgeois system. Estimates show that the "free" labor movement counted 35 union federations and 2,351 local organizations, with a total of 91,207 members in 1886; by 1890, these figures had risen to 59 federations, 3,305 local organizations, and 237,039 members (Moses 1982, p. 78).

It was also becoming apparent at the end of the 1880s that Bismarck's Anti-Socialist Law and his welfare legislation had failed to bring about labor peace. The May 1889 strikes by the Ruhr miners, which spread to other mining areas of Germany, caused work stoppages by an unprecedented number of miners. The large number of strikers evidenced the fact that the workers recognized that the government supported the interests of the employers and that only social democracy defended the workers' welfare. This is why, in spite of Bismarck's restrictive laws, the electoral base of the Social Democrats and union membership went on expanding in the period 1878–90. Yet, out of a labor force of 8 million persons, organized workers were only about 150,000 in 1890 (Moses 1982, p. 83).

The Anti-Socialist Law was repealed by the Reichstag on January 25, 1890. This did not mean that the new emperor, William II, dismissed Bismarck and his legislation because the crown had decided to tolerate social democracy. William simply decided to eradicate social democracy by more subtle means. The authoritarian ways of Bismarck had failed. Therefore other methods had to be found by the leaders of the Wilhelmine Reich to oppose effectively Socialist ideas.

THE "FREE" TRADE UNIONS AND SOCIAL DEMOCRACY

The antagonism toward Socialist ideas and the Socialist trade movement remained unchanged after Bismarck left the political scene. This antagonism not only lasted until 1914; it also manifested itself during the years of the Weimar Republic and facilitated the coming to power of the National Socialists. The ruling classes in Germany continued to perceive social democracy as a dangerous revolutionary movement that was expanding on two fronts. German officialdom never learned to distinguish between the revolutionary tone of the SAPD's platform and the reformism of its actual policies. The adoption by the SAPD of the Marxist Erfurt program of 1891 appeared to confirm the belief of the authorities that the party sought to overthrow the existing social system; Bebel's prediction that the party would obtain sufficient votes in 1898 to appropriate political power filled them with apprehension; the industrialists in turn observed with dismay the growth of the Socialist trade union movement. Their fear reflected the idea that "behind every strike lurked the Hydra of revolution."

The emperor's trade union policies were not to differ markedly from those of Bismarck. They could be designated as "carrot and stick" policies. On the one hand, new legislative protection measures were passed to safeguard the health and work ability of most workers. The government enacted new legislation that regulated the length of the workday for women and children; the law also provided that when long hours could endanger the health of adult male workers, the *Bundesrat* could impose a limit on the number of daily work hours. The law regulated the length of rest periods, the way wages were to be paid, and conditions of dismissal.

On the other hand, the government tried to restrict the right of association, which had existed since 1869. One way it tried to do this was by increasing the penalties provided by the penal code for attempts to coerce workers to join a trade union or for attempts to prevent workers from leaving a trade union. The government also attempted to amend existing legislation in order to allow an employer to sue an employee for damages whenever the employee had left his or her work prior to the time stipulated in the employment contract; the employer could regard this quitting as a breach of contract for which he could recover an amount equivalent to wages for up to six weeks of work. Workers could demand similar compensation from an employer if the latter dismissed them before the end of the contractual work period. The idea behind the proposed amendment was to make strike action difficult for employees by giving the employer a right of action for damages against the striking employees. The proposed bill was defeated in the Reichstag, but it clearly showed that the government was supporting the interests of the employers.

The emperor then abandoned the policy of trying to win workers over to his side through improved welfare legislation. His government continued to introduce bills in the Reichstag in order to restrict the legal activities of labor leaders. The hostility of the government toward the "free" unions surfaced again in 1906, when the minister of the interior,

Count Posadowsky, introduced a bill that purportedly gave legal recognition to those trade unions that would declare their conformity with the existing social system. The idea was to strengthen the Christian trade unions at the expense of the "free" organizations. The proposed legislation also stipulated that unions carrying out strikes that endangered "national security" or threatened the supply of "essential services" could be deprived of their legality and of their assets. The bill was defeated by the vote of left-wing liberals, of the Center party, and of the SAPD deputies.

The imperial law on "political" associations of 1908 provided that these associations could only hold meetings if these had been previously allowed by the police. It provided that persons under the age of 18 could not be lawful members of these associations and that these associations could only use the German language at their functions. The "free" unions protested this law because they were considered to be political associations and thus subjected to police surveillance of their meetings. The law made it also difficult for these trade unions to organize Polish or Italian workers whose knowledge of the German language was inadequate.

During the decade 1890 to 1900, the "free" unions succeeded in establishing a centralized organization under the leadership of Carl Legien, an organization that would become equal to the Socialist party in the fight for better terms of employment, or what Legien referred to as *Sozialpolitik*. The achievement of equality with the SAPD by the leadership of the "free" unions in matters that were regarded as political was a peculiarity of the German labor movement that was not duplicated in Spain, where the same persons represented both the political party and the trade unions.

In 1889, the founding congress of the Second International in Paris had called for an eight-hour workday and had requested the workers of all countries to demonstrate in support of the eight-hour day on every May 1. When the workers of Hamburg responded to this appeal on May 1, 1890, the employers reacted to the work stoppages with a lockout that lasted one month. All other strikes at that time in Germany were broken off so that all available resources commanded by labor could be directed to Hamburg. In August, five leaders of the Hamburg workers requested a conference of all German trade unions. Such a conference was held in Berlin on November 16, 1890. The delegates agreed to form a commission that would in turn organize a general trade unions congress. The delegates also supported the idea of developing a centralized form of organization for the entire "free" labor movement.

A General Commission of the Trade Unions of Germany was established to draft an organizational statute and to prepare the all-trade unions congress. The delegates at the conference followed two different lines of thought. The centrists favored the creation of a powerful centralized trade union organization that would lead all organized workers in the struggle against capital. The localists preferred to have the Socialist party lead this fight, the unions being subordinated to the political party. While the localists gave emphasis to the political struggle, the centrists favored the economic struggle under the leadership of a powerful, autonomous labor organization.

The chairman of the provisional General Commission was the young Carl Legien, who supported the centrist position in the commission's organ, *Das Correspondenzblatt*. In this newspaper, Legien attacked the views of both the localists and the leaders of the Hirsch-Duncker unions. He believed that because German law prohibited the affiliation of a trade union with a political party and because the Anti-Socialist Law had lapsed, the correct tactic to follow was to build strong and separate trade union and political wings of the labor movement.

On April 25, 1891, the General Commission published an organizational plan for the "free" trade unions. Unions were grouped into craft associations, or *Zentralverbaender*; related craft associations formed a *Union*, which had a common executive body consisting of the chairmen of the various *Zentralverbaender*. The *Union* was to plan and to finance activities of the affiliated craft associations, to publish a newspaper of common interest, to fund strikes when the craft associations lacked the resources, to compile statistical data, and to administer affiliated labor exchanges and hostels. Coordinating the *Unionen* was the General Commission, elected by a biennial trade union congress. Although these organizations were to remain independent of any political party, they would not be apolitical in the sense that they would all be engaged in an economic struggle to improve the work and living conditions of the workers. For Legien, trade unions had to engage in what he called *Sozialpolitik*.

In order to have the statute on organization approved by the trade union chairmen before the workers' congress met, Legien called a conference of the latter at Halberstadt to take place on September 7, 1891; 42 delegates representing 39 trade unions met. In spite of general skepticism about the proposed statute, the delegates supported it.

The congress itself was held from March 14 to 18, 1892, also at Halberstadt. On this occasion, Legien spoke again in favor of a centralized organization of trade unions established on a craft basis. There was a great deal of debate for and against Legien's proposal. Finally, the delegates only recommended the centralization of related craft organizations. The General Commission was retained but, against Legien's wishes, no special strike fund was established for the commission to administer.

The SAPD newspaper *Vorwaerts* criticized the establishment of a centralized trade union body that would compete with the Socialist party's leadership. At the Cologne congress of the Socialist party held in November 1893, August Bebel attacked Legien's proposals and argued that only the party could offer the workers significant social and economic improvements. The SAPD delegates took the view that the trade unions had to remain subordinated to the party and that the trade unions alone could achieve little for the labor movement.

In September 1894, the General Commission proposed to its affiliated unions that a trade union congress should be held to debate the role of the trade unions regarding possible changes in the law on associations, factory inspection laws, and other matters dealing with *Sozialpolitik*. The proposal was attacked by *Vorwaerts*. This congress met in May 1896 in Berlin.

At the congress, a number of delegates opposed the commission's proposal. The delegates, once again, followed two lines of policy. The metalworkers opposed the federal structure proposed by the General Commission and wanted to abolish the latter. The woodworkers supported the commission's proposals. A majority of the delegates upheld the existence of the General Commission and retained Legien as its chairman. The congress did not approve, however, of the creation of a strike fund to be managed by the commission. The latter's retention as a permanent feature of the Socialist labor movement was, however, a victory for Legien.

At the SAPD conference of October 1896 in Gotha, Legien asserted again the right of trade unions to engage in *Sozialpolitik*. Legien's theme was that the trade unions were not established to serve as mere tools of the Socialist party but were to act independently of the party in the struggle to transform society.

Two years later, a sudden change in the government's policy made it easier for the General Commission to follow its own *Sozialpolitik*. The government, in order to retain the support of the National Liberals and of the Catholic Center party, removed the ban of political activity imposed on trade unions. This was done largely to help the Center party develop a Christian trade union movement that the government hoped would oppose that of the Socialists.

The General Commission found no difficulty in acting as a political body and pursuing at the same time the class struggle in conformity with Marxist theory. In due course Bebel had to accept the fact that the "free" unions would act independently of the party. Reversing himself in 1900, Bebel recognized that the political neutrality of the trade unions was consistent with Marxist views and even hoped that the three labor movements—the "free" unions, the Christian unions, and the Hirsch-Duncker unions—would cooperate in order to obtain better welfare legislation (Moses 1982, p. 137).

The roots of the Christian trade union movement go back to the late 1860s, when Bishop Ketteler encouraged the formation of workers' associations that were to strive for both higher wages and the moral and religious uplifting of workers. Before long, a number of such associations were established, mainly in the Rhineland and in Westphalia. In 1875 these associations were demanding an eight-hour workday in the mines, a ten-hour day in the factories, and limitations on female work in the factories. The movement stagnated until 1891, when the encyclical of Pope Leo XIII was published. Although this encyclical, *Rerum Novarum*, defended the institution of private property, it criticized the excesses of capitalism; it encouraged the formation of workers' associations, advocated the right of association, and did not forbid strikes. This encyclical gave new impetus to the Catholic trade union movement.

The Protestant church also encouraged workers to form denominational associations. Both Christian movements advocated a peaceful relation between employers and workers and the acceptance by workers of the existing social order. The Christian trade unions rejected the idea that social democracy represented the only true labor movement in Germany. Their common rejection of social democracy brought Catholic and Protestant unions closer.

The first Christian trade union associations appeared in 1894. In May of that year, the German Railwaymen's Association was founded, followed in August by the Christian Miners Association. The bylaws of these associations stated that their purpose was to raise the social and moral conditions of the workers on a legal and Christian basis, proclaimed their loyalty to the *kaiser* and to the empire; and rejected any involvement in political or religious problems. The Christian Textile Workers Association was established in December 1898; in the following year, the Association of Christian Masons and Allied Vocations and the Christian-Social Metalworkers Association were established.

In 1899, the first general congress of Christian trade union associations was held at Mainz. This congress declared that the represented trade unions would be nondenominational, although they would be based on Christian beliefs, that they would remain independent of any political party, and that they would act to improve the physical and spiritual conditions of the workers. A second congress was held one year later, the attending delegates representing more than 80,000 members (DGB 1973, p. 30). A General Federation of Christian Trade Unions in Germany was created to coordinate the activities of the various associations and was given the responsibility of supporting any association engaged in a labor dispute.

The Christian trade union movement rejected both the capitalist system and Marxist theory. It purported to assist the worker to obtain higher real wages, capital assets, and co-ownership of the means of production. It claimed that the state had the duty to intervene in the economy to protect workers against hunger and misery.

The Christian trade unions had to struggle to achieve a nondenominational form of organization. The "free" trade unions also had to struggle to obtain independence from and equality with the Social Democratic party. A principal reason for conflict between the "free" trade union leadership and the radical left of the SAPD was the assertion of the latter that the nonrevolutionary policies of the trade unions were prolonging the survival of the existing bourgeois society. In their view, the trade unions were to prepare the workers for the breakdown of the capitalist system, and in all matters of policy, the unions had to be subordinated to the party. This argument was supported by the localist union leaders, who, under the leadership of Dr. Raphael Friedeberg, rejected all reformist trade union policies and advocated a revolutionary couse of action. SAPD leaders such as Ignaz Auer and Karl Kautsky were suspicious of the motivation of trade union leaders in their struggle for trade union independence from the Socialist party and tended to support the localists.

The conflict between the trade union centrists and the radical left of the party coalesced around two main issues: the workers' observation of May Day and the use of the general, or mass, strike as a political tool.

The SAPD had resolved at its conference in Halle in 1890 to abide by the resolution of the Second International, which urged all workers to demonstrate in favor of an eight-hour workday on every May 1. The SAPD delegates added an important proviso to this resolution; if a work stoppage on May 1 should cause workers difficulties the latter should instead hold their demonstrations on the first Sunday of May. At the 1896 party conference in Gotha, the delegates agreed that the financial burden of May Day demonstrations should be shouldered by the trade unions.

The unions were not happy with the party's resolution. Opposition to it strengthened when the Amsterdam Congress of the Second International commanded all proletarian organizations to strike on May 1. The General Commission proclaimed that this order was inconsistent with the interests of the "free" trade unions. The opposition of the General Commission to the order of the Second International was criticized at the SAPD conference in Jena in 1905. The conflict between the party and the trade unions was only solved in 1907, when, at the SAPD conference in Essen, the party leadership practically accepted the trade unions' position and agreed that the holding and the financing of May Day demonstrations would be decided locally through a joint decision of the local party and union organizations.

Equally divisive was the debate over the general, or mass, strike. At the 1903 SAPD conference in Dresden, Friedeberg had made a motion to the effect that the general strike should be fully debated at the next conference of the party. Although the motion was defeated, it received the support of known party theoreticians, such as Karl Kautsky, Rosa Luxemburg, and Klara Zetkin.

Until 1905, both the party and the unions tried to avoid debate over the desirability of a general strike. The Russian Revolution of 1905 and extensive strike activity in Germany in that year strengthened the interest of radical Socialists in the mass strike. Rudolf Hilferding, an Austrian who, like Kautsky, was active in the SAPD, proposed that the party consider the mass strike as a means of ending the country's existing social system. The trade union leadership, aware of the financial cost generated by the existing strikes and fearing strong government repression against the unions, felt that the mass strike was a dangerous tactic that the party should not use for purely political reasons. Many party leaders agreed with the trade union leadership.

The more radical elements within the party, however, disagreed with the trade union leaders and with most of the party's bureaucracy on this issue. Radicals such as Rosa Luxemburg, Klara Zetkin, and Karl Liebknecht (the son of Wilhelm Liebknecht) urged the party to embrace revolutionary tactics and to use the mass strike to fight Prussian rule. Karl Kautsky, initially a member of the radical group, tried as of 1905 to follow a middle course between the reformism-revisionism of the party's conservative bureaucracy and the radicalism of its left wing. In his view, the SAPD was a "revolutionary, but not revolution-making party." Still, Kautsky argued that in the case of conflict between the party and the trade unions, the former should prevail.

The argument in favor of the mass strike was strongly opposed by Legien, who feared that if the party accepted the mass strike as a useful tactic, then workers would have reason to believe that retention of trade union membership was no longer necessary to bring forth a social revolution. Legien decided that the trade unions' position on the issue of the mass strike had to be clarified before the party would vote on the matter. At the trade union congress held in Cologne, May 22–27, 1905, the delegates voted against the mass strike tactic and concluded that "the congress holds the general strike as it is championed by anarchists and such people lacking any experience in the field of the economic struggle to be unworthy of discussion; it warns the working class against allowing itself from being deflected from the day to day work of strengthening worker organizations by listening to and spreading such ideas" (Moses 1982, p. 154).

Stung by the strong position taken by the trade union leadership, Bebel reminded the delegates at the party's 1905 conference in Jena that the party was the highest authority on political matters within the labor movement. Bebel, using the term *Massenarbeiteinstellung*, "mass work stoppage," instead of the term "mass strike," called for the party control of such a strike and for its acceptance as a reasonable tactic, while reasserting party superiority over the trade unions in the solution of this question. Both the revisionist Eduard Bernstein and the radical Rosa Luxemburg supported Bebel. Kautsky cautioned that the use of the mass strike in Germany demanded a revolutionary situation. The final vote strongly supported Bebel's resolution.

Starting in November and extending until early 1906, workers throughout Germany engaged in repeated work stoppages to protest suffrage restrictions at the provincial level. The cost of these political strikes induced the Socialist party leadership to enter into a secret agreement with the trade union leadership. The agreement, signed in February 1906, stipulated that the party would bear the financial burden of political strikes, while the trade unions would be responsible for financing economic strikes. The party also agreed to prevent mass strikes in most instances.

At the party's conference of September 1906 in Mannheim, Bebel argued that the mass strike was not feasible without the cooperation of the trade unions. Trying to prevent a rupture between the SAPD and the "free" unions, Bebel had the following resolution passed by the delegates: "The party conference confirms the Jena resolution on the political mass strike asserting that the resolution of the Cologne trade union congress does not contradict the Jena resolution.... The trade unions are indispensable for the raising of the status of workers within bourgeois society. They are not of secondary importance to the Social Democratic Party..." (Moses 1982, pp. 160, 161). Despite the contradictory affirmations of this resolution, it was passed by a great majority of the SAPD delegates. It represented a victory for the General Commission because the "Mannheim resolution" gave it equal status with the party. Kautsky, who had proposed a resolution calling for the supremacy of the party over the trade unions, saw the radical position defeated. As Moses (1982) observed: "The unions had achieved the right of codetermination within the labour movement..." (p. 162).

THE OUTBREAK OF WORLD WAR I

On the eve of the war, the government of the Reich still viewed social democracy and its trade unions as internal dangers to the Wilhelmine state. The German government probably felt that war with the Allies would strengthen the Bismarckian-Wilhelmine state against the forces of social democracy.

The right-wing SAPD delegates in the Reichstag were also victims of the war fever but for a different reason; they believed that their support of the war would induce the government to grant them needed democratic reforms. They overlooked the fact that the government had granted military officers exceptional powers under Article 68 of the Reich constitution, so that in the event of war they could enforce internal "public security." Under these contingency powers, military officers were to arrest Socialist agitators and even SAPD delegates to the Reichstag should the Social Democrats endanger the public order at a time when the empire was engaged in war. The Wilhelmine government simply intended to destroy social democracy in Germany under the guise of a war-imposed necessity. Bebel understood quite clearly the intention of the government and felt that there was nothing the Socialists could do to prevent Germany from entering a war.

Legien also believed that any propaganda in favor of the general strike as an antiwar measure would only bring harm to the trade unions. Apprehending that the government was about to dissolve the unions and to confiscate their assets, the General Commission contacted the Ministry of the Interior to offer the unions collaboration in the war effort. The ministry replied that as long as the unions would not cause any difficulties they would not be dissolved; as the minister replied, "We are happy to have large organizations of the working-class upon which the government can depend in the event support is necessary" (DGB 1973, p. 39). On August 2, 1914, the General Commission agreed to suspend all economic strikes for the duration of the war. The "free" trade unions' commitment to a wartime "civic truce," or *Burgfrieden*, ensured their survival and safeguarded their assets. It also barred the SAPD from taking any position hostile to the war when it met on August 3. The General Commission had acted without the consent of the party; this had been done in the hope that the collaboration of the trade unions in the war effort would be recognized and rewarded by the elite classes and would allow the working class to be fully integrated into the rest of German society.

Carl Legien saw in the *Burgfrieden* not only a way to strengthen the Reich militarily and economically in a war perceived initially by most workers as one of self-defense but also as a practical way that would allow the further growth of the "free" trade unions. For Legien, this growth would gradually and inevitably introduce socialism in Germany. The belief that socialism could be slowly introduced with the help of the state clashed with the Marxist ideology of the radical Socialist deputies in the Reichstag, who advocated opposition to the war. Legien's policy, however, was accepted by most of the SAPD representation in that body, so much so, that by December 2, 1914, Karl Liebknecht was the only Socialist deputy who voted against war credits.

Legien continued to cling to the belief that socialism could be implanted in Germany by extracting concessions from the imperial state. His belief was shared by a majority in the Socialist party. The minority, who felt that the Reich had engaged in an imperialist war of aggression and who were faithful to the idea that socialism could only be established through revolution, were to abandon the SAPD in 1917 and form an Independent Social Democratic party. Legien remained hostile to this minority,which he considered to be formed by dogmatic *Literaten*, men who valued more remaining loyal to Marx's or to Lassalle's views than dealing with the reality of *Sozialpolitik*. For Legien, the only practical way of moving toward socialism was to expand the trade unions to a level, where, because of their size alone, government and employers would have to accept the demands of organized labor.

Legien's tactics were successful in 1915. A new Law on Associations no longer held trade unions to be political associations. Trade unions obtained legality. New labor legislation provided that in each factory a "works' committee" would meet with management in order to examine and settle workers' grievances; if the particular problem could not be solved at the factory level, it would be heard by arbitration courts made up of an equal number of representatives of both management and labor.

For most German workers, it appeared in 1915 that it was the General Commission and not the Socialist party that was successfully working for their full integration into German society. They tended to place more faith in the state-friendly tactics of Carl Legien than in the predictions of revolutionary Marxism. This was still the situation in 1916.

As the war continued, as the economic conditions of the workers deteriorated, as many Germans started realizing that their government was not engaged in a war of self-defense, and as many workers perished on the battlefronts, the trade union rank and file started to question the wisdom of their leaders.

NOTES

DGB. 1973. *Die Deutsche Gewerkschaftsbewegung*. Düsseldorf.

Droz, J., ed. 1976. *Historia General del Socialismo*. Vol. 1. Barcelona: Ediciones Destino.

Grebing, H. 1980. *Geschichte der Deutschen Arbeiterbewegung*. Munich: Deutscher Taschenbuch Verlag GmbH.

Guttsman, W. L. 1981. *The German Social Democratic Party, 1875–1933*. London: Allen & Unwin.

Moses, J. A. 1982. *Trade Unionism in Germany from Bismarck to Hitler*. Vol. I. Totowa, N.J.: Barnes & Noble.

BIBLIOGRAPHY

Balser, F. *Sozial Demokratie 1848/9–1963. Die erste deutsche Arbeiterorganisation*. Stuttgart, 1962.

Bartel, H., ed. *Marxismus und deutsche Arbeiterbewegung*. Berlin, 1970.

Bronder, D. *Organisation und Fuehrung der sozialdemokratischen Arbeiterbewegung im deutschen Reich, 1890–1914.* Göttingen, 1952.

Conze, W. and D. Groh. *Die Arbeiterbewegung in der nationalen Bewegung. Die deutsche Sozialdemokratie vor, waehrend und nach der Reichsgruendung.* Stuttgart, 1966.

Desai, A. V. *Real Wages in Germany, 1871–1913.* Oxford, 1968.

Domann, P. *Sozial-Demokratie und Kaisertum unter Wilhelm II.* Wiesbaden, 1974.

Flechtheim, O. *Die KPD in der Weimarer Republik.* Frankfurt, 1969.

Grunenberg, A. *Die Massenstreikdebatte.* Frankfurt, 1970.

Potthoff, H. *Die Sozialdemokratie von den Anfaengen bis 1945.* Bonn, 1973.

Ritter, G. A. *Die Arbeiterbewegung im Wilhelminischen Reich.* Berlin, 1963.

Ryder, A. J. *The German Revolution of 1918.* Cambridge, 1967.

Wachenheim, H. *Die deutsche Arbeiterbewegung, 1844 bis 1944.* Cologne, 1967.

5

The German Trade Unions in the Twentieth Century: From the ADGB to the DGB

THE REVOLUTION OF 1918

In 1914, the Socialist party was divided into a number of factions. The extreme right wing of the party regarded the German war effort as a true revolutionary movement furthering the interests of international socialism. They denounced Britain as the leader of reaction. This group, which published its views in the journal *Die Glocke* edited by Alexander Helphand, who wrote under the pseudonym "Parvus," advocated the establishment of "organizational socialism" in victorious Germany and the formation of a bloc of Central European nations under the leadership of Germany. Their views were those of a nascent German Fascism. A more moderate group, writing in the *Sozialistische Monatshefte*, also claimed that Central Europe would have to be directed by Germany following a German victory.

The Left of the SAPD was also split into two groups. The prewar Left was formed by people who felt that the Socialist delegates in the Reichstag who had voted in favor of war credits had betrayed the Socialist cause and that the war was one of imperialism that would hurt the working class. Rosa Luxemburg, Karl Liebknecht, Klara Zetkin, and Franz Mehring advocated the seizure of power by the workers. On January 1, 1916, a number of Social Democrats who supported Luxemburg and Liebknecht formed their own *Internationale Gruppe*, which published the journal *Spartacus*; this group was to become known as the Spartacists.

The majority within the Left followed, together with the centrists in the party and the revisionists, pacifist views and democratic principles. They advocated a negotiated peace and believed that the Wilhelmine government had engaged in a war of expansionism.

Between the Right and the Left stood the majority Socialists, whose leaders were Friedrich Ebert, Philip Scheidemann, and Eduard David. This group strove to obtain a national democracy through negotiation with the army and with the government. Most of the Social Democrats in this group rejected the war of expansionism, although individuals such as Gustav Noske and Eduard David sympathized with economic imperialism in the East. Members of this group voted religiously in support of war credits and adhered to the *Burgfrieden* of 1914. It is not astonishing that Carl Legien supported this group.

The rising opposition of workers to the war, the likelihood that warfare was to continue after Germany announced in January 1917 the resumption of unrestricted submarine attacks, and the inability of the majority Socialists to compromise with the radical minority in the party all led to an inevitable split of the SAPD.

The first organized opposition within the German Socialist party can be traced back to April 1915, when Franz Mehring and Rosa Luxemburg founded the journal *Internationale* in which they voiced their strong opposition to the policies of the majority. A more moderate opposition group formed by Eduard Bernstein, Karl Kautsky, and Rudolf Breitscheid started its own journal, the *Sozialistische Auslandspolitik Korrespondenz*, later named *Der Sozialist*.

In March 1916, the "opposition" Socialist delegates to the Reichstag formed their own group in the imperial parliament under the name Sozialdemokratische Arbeitsgemeinschaft, the Workers' Social Democratic Association. On February 9, 1917, the leaders of this latter group called for political action independent of the SAPD. Local Socialist organizations in Berlin, Leipzig, Braunschweig, Bremen, and Halle joined the Arbeitsgemeinschaft to form the German Independent Social Democratic party, or *Unabhaengige Sozialdemokratische Partei Deutschlands* (USPD). Kautsky, the Marxist theoretician, joined the USPD, having attacked the majority Socialists in his *Neue Zeit* for supporting the war and its expansionist aims and for cooperating with the regime of the *Kaiser*. Kautsky argued that workers could obtain political power only within a democratic political system; cooperating with the Wilhelmine state, which was not democratic, meant the abandonment of the goal of proletarian rule. Kautsky feared, however, that the division of the Social Democrats had weakened labor's chances of obtaining a postwar democratic state.

The minority Socialists were not the only ones to oppose the war in Germany in 1917. German workers who had been willing to support a war of self-defense against Russian aggression in 1914 demanded peace and more food in 1917. The government's announcement that the bread ration would be reduced caused metalworkers in Berlin and in other cities to strike; about 1 million workers were out on strike by January 1918.

In July and August of that year the miners of Upper Silesia struck in order to obtain an eight-hour workday. In October, sailors refused to obey their officers' orders when the German navy was ordered to attack the British fleet. The workers and the sailors did not identify with the Socialist party or with any other party. What they wanted was an immediate end to the war, more food, the release of political prisoners, and a bourgeois democracy.

The first Workers' and Soldiers' Councils with revolutionary powers were set up in Kiel on November 4, 1918, by rebelling sailors. A few days later, all of the German navy's sailors had followed the example of those in Kiel. The revolt extended to Munich by November 7. William II abdicated on November 9, and Prince Max von Baden handed the chancellery to the chairman of the majority Socialists, Friedrich Ebert. Another majority Socialist, Philip Scheidemann, proclaimed Germany to be a republic from a window of the Reichstag, shortly before Karl Liebknecht announced to his followers the establishment of the "Social Republic of Germany."

German social democracy, instead of joining the revolutionary movement, did all it could to contain and control it. The reformist Social Democrats tried to build a democratic and peaceful Germany to replace the feudal, imperialistic, and militaristic Wilhelmine empire. This was to be done peacefully, through the parliamentarian process and by means of universal suffrage. In the months after November 1918, the most pressing problems faced by the Social Democratic majority centered on how to prevent the revolutionary councils from gaining political power and how to place this power in the hands of a democratically elected constituent assembly.

On November 10, about 3,000 representatives of the Berlin Soldiers' and Workers' Councils assembled in the city's Busch Circus and gave their support to the government formed by Friedrich Ebert. This government, known as the Council of the People's Commissars, the *Rat des Volksbeauftragten*, included three representatives of the majority Socialists (Ebert, Scheidemann, and Landsberg) and three independent Socialists (Haase, Dittmann, and Barth). An Executive Committee of the Councils of Berlin, (*Berliner Vollzugsrat*) was charged with the task of supervising the government.

The Soldiers' and Workers' Councils, formed spontaneously in Germany during the last months of the war, had little resemblance to the Russian soviets. They were not established according to a careful plan, and most of them shared the ideology of social democracy; the councils were not dedicated to establishing in Germany a Soviet-type society.

Still, Friedrich Ebert considered these councils to be the product of disorder, reflecting the will of a minority of Socialists. For Ebert, a German Socialist republic could only be obtained through peaceful and legal means. His distrust of the councils is shown by the fact that already on November 10, he contacted the military adjunct chief of staff, Groener, who assured Ebert that the army would prevent the outbreak of violence as long as the new government would try to maintain order and safeguard the authority of military officers.

Ebert also favored the maintenance of labor peace through joint agreement between the trade unions and the employers. The most important of such arrangements was the Stinnes-Legien Agreement of November 15, which one month later was institutionalized into the Central Work Community, the *Zentralarbeitsgemeinschaft* (ZAG). This was a new organization formed by both the representatives of the Rhenish-Westphalian heavy industry and by the pertinent trade unions. The organization had a Central Executive Committee, Industry or Branch Executive Committees, and lower level groups formed by representatives of both management and labor.

Most German workers trusted the Social Democratic government and hoped that Ebert would be able to achieve a meaningful transformation of society and economy without the use of violence. The radical Left in the Socialist camp still believed that a social revolution should follow the political change; this group, however, was weakened by factionalism and by sharp differences in views. Within the USPD, some supported the formation of a constituent assembly supported by the Workers' Councils, while others were impatient for the establishment of the dictatorship of the proletariat.

A National Congress of the Workers' and Soldiers' Councils met in Berlin from December 16 to 19, 1918; the majority in this congress approved a resolution setting the elections for a constituent assembly on January 19, 1919. This was a victory for the Social Democratic Majority.

A few days after the Berlin congress, a naval division that had come to Berlin from Cuxhaven to protect the revolutionary government mutinied in Berlin. The sailors occupied the Chancellery and arrested Ebert; order was reestablished after the intervention of units of the old army under the command of General Lequis. This caused the independents in the government to resign; they were replaced by three majority Social Democrats: Gustav Noske, Rudolf Wissell, and Paul Loebe. At the same time the Spartacists left the independents to form, at the end of December, the Communist Party of Germany, *Kommunistische Partei Deutschlands* (KPD).

Tensions among the government, the Spartacists, and the KPD were rising; the government's dismissal of the chief of Berlin's police force, a man very popular among the workers, served as the justification for the extreme Left to rise against the government on January 6, 1919. Members of the KPD and of the USPD occupied the offices of the journal *Vorwaerts* and called for a general strike in Berlin. Noske proceeded to crush this revolt with the aid of a "free corps" constituted by former soldiers hostile to the republic. Rosa Luxemburg and Karl Liebknecht were assassinated on January 15. Their murders were followed by strikes and disorders throughout Germany, a "Republic of Soviets" being proclaimed in Munich that lasted from April 7 to May 2.

The Ebert government tried at all costs to maintain law and order. The establishment of the ZAG appeared to have given the government some success in labor-management relations. Labor had obtained the eight-hour workday and the right to organize.

The "people's commissars" appeared otherwise actually reluctant to use the November 1918 popular victory to reshape their society into a Socialist utopia. Their eagerness to draft a new constitution, which in many ways continued the traditions of the old empire, revealed their apprehension that the revolution of 1918 could establish Bolshevism in Germany.

LABOR IN THE WEIMAR REPUBLIC

The "free" trade union leaders showed their willingness to cooperate with employers and to operate within the existing capitalist system when they signed the Stinnes-Legien Agreement. The labor unions obtained many immediate benefits from this agreement. The employers agreed to recognize the unions and to bargain with them, to disband "company unions," not to discriminate against union members, to establish shop committees in plants employing more than 50 workers, and to introduce the eight-hour workday. The signing of the agreement by labor leaders at a time when most workers demanded the socialization of industry revealed their dislike for a totally new economic system.

Because of its attachment to a basically traditional society, the General Commission was harshly criticized by the USPD, by the Spartacists, and by the Metalworkers Union. The Metalworkers Union accused Legien of opposing the workers' revolutionary goals and of sympathizing with class collaboration and withdrew from the ZAG in October 1919. Too many German workers were disappointed by the cooperation of their leaders with the prewar elites. They could not understand why the General Commission opposed political strikes organized by the USPD and by the Communists in the early months of 1919. They resented the use of troops against the strikers and tried to oust the SAPD government. In a number of cities workers closed down trade union offices and expelled the officials.

Trade union leaders, however, supported the Socialist government and hoped that it would follow a policy of parliamentary reformism. However, when worker dissatisfaction with existing economic and political conditions increased, causing a strengthening of the USPD and of the USPD-controlled trade unions, conservative labor leaders started to question the wisdom of their alliance with the SAPD.

At the Nürnberg Congress of June 30 to July 5, 1919, the delegates repudiated the Mannheim Agreement of 1906 and affirmed the trade unions' neutrality in party politics. Labor leaders felt they could no longer consult with various working-class parties and that their principal concern was to unite the workers, regardless of their political or religious views. The Nürnberg consensus was that trade unionism would continue to exist regardless of the forms of existing economic and political systems. As far as the present was concerned, the delegates chose the parliamentary rather than the radical council system. They showed a greater concern for immediate gains for the working class than for an eventual radical transformation of society. These German labor leaders in effect rejected the overthrow of the existing political-economic system and manifested their conformity with the bourgeois order.

In order to achieve a more centralized organization, the General Commission was replaced by a new organization, the General Federation of German Trade Unions, or *Allgemeiner Deutscher Gewerkschaftsbund* (ADGB), whose statute and goals were written by a commisssion headed by Theodor Leipart, future president of the ADGB.

The Weimar constitution explicitly allowed the establishment of trade unions. Article 159 provided for freedom of association but did not guarantee the right to strike. This right, however, was implicit in that article as long as the strike did not amount to the violation of a contract. Article 165 established the principle of labor-management codetermination in the decision-making process of the firm. It read:

> Laborers and employees are called upon to take part on equal terms and together with the employers in regulating conditions of work and wages and also in the general economic development of productive forces. The organizations on both sides and agreements between them shall be recognized. Laborers and employees shall be legally represented on the Workmen's Councils of the Enterprise as well as in the District Workmen's Councils (*Bezirksarbeiterraeten*) organized for each economic area, and on the Reich Workmen's Council (*Reichsarbeiterrat*). The District Workmen's Councils and the Reich Workmen's Council shall combine with the representatives of the employees and other interested elements of the population to form District Economic Councils (*Bezirkswirtschaftsraete*) and a Reich Economic Council (*Reichswirtschaftsrat*) for the purpose of performing all economic tasks and of cooperating in carrying out the socialization laws.... (Moses 1982, pp. 300, 301)

At a minimum, this article recognized the unions as negotiating part-
ners with managers; it implied that once an agreement had been arrived
at by both unions and managers, it could no longer be modified or questioned by the state.

Under a Works Council Act drafted by the General Commission,
works councils (*Betriebsraete*) were to be organized in firms with more
than 50 employees or more than 300 workers. These works councils were
to be established as part of the ZAG agreement. They were to prevent
the "bolshevization" of German workers, and their functions were to be
carefully limited by law. In a given firm, the works council could negotiate with the firm's managers regarding such matters as wages, hours of
work, apprenticeship regulations, pension funds workers' welfare
schemes, and the like. They were not designed to replace the trade
unions, and, unlike the unions, the works councils could not represent a
given trade at the national level.

The ADGB succeeded in retaining control over most works councils
until 1924, when the economic crisis and hyperinflation induced many
workers to join Communist or syndicalist organizations.

The beginning of the Weimar Republic was accompanied by political and economic turmoil, the disturbances reflecting the reaction of
many Germans to military defeat and to the terms of the Versailles Peace
Treaty. The republic faced serious danger on March 13, 1920, when two
men of the political Right, Wolfgang Kapp, the founder of the Fatherland
party, and General Walter Luettwitz led 6,000 troops to Berlin in order
to overthrow the government.

The rebel forces seized the Chancellery and a number of public buildings in Berlin, and Kapp was proclaimed by his men to be the new chancellor. Chancellor Gustav Bauer and his cabinet promptly left Berlin. The
Reichswehr took a position of neutrality in the coup. Labor was left alone
to oppose the military dictatorship.

The ADGB decided to call a general strike to oppose the Kapp putsch.
It invited the leaders of the Berlin trade unions, the salaried employees
union AFA, and representatives of the SAPD, the USPD, and the KPD to
form an alliance for the purpose of carrying out a joint general strike.
Both the USPD and the KPD refused to participate in such an alliance.
Two independent strike committees were formed. One was to organize
the general strike throughout Germany; this was the committee
representing the ADGB and the AFA. It received the support of the
Hirsch-Ducker unions. The other committee was formed mostly by members of the USPD and the KPD.

By March 15 the general strike had extended throughout most of Germany. Kapp reacted to these events by trying to persuade the "free" labor leaders to join him in a political coalition that would embrace both

the political Right and the Left. When the ADGB refused to join his forces, Kapp promptly ordered the execution of the strike leaders.

Kapp's coup started to disintegrate on March 16; most of the German provinces remained loyal to the Bauer government and, on that day, the National Association of German Industrialists declared its support of the unions. Unable to cope with the strike, Kapp decided to "resign" on March 17, and on the following day his troops abandoned Berlin. The government leaders in Stuttgart called for an end of the strike.

The "free" union leaders, however, refused to end the strike or to allow the Bauer government to take effective command until that government accepted a nine-point program of reform. The ADGB leadership demanded (1) decisive influence of the unions in the formation of national and state governments and in the enactment of new social and economic legislation, (2) the immediate disarming and punishment of all troops that had participated in the putsch, (3) the immediate resignation of a number of ministers, Noske being one of them, (4) the immediate purge of counterrevolutionary officials in the public service and in the factories, (5) the democratization of all administrative services, (6) new social laws to guarantee workers, salaried employees, and civil servants social and economic equality, (7) the immediate socialization of mines and of electric power and the nationalization of the coal and potash syndicates, (8) the enactment of an expropriation law directed against property owners who did not release available foodstuffs or who did not manage their property in the interest of the public, and (9) the takeover of security forces by organized labor (Braunthal 1978, p. 43).

Although the government did not accept this program, it agreed to a more limited one on March 20. On that day, the ADGB announced the end of the general strike; the USPD agreed to the end of the strike only three days later after it received assurances that the strike would be renewed should the government fail to comply with the conditions of the agreement with the unions.

The government did not honor this agreement, but the general strike was not renewed. When Chancellor Bauer resigned, the labor leaders demanded the formation of a Socialist-labor government, a government that would include representatives of the SAPD, the USPD, and the trade union federations but that would exclude KPD members. While a majority in the USPD rejected this plan, the KPD accepted it and declared itself ready to become a "loyal opposition." The plan was then dropped by the "free" trade unions. President Ebert then asked Legien to form a new government; when the latter declined, Rudolf Wissell of the ADGB was asked to form a cabinet; Wissell also declined. The Socialist Hermann Mueller then agreed to form a new cabinet on March 27 that would represent the SAPD and the Democratic and the Center parties. Labor had agreed to the restoration of a liberal bourgeois government and to the retention of the capitalist system.

Workers in the Ruhr and in other areas of Germany were dissatisfied with the outcome of the Kapp putsch. They refused to surrender their weapons to the authorities until a labor government would be formed; in the Ruhr, workers formed armed "defense battalions" led by Communists and occupied a number of cities. The government used the Reichswehr to crush the workers' insurgency.

Labor's political power had peaked in 1920; Legien could have formed a labor government in that year. The unwillingness of labor leaders to lead the country was to weaken the political strength of organized labor during the rest of the 1920s and undoubtedly helped the National Socialist cause in the early 1930s.

The National Socialist movement was also strengthened by the policy followed by German industrialists in the early 1920s. The industrialists had decided to end their cooperation with the trade unions and to weaken them by allowing hyperinflation to take its course; they also utilized the Franco-Belgian invasion of the Ruhr in January 1923 and the passive resistance movement on the part of German miners to fortify their position vis-à-vis the unions. The Ruhr crisis stopped coal production in Germany, forced the country to import coal from Britain, and caused widespread unemployment. The German industrialists' policy was based on the expectancy that the French would finally recognize Germany's inability to fulfill its obligations and that the burden of the Versailles Treaty would be reduced; once this was achieved, full production would resume with the advantage of lower real wages. Industrialists expected that this policy would induce the government to limit its social legislation and to grant more freedom to private enterprise. The employers, realizing that inflation had impoverished the trade unions and that massive unemployment had weakened them, felt that the moment had come to abandon the ZAG and all cooperation with the unions.

The French occupation of the Ruhr clearly revealed that employers were little concerned with the welfare of organized labor. It sharpened the conflict between industrialists and workers. Whereas the latter pleaded for greater intervention on the part of the state in the economy, the former stood for more liberal government policies. The employers advised the political leaders to extend the legal workday so that the foreign debt could be paid out of the additional effort of the working class; the unions wanted a reform of the tax system that would particularly reach the real income of the wealthy classes.

Unable to reach an agreement with French Premier Raymond Poincaré, Chancellor Cuno resigned on August 13, 1923 and was replaced by Gustav Stresemann, head of the People's party. The new government included SAPD ministers in the hope of effectuating a split between moderates and radicals in the labor movement. Passive resistance in the Ruhr ceased on September 26, and mine owners started dictating conditions of work as if the unions did not exist. Underground workers were required to work 8 1/2 hours a day, while the length of the workday was extended to between 10 and 12 hours for those working aboveground. Employers embraced once again the idea that they were "masters in their own house." Unemployment in the Ruhr continued to stand at between 1.4 and 2 million workers (Moses 1982, p. 352).

Weakened by inflation and large unemployment, the ADGB did not participate in national politics for the remainder of the decade. Following the merger of the right wing of the USPD with the SAPD in 1922, the ADGB chose to support the Socialist party at election time and to concentrate on economic problems.

Although the Socialist unions had participated directly in the fights carried out in the national political arena in times of the revolution and of the Kapp putsch, these activities constituted a brief departure from the conservative and reformist policy so dear to Carl Legien and Theodor Leipart. The advent of the Great Depression in 1929 was to force the ADGB to participate once again in national politics.

Between September 26, 1923 and the end of December of that year, the ADGB lost more than 1.2 million members (Moses 1982, p. 354). Inflation had wiped out its resources, and it was impotent when the employers reneged on their promise to introduce the eight-hour workday. Cooperation between the unions and the industrialists had vanished. The ADGB simply recognized an existing fact when it announced its withdrawal from the ZAG on January 16, 1924.

The leaders of the ADGB continued to reject the Communist belief in the necessity of a violent revolution; the trade union leaders stuck to the tactic of gradually expanding the social and economic living standards of the workers by operating within the existing capitalist system and by trying to democratize the latter. They attached great significance to obtaining codetermination rights in the management of enterprises. An increasing degree of worker participation in management was seen as the best way to move toward economic democracy and socialism. Given a sufficiently large power base, the ADGB leaders hoped to be able to obtain economic democracy by nonviolent methods. Their optimism reflected the belief of Rudolph Hilferding that in the Weimar Republic the state no longer served exclusively the interests of the capitalists.

The reformism of the ADGB was opposed by the Moscow-inspired KPD. The Communist International had branded the left wing of social democracy as the chief enemy of the workers. Stalin had noted that "Fascism is the fighting organization of the bourgeoisie which relies on the active support of Social Democracy. Objectively, Social Democracy is the moderate wing of Fascism..." (Moses 1982, p. 363). The ADGB pursuit of economic democracy, and therefore its conformity with the relaxation of the class struggle, was attacked by the Communists, who asserted that the advent of monopoly capitalism had intensified the class struggle. According to the KPD leaders, monopoly capitalism made it impossible for capitalists and workers to cooperate in production. The only way to fight for the interests of the workers was to destroy capitalism.

The increasing hostility shown by German industrialists to the ADGB appeared to confirm the Communist claim. In the late 1920s, industrialists attacked in many pamphlets the idea of economic democracy. Fearing that the Social Democrat chancellor, Hermann Mueller, would propose new Socialist legislation, in 1928, employers claimed louder than ever that what the ADGB tried to achieve was a social revolution in Germany that would bring an end to German economic growth. It was because of such fears that German industrialists were to embrace so readily Nazi propaganda.

A national unemployment benefits system had been set up in 1927 under Article 163 of the constitution stating that the Reich would provide work and resources to all of its citizens. In March 1930, the cabinet decided that public expenditure had to be reduced and that taxes had to be raised to finance rising relief costs and to compensate for declining revenues. The ADGB and the Socialist party advocated the increase in benefits paid to the unemployed; the People's party and other conservative parties urged a cut in such benefits. Heinrich Bruening, the leader of the Catholic Center party, proposed to increase certain taxes in order to maintain temporarily the rates of unemployment benefits. The ADGB opposed this compromise and warned the Socialist delegates in the Reichstag that their support of the Bruening proposal would subject the party to the loss of many votes at the next election. Rudolf Wissell, minister of labor, supported the ADGB position, while Chancellor Mueller opposed it. When the SAPD *Fraktion* in the Reichstag decided to support the ADGB position, Chancellor Mueller and his Socialist ministers resigned.

The ADGB had refused to compromise over an issue vital to the workers, fearing that if it accepted the Bruening proposal, it would have to accept further legislation adverse to the interests of the working class. By standing firm on its policy, however, it had ousted from power a political ally and facilitated the formation of a more conservative government. The new chancellor was Heinrich Bruening of the Center party, and he appointed to his cabinet only members of conservative parties.

Bruening's principal goal was to stabilize the value of the mark. In order to achieve currency stabilization, the chancellor tried to balance the budget by drastically reducing public expenditure and by raising taxes. The fact that such deflationary policy increased unemployment to 15.7 percent of the German labor force did not disturb him. Bruening believed in laissez-faire political economy. Cuts in public spending were to affect the social security system as well as public contracts. The pensions and salaries of civil servants were reduced. Public works were stopped. As increasing taxation and declining demand reduced the income generated by the private sector, the government reduced public spending even further.

The German economy started following a downward spiral at the very same time when depression plagued the world economy. This did not bother Bruening, who, in his attempt to balance the budget, ruled by means of emergency decrees. His disastrous economic policy benefited the NSDAP, whose presence in the Reichstag increased spectacularly after the elections of September 1930. The Nazi gains reflected the fact that the German middle class no longer trusted the parliamentary system.

Meanwhile, both the SAPD (better known as the SPD since 1922, the *Sozialdemokratische Partei Deutschlands*) and the ADGB decided to support Bruening out of apprehension that new elections could establish a Fascist government. The ADGB leaders still hoped that the economy would improve and that the danger presented by the extremist parties, the NSDAP and the KPD, would subside. The economy did not improve. Industrial output and trade continued to decline, banks failed, and unemployment rose to 6 million in early 1932. Through emergency decrees the chancellor went on reducing public spending to compensate for declining revenues.

The unions protested vigorously Bruening's decrees, but to no avail. At interviews with the president and with the chancellor on February 26, 1931, union leaders expressed their dismay at the failure of the government to take strong action to alleviate unemployment. On April 23 and May 30, the "free" labor unions asked for a 40-hour work week, an increase in the workers' purchasing power, the preservation of existing social security benefits, and higher taxes on high incomes. The government ignored such demands. On June 5, Bruening issued a new decree ordering new cuts in government expenditures, wages, and prices. The chancellor refused to meet with labor leaders or with SPD representatives.

Labor leaders started to attack Bruening, claiming that he only listened to the employers and that he remained indifferent to the threat presented by an expanding NSDAP. Bruening stuck to his deflationary policy. On December 8, new cuts in salaries, wages, prices, and interest rates were ordered. Aware of the Fascist dangers, the unions and the SPD continued to support Bruening. Labor leaders, aware that union resources were near depletion and that 45 percent of the union membership was unemployed, refrained from any strike activity. As the threat from the political Right increased, the "free" unions and the SPD created a paramilitary front, the "Iron Front," composed of union members who were to fight for the defense of the republic should a Fascist putsch materialize.

The unions and the SPD still supported the Bruening government in 1931. In that year, the ADGB's director of the organization's research and statistics division, Wladimir Woytinsky, formulated a plan to counter rising unemployment. Woytinsky's program was interesting because it announced Keynesian counterdepression policy. Fritz Tarnow, the president of the Woodworkers Union, and Fritz Baade, an SPD economist, supported this plan; it was presented to the ADGB Executive in December 1931 under the title Program for the Creation of Jobs, better known as the WTB plan, after the initials of its creators.

The central idea of the WTB plan was the creation of a Central Office for Works Procurement that would be managed in part by union representatives; it would provide employment connected with new public works covering highway improvements, low-cost housing, and so on. The plan contemplated the creation of 1 million jobs to be financed by a Reichsbank loan, borrowing in the private capital market, by a reduction in unemployment insurance payments, and by the taxes paid by those obtaining jobs. The plan was approved by the ADGB on February 16, 1932.

In September 1932, the SPD *Fraktion* in the Reichstag introduced a bill calling for a public works program of 1 billion marks and for the nationalization of key industries. The conservative majority voted down the proposal. A similar bill introduced by the minister of labor, Adam Stegerwald, calling for an expenditure of only 135 million marks on new public works was also defeated.

President Hindenburg dismissed Bruening in May 1932 and appointed in his place the archconservative Franz von Papen. This appointment ended the SPD-ADGB policy of toleration of a conservative government. Von Papen formed a cabinet of aristocrats with strong anti-Socialist and antilabor feelings. He promptly dismissed the Reichstag and ordered the lowering of wages and of unemployment benefits.

The Left had retained political power only in Prussia, and von Papen decided to eliminate this last bastion of socialism in Germany. A coup was carried out against the SPD-dominated Prussian government. Von Papen threatened to use the Reichswehr if the Prussian police dared to oppose his action. Von Papen's coup induced workers throughout Germany to assemble in "Iron Front" units that waited for instructions from their union leaders. These leaders remained silent.

Otto Wels, the leader of the SPD, had warned the unions about taking action against the central government; Wels, fearing that a general strike could result in a civil war that would delay the July 31 elections to the Reichstag, elections that could bring gains to the SPD, urged the unions to remain passive. The union leaders agreed that a general strike should not be called. The ADGB remained true to its traditional cautious policy; it was unwilling to cause a civil war and preferred to wait passively for future developments. Disappointed rank and file members flocked to either the NSDAP or the KPD.

The von Papen coup against the Socialist Prussian government was an initial step toward Fascism. It was the first illegal act undertaken by the German government with the aim of weakening the existing democratic system. The trade unions, the only group in Germany that could have rallied the masses against such behavior, failed to demonstrate their opposition. Von Papen resigned in November and was replaced by his minister of defense, General Kurt von Schleicher, the leader of the Reichswehr.

Von Schleicher had informed the unions that he would welcome the unification of all union organizations into one single, apolitical labor front that could counteract the Nazi threat. As minister of defense, von Schleicher had invited three ADGB leaders and two representatives of the moderate faction of the NSDAP to discuss jointly with him the possibility of forming a corporative state (Braunthal, 1978, p. 71). The union leaders met with von Schleicher and the Nazis and showed interest in corporatism and in cooperation with the NSDAP. This reveals how strongly the unions had abandoned Socialist ideology and the belief in the class struggle. The Nazi leader Gregor Strasser who sympathized with the AGDB public works plan assured the "free" unions that the NSDAP would support them if they cut ties with the SPD.

On November 28, von Schleicher invited the ADGB leaders Leipart and Eggert to meet with him to discuss labor problems; SPD leaders were excluded from the meeting. The hope union leaders entertained that von Schleicher, once appointed chancellor, would be more sympathetic to the trade unions than his predecessor vanished when von Schleicher appointed to his cabinet the same ministers who had served von Papen, with two exceptions.

LABOR UNDER NAZI RULE

Von Schleicher's administration was short-lived. President Hindenburg dismissed von Schleicher on January 28, 1933. Two days later, Adolf Hitler was sworn in as Germany's new chancellor.

On the same day, workers staged anti-Nazi demonstrations in a number of German cities. The KPD asked the SPD, the ADGB, and the AFA to join it in a general strike. Theodor Leipart, head of the ADGB, was asked by union leaders whether he would issue directives for such a strike. Leipart did not commit himself to such action. Although ADGB workers expected to receive orders to strike at any moment, no such orders were ever issued. The union leadership remained passive, hopeful that an agreement could be reached with the NSDAP. A proposal to merge the "free," liberal, and Christian trade unions into a single labor federation to oppose Nazi power never went into effect.

A secret agreement between von Schleicher and Leipart to organize a coup against Hitler with the help of the Reichswehr and of the unions was divulged to the Nazis; soon thereafter, the Reichstag building was set afire, an incident that allowed the Nazis to justify acts of terror against their opponents. On March 8, the paramilitary SA attacked the ADGB building at Bernau.

Senior labor leaders tried to appease the Nazis. They talked of a complete disassociation of trade unions from political parties. On March 21, Leipart wrote to Hitler that the ADGB was separating from all political groups and would not participate in politics; on March 29, Leipart announced that the ADGB was cutting all ties with the SPD and was ready to cooperate with employers. On April 9, he recognized that trade unions were subordinated to the will of the state. In spite of these assurances, Leipart received no answer from Hitler.

At that time, a number of NSDAP leaders, among them Goebbels and Robert Ley, the future leader of the Nazi German Labor Front, advised Hitler that organized labor had to be crushed in order to prevent a possible future rivalry between a labor federation and the NSDAP. Hitler agreed with these views. On May 2, 1933, at 10 A.M., SS and SA units arrested a number of trade union leaders and occupied trade union offices. On the thirteenth, they confiscated all trade union property. The "free" trade unions were not the only victims of Nazi violence; the Christian and the Hirsch-Duncker unions had a similar fate.

In 1936, the Spanish trade unions decided to fight right-wing dictatorship; poorly armed and poorly organized they resisted for four years the better equipped troops of General Franco. The well-organized German Social Democrats and their trade unions not only were unable to take significant action to stop the onslaught of Fascism but until the very end tried to accommodate the Nazis, discarding in the process their own ideology.

The first attack by the Nazis on democratically organized labor had come as early as April 1933, when the government enacted a Law Relating to Industrial Representation, which allowed the authorities to depose works council members and replace them with NSDAP members. The

Nazis then justified the dissolution of the trade unions on the grounds that such action was necessary to prevent the spread of Bolshevism in Germany.

As a substitute for the trade unions, the Nazi government created a giant organization, the German Labor Front, or *Deutsche Arbeitsfront* (DAF), led by Robert Ley. A law of May 19, 1933 abolished all collective agreements. Thirteen "labor trustees" were then appointed by Hitler who were to establish wages and conditions of work for the entire country. A law of January 20, 1934 established the *Fuehrerprinzip*, or "leadership principle," for industrial and commercial enterprises; this principle commanded employees and workers to follow the dictate of their employer, the employer having to comply in turn with the directives issued by the government. The National Socialist government viewed workers as "soldiers in the service of the state" and abolished their right to select their place of employment. In the words of Grebing (1969):

> Under the national-socialist regime the entrepreneurs, the urban middle class and the farmers considerably increased their material security and social prestige; the organization of the economy on corporate lines even brought them a measure of recognized representation similar to that of professional organizations. The workers on the other hand were the only section of the population which was not directly represented: they were "looked after" and kept dependent like members of an army; nor did their material conditions appreciably change. (p. 142)

Conditions of full employment, the maintenance of the pre-1933 social security programs, propaganda, and the mounting use of terror discouraged any anti-Nazi demonstrations by dissident workers. With their leaders in custody, murdered, or in exile, it was difficult for workers to form resistance organizations against the NSDAP regime. The SPD party had been declared illegal on June 22, 1933, and many of its leaders, as well as those of the KPD, disappeared in concentration camps and prisons.

Social Democratic students and young workers defied danger and organized resistance groups under the guise of athletic or debating clubs. From the very beginning of National Socialist rule, small Socialist and Communist groups distributed leaflets and pamphlets attacking the NSDAP. In time, Gestapo terror ended their existence.

The coming of World War II gave new hope to former labor leaders, inside and outside prisons. Renewed resistance against Nazi rule was led by young labor leaders who had been released from jail; Wilhelm Leuschner, minister of the interior of Hesse between 1928 and 1933 and a deputy chairman of the ADGB in 1932, Jakob Kaiser of the Christian Trade

Unions, and Max Habermann of the German National Shop Assistants' Union started formulating the principles of a future unified German labor movement. Carlo Mierendorff and Theodor Haubach were released from concentration camps and started immediately to build Socialist resistance against the Hitler government; the Catholic labor movement with Nikolaus Gross, Otto Mueller, Bernhard Letterhaus, and H. J. Schmitt also engaged in resistance activities. So did the Communists, led by Harro Schultze-Boysen and Arvid Harnack.

Following the suppression of the trade unions by the Nazi government, the SPD Executive established a "foreign delegation" of six of its members in Prague. After the dissolution of the SPD in June, the foreign delegation constituted themselves the SPD Executive in exile. Among the members of the Prague delegation were Otto Wels, elected SPD chairman in April 1933, Hans Vogel, deputy chairman, Friedrich Stampfler, editor of the journal *Vorwaerts*, and Erich Ollenhauer, chairman of the Socialist Youth. In 1937 this group moved to Paris, and in 1940 members of the group fled either to London or to the United States. Otto Wels died in 1939; Rudolf Hilferding died in a Gestapo prison in Paris in 1944.

Whether in exile or still in Germany, SPD leaders tended to agree on certain basic ideas relating to the nature of the party in a post-Hitler world. They agreed that the party should no longer be a one-class party; it was to be a party appealing to all Germans, a party functioning within a democratic Germany and a democratic Europe; Marxist concepts were ignored. The SPD was to be a nationwide party fighting for the improvement of the living conditions of all Germans.

THE GERMAN LABOR MOVEMENT SINCE 1945

The main architect of the post–World War II labor movement in Germany was Hans Boeckler. In 1927 he had been president of the Rhineland-Westphalia District of the ADGB and in 1928 he was elected Social Democrat delegate to the Reichstag. After the end of the war, Boeckler contacted the British military government in order to obtain its support for the reconstitution of trade unions in the British zone of occupation. The organization of labor in this zone proceeded much faster than in the American and French zones of occupation.

In the British zone, Boeckler was allowed to establish a Provisional Zonal Executive and a Zonal Secretariat. Members of the executive were Hans Boeckler, Hans Boehm, Wilhelm Doerr, Hans Jahn, Albin Karl, and Franz Spliedt. A first Zonal Trade Union Congress was held at Bielefeld, August 21–23, 1946. This congress was attended by 375 delegates representing more than 1 million members. The British authorities then gave their permission to the German labor leaders in their zone to organize labor free of British interference.

Boeckler proceeded to organize labor according to his plans. Sixteen industrial unions were formed. Boeckler's insistence on establishing a new German trade union organization based on industrial unions induced the White Collar Workers' Union, or *Deutsche Angestelltengewerkschaft* (DAG), to form its own independent organization.

Unsuccessful attempts to cooperate with the German Confederation of Free Trade Unions in the Soviet zone of occupation, the *Freier Deutscher Gewerkschaftsbund*, led to a complete separation between the trade unions in the zones of the Allies and the trade unions in the Russian zone. The authorities in the American and French zones had, meanwhile, allowed trade unions in their areas to be established in conformity with the example set in the British zone.

A congress of all trade unions within the German Federal Republic, excluding the DAG, took place in Munich in October 1949. The congress was attended by representatives of labor movements in a number of other European countries. The *Deutscher Gewerkschaftsbund* (DGB) was formally established at that congress. This German Trade Union Federation covered the entire area of the German Federal Republic. It included the already established 16 industrial unions that surrendered to the DGB part of their functions and part of their income. Hans Boeckler became the first president of the DGB.

The industrial trade unions within the DGB, the *Industriegewerkschaften* (IG), embraced all the skilled and unskilled workers in an industry, as well as the salaried staff without membership in the DAG. In 1964, the DGB counted about 6.4 million members who belonged to the following industrial unions: metal; public services, transport, and communications; chemicals, paper, and pottery; mining and power; building, stone, and soil; railways; textiles and clothing; postal services; food, entertainment, and hotels; printing and paper; wood and timber; commerce, banks, and insurance; education and science; leather; horticulture, agriculture, and forestry; and the arts.

Boeckler's wish to bring all German trade unions under a single federation was not fulfilled. Compared to the size of the DGB membership, the size and significance of independent labor organizations were, however, quite limited. The White Collar Workers' Union had a membership in 1964 of about 475,000; the Union of German Civil Servants, the *Deutscher Beamtenbund* (DBB), counted about 700,000; the Union of Police Officers, the *Gewerkschaft der Polizei*, and the Christian trade unions were even smaller.

The DGB's Principles of Economic Policy, formulated in 1949 in Munich, stipulated the following:

The unions, being the organizations of manual workers, salaried employees and civil servants work for the economic, social and cultural interests of the working population. They support an economic system which will do away with social injustice and material poverty, and offer work and a livelihood to everyone willing to work.... Starting from this premise, the unions make the following basic demands:

I. An economic policy which, while preserving the dignity of all free men, will secure full employment for all those willing to work; the most efficient use of all national productive resources, and the satisfaction of the most important national economic needs.

II. Co-determination by organized labour in all economic, social and personnel aspects of management.

III. Nationalization of key industries, particularly mining, iron and steel, chemicals, power, essential transport and banking.

IV. A fair share for all in the total national economic product, and adequate provisions for those unable to work because of age, disablement and sickness.... (Grebing 1969, p. 175)

It will be noted that these principles totally avoided mentioning the necessity of a social revolution. They did not refer to Marxist or non-Marxist Socialist dogma. Instead of social revolution, these principles advocated codetermination by both managers and workers of the economic decision-making process in a neocapitalist system.

This politicoeconomic orientation of the German trade unions in 1949 must be understood in terms of two developments. First, in the late 1940s, most people in the Federal Republic supported a capitalist economic system. Second, the SPD had abandoned for all practical purposes basic Socialist ideology.

The post-1948 German "economic miracle" and the awareness of much lower living standards in the "other" Germany strengthened the acceptance of capitalist institutions in the Federal Republic. As living standards rose, the popular sympathy extended to the trade unions in 1945 rapidly diminished. Trade union leaders in the late 1940s faced the old choice of either striving for the transformation of society or of adjusting to existing conditions; as in the past, they chose gradual reformism rather than revolution. In this they echoed the feelings of the SPD leaders who tried to transform their party into a nationwide party whose base would no longer be limited to the working class. In order to do so they had to purge their party's platform of Marxist doctrines and reasoning. According to the SPD leader Kurt Schumacher, the SPD had to develop its own ideology, so that the new SPD could appeal to workers and nonworkers alike.

This conception of the postwar SPD was embodied in its Godesberg Program of 1959. This program stated that "the Social Democratic

Party. . .is a community of men holding different beliefs and ideas. Their agreement is based on the moral principles and political aims they have in common. . ." (Grebing 1969, p. 166). This statement clearly indicated that the SPD no longer followed any Socialist ideology.

The DGB goal of codetermination in the firm's decision-making process was partially fulfilled in 1951, when the German federal government enacted the *Mitbestimmungsgesetz*, the "codetermination law," which covered the coal mining, iron, and steel industries. This law, still operative today, applied the principle of parity codetermination, *"paritaetische Mitbestimmung,"* to a limited number of industries.

The origins of this law go back to 1946, when the British military government tried to deconcentrate the coal, iron, and steel industries of the Ruhr. A German, Heinrich Dinkelbach, was given the responsibility of carrying out the program of decentralization and of breaking down large enterprises into smaller, competitive firms. Trade union leaders were demanding at that time the nationalization of all heavy industries in the Ruhr. Dinkelbach, in an effort to stop the unions from pressing for nationalization, offered the unions equal seating on the board of directors, the *Aufsichtsrat*, of the new companies that were to be formed. Furthermore, the unions were to be able to appoint for each firm a labor director, the *Arbeitsdirektor*, who would also be a member of the executive board, the *Vorstand* (Lieberman 1977, p. 60).

The union leaders accepted the Dinkelbach plan with enthusiasm. Industrialists and their managers opposed the idea, claiming that codetermination was inconsistent with a free enterprise system. The Dinkelbach plan, as implemented originally only in the British zone of occupation, was, however, very successful and brought an era of peaceful labor-management relations that allowed the steel industry in the Ruhr to rebuild a full year ahead of Germany's receipt of Marshall Plan aid.

After the formation of the German Federal Republic, a codetermination bill applicable only to the coal, iron, and steel industries became law in 1951 in spite of employers' opposition to it. The law provided that the board of directors, the *Aufsichtsrat*, of any firm covered by this law would consist of 11 members. Five were to represent the shareholders, five to represent the employees and their unions, and one member to be neutral. A labor director responsible for social and personnel problems and representing the unions would be part of the executive board, the *Vorstand*.

In 1952, the Bundesrat of the German Federal Republic passed a Works Constitution Act, the *Betriebsverfassungsgesetz*, which applied to private employment in general. This law disappointed the unions because, unlike the law of 1951, it related only to the firms' workers and employees, not to their unions. It provided a milder form of codetermination by stating that "the employer and the works council shall work together in a spirit of mutual trust under the applicable collective agreements in co-operation with the trade unions and employers' associations represented in the undertaking, for the good of the undertaking and its employees, having due regard to the interests of the community" (Cullingford 1976, p. 65).

A third law, enacted in 1955, extended the *Betriebsverfassungsgesetz* to employees in the public sector. It was replaced in March 1974 by a new *Bundespersonalvertretungsgesetz*, which aimed to extend a limited form of codetermination to public service employees.

The 1952 *Betriebsverfassungsgesetz* applied to all privately owned firms operating with five or more employees (ten or more in agriculture and forestry). All covered firms were required to have the following:

(1) A works council *(Betriebsrat)* consisting of employees and workers secretly appointed and serving for two years. (2) A works assembly *(Betriebsversammlung)* composed of all employees and dealing with any problem relating to the firm and its employees not covered by a collective bargaining agreement. (3) An economic committee *(Wirtschaftsausschuss)* existing only in firms of more than 100 permanent employees. This committee was to act as a liaison body trying to develop better relationships between workers, works council and the employer. (4) In corporations, one-third of the board of directors *(Aufsichtsrat)* had to represent the employees, the other two-thirds representing the shareholders.

While syndicalists have advocated increased workers' control in an enterprise as a way to weaken and eventually to destroy the capitalist system, neither the ADGB in the past nor the DGB in the present ever demanded workers' participation in the decision-making process of the firm to facilitate the breakdown of the democratic bourgeois system.

In the 1960s, DGB leaders pressed the government to pass legislation that would introduce parity codetermination throughout the economy. This type of codetermination was opposed by the employers' federation, by the conservative Christian Democratic party (CDU/CSU), and by the Free Democrats (FDP), the allies of the SPD. As a delaying tactic, the Bundesrat referred the study of the implications of parity codetermination to a special commission of nine university professors, headed by Biedenkopf. The commission's report, published in 1970, stated that the board of directors of a firm cannot operate efficiently unless its decisions are supported by a clear majority of the board. The report also recognized that it was necessary to involve the workers in the decision-making process because ultimately their jobs depend on such decisions. The report advised that workers should be represented on the board of directors in a ratio of 5 to 7 in favor of the shareholders. The report disappointed the DGB.

Walter Arendt, former head of the Mine Workers Union, became minister of labor and social affairs in the SPD/FDP coalition government of 1969. Arendt had had a great deal of experience with the system of parity codetermination and sympathized with it. He introduced in October 1970 a draft bill that practically mandated parity codetermination for all German firms. The bill met such strong opposition that a revised bill was introduced by Arendt two months later. The new draft bill was no longer a measure facilitating the application of parity codetermination to all firms in the country. It was, rather, a revision of the Works Constitution Law of 1952.

The DGB was uncertain about the policy it should follow. If it went on pressing for parity codetermination it could endanger the position of its political ally, the SPD-FDP coalition. On the other hand, it was very difficult for the DGB to abandon completely the long battle it had fought to obtain *paritaetische Mitbestimmung*. In 1971, the DGB made the surprising decision of appealing to the parliamentary opposition, the Christian Democrats, for aid in realizing its goal of parity codetermination. It appealed particularly to a former minister of labor and social affairs, Hans Katzer, who, although a CDU member, was known to be a reformist with ideas farther to the left than those of most Social Democrats. The 1971 CDU congress adopted, however, a codetermination formula that was not very different from that proposed by Biedenkopf. It adopted the 6:2:4 model: The *Aufsichtsrat* of a firm would have six representatives of the shareholders, four representatives of the employees and workers, and two neutral members.

At the end of 1971, Arendt's amended bill became law. This law strengthened the powers of the works councils without unduly restricting the ability of owners or their representatives to manage the firm. Works councils could make certain that new jobs in the firm would first be offered to existing employees in the firm. They also participated in decisions affecting work processes and the work environment. Under this law, foreign workers could be elected to the works council. The law also established a conciliation board, the *Einigungsstelle*, made up of an equal number of representatives of employers and employees and chaired by a neutral president; this board was to hear matters subject to dispute within the firm.

The enactment of the Works Constitution Act of 1971 did not allay the DGB's eagerness to obtain parity codetermination. It was not alone in presenting new codetermination plans to the government. Government officials were plagued by a number of such proposals submitted by various groups, such as the SPD, the CDU, the DAG, the Protestant church (EKD), the Catholic employers (BKU), and so on. The issues became more complicated when these plans started distinguishing various categories of employees; they referred to employees in position of authority, the "leading employees," or *leitende Angestellte*; to regular white-collar employees, or *Angestellte*; and to semiskilled workers or unskilled workers, or *Arbeiter*. The legality of parity codetermination was then challenged by a constitutional lawyer from Berlin, Scholz, and by a professor from the University of Giessen, Raiser.

In spite of these difficulties, the SPD chancellor, Helmut Schmidt, succeeded in 1976 in having a bill enacted into law that came very close to providing for parity codetermination in firms with more than 2,000 employees. At first reading, the bill seemed to extend the parity codetermination provisions applicable to the coal, iron, and steel industries to large firms with a labor force exceeding 2,000. Indeed, the ratios between representatives of shareholders and representatives of employees forming the *Aufsichtsrat* were as follows: for firms up to 10,000 employees, 6:6; for firms with from 10,000 to 20,000 employees, 8:8; and for firms with over 20,000 employees, 10:10.

This law, however, provided that in the case of a deadlock vote by the *Aufsichtsrat*, the shareholders' vote would prevail. Further, in the case of boards of directors with ten worker representatives, seven had to be chosen from the shop floor and the staff of the firm, and one of these had to be a *Leitender Angestellter*. This "leading employee" was a salaried employee whose duties involved the power to make a final decision. This "leading employee" had to be elected by other "leading employees" in the firm. The unions were naturally apprehensive of the possibility that the *Leitender Angestellter* could be a junior executive who would identify with the interests and views of the shareholders.

The other three worker representatives had to be union officials, elected by the firm's employees, but who were not on the payroll of the firm. The executive board, or *Vorstand*, was to be appointed by the board of directors, and one of the members of the *Vorstand* had to be the labor director, a union official.

Thus, as of 1976, there were three different forms of codetermination in the German Federal Republic:

1. Under the Mitbestimmungsgesetz of 1951, parity codetermination was mandatory in the coal, iron, and steel industries.
2. Under the *Betriebsverfassungsgesetz* of 1971, employees and workers obtained a one-third representation on the board of directors of firms of less than 2,000 employees and workers.
3. Under the Works Constitution Law of 1976, parity codetermination applied with certain restrictions to firms with more than 2,000 employees and workers.

The DGB constitution states that the German Trade Union Federation will operate independently of government, political parties, religious bodies, and employers' associations. Independence of political parties cannot mean political abstinence. The DBG must represent workers' interest not only vis-à-vis employers but also vis-à-vis the government and other institutions in society. Besides these political responsibilities, the DGB also has a number of organizational duties, such as unionist schooling, legal aid services, public relations, and the coordination of trade union activities. These various tasks and objectives are expressed in a basic program and in an action program.

Presently, the DGB's total membership has reached about 7.7 million members of the industry-based unions belonging to the DGB.

The structure of the DGB parallels the administrative structure of the German Federal Republic. The federation is administratively divided into three levels: federal (*Bund*), state (*Landesbezirke*) and county (*Kreis*).

At the federal level, the DGB's organs are the Federal Congress (*Bundeskongress*), the Federal Executive Council (*Bundesausschuss*), the Federal Executive Board (*Bundesvorstand*), and the Auditing Commission (*Revisionskommission*). The Federal Congress is the DGB's supreme organ; it meets regularly every four years, apart from extraordinary congresses, and is made up of delegates from member unions. Additional congress participants, in consultant or observer capacities, are the members of the Federal Executive Council, the Federal Executive Board, the Auditing Commission, the *Landesbezirk* presidents, and three representatives for each of the following special interest groups: salaried staff, wage earners, civil servants, women, and youth. The Federal Congress lays down the guidelines of trade union policy, studies constitutional changes, and formulates the basic program.

Between federal congresses, the highest organ is the Federal Executive Council, composed of 135 members. These are drawn from the Federal Executive Board, the nine state district presidents, and delegates of member unions. The council meets every three months and supervises trade union policy, rules on application for membership by outside trade unions, or on the expulsion of a member union and decides on the federation's budget allocations.

The Federal Executive Board consists of the presidents of the member unions and of various federation officers, for example, the president of the DGB, two vice-presidents, and six other elected officials. The Duesseldorf-based Federal Executive Board Administration, the *Bundesvorstandsverwaltung*, is subdivided into nine Federal Executive Board departments (*Vorstandsbereiche der Geschaeftsfuehrenden Bundesvorstandsmitglieder*) with 22 subdepartments. The Federal Executive Board meets once a month; its tasks are to monitor adherence to the DGB constitution, ensure cooperation within the federation, and convene the Federal Congress.

The structure is paralleled at the state (*Land*) and county (*Kreis*) levels.

In 1963 the DGB adopted a basic program, still in effect today. This program states in part:

> The trade unions...strive and will continue to strive for a social order in which human dignity is fully respected, and they demand the full realization in all parts of the Declaration of Human Rights of the United Nations.... It will continue to be the goal of the trade unions to play their part in the further consolidation of a social and constitutional state and of a democratic form of society. In pursuing this goal the trade unions will act as an integrating factor of democracy, and will represent an indispensable force in democratic development in the political, economic and cultural fields. Free and independent trade unions can exist and be effective only within a democracy. For this reason the German Trade Union Federation (DGB) and its affiliated unions resolutely oppose every totalitarian and reactionary manifestation, and will resist any and every attempt to restrict or annul any of the basic rights guaranteed by the Basic Law of the Federal Republic.... (DGB, p.20)

The action program adopted by the DGB in June 1979 listed the following demands: right to work and secure jobs, shorter working time and longer vacation time, higher wages and salaries, a more just distribution of wealth, an improved taxation and public finance policy, greater social security, greater old age security, expanded codetermination, equal educational opportunities, and better protection of resources and of the environment.

It is to be noted that further socialization or nationalization of industry was completely left out of the basic and action programs. Neither demanded that workers obtain the full value of their labor. They did not establish as a goal a social revolution or the "dictatorship of the proletariat." As a matter of fact, the DGB expressly stated its opposition to any dictatorial rule in its programs. The basic program stipulates that "the problems of our age can be solved only by constructive, joint cooperation of peoples, nations, and states. The goal is a political and economic community of the free and democratic peoples of Europe and their close association with the free peoples of the world" (DGB p. 21).

CONCLUSION

Even though the roots of the German trade union movement are tied to political parties formed by men influenced by Marxist ideology—Lassalle, Bebel, and Liebknecht—German trade union leadership soon embraced conservative, pragmatic policies that favored lawful reformism instead of violent revolution. This conservatism strengthened as the membership of the "free" trade unions expanded. At their national congress in Cologne in May 1905 the trade unions not only denounced the use of the mass strike; they even rejected any discussion of it. When the great Marxist theoretician Karl Kautsky urged a debate regarding the use of the mass strike, the trade union leaders labeled him a *"Nurpolitiker,"* a man interested only in the political aspects of the labor movement and not in its economic aspect (Steenson 1978, p. 147).

In the days of the Weimar Republic, and since 1945, Germany's trade unions have shown a willingness to act within the capitalist framework. Looking at the period that has lapsed since the end of World War II, it must be recognized that the labor movement in the German Federal Republic has become one of the most successful in the world even though it operates within the neocapitalist economy founded by Ludwig Erhard in 1948. German trade unions committed themselves, both in the 1920s and since 1945, to the realization of their objectives by peaceful, legal means. To do so effectively, trade union leaders had to bargain with their opponents on equal terms. This required trade union officials to be as knowledgeable and skilled as the representatives of the shareholders. In order to improve the knowledge and skills of its officials and members, the DBG founded an Economic Research Institute *(Wirtschafts und Sozialwissenschaftliches Institut)*, in Düsseldorf. This institute is staffed by top economists, statisticians, and social scientists. The DGB has also founded a number of educational institutions *(Bundesschulen)* and academies *(Akademien)*.

The DGB's willingness to cooperate with the other sectors of the neocapitalist West German economy is also evidenced by the fact that any reference to Socialist dogma was expunged from its action program in 1963. Like the SPD, the DGB tried to appeal to German workers, salaried employees, and public servants in general, regardless of their political convictions. The DGB simply proclaimed its efforts to obtain a just, humane, and democratic society. If some people have interpreted these efforts as meaning a quest to attain a Socialist society, they would have to conclude that, for the DGB, the attainment of socialism had to be achieved by "gradual evolution." The concentration of DGB policies on obtaining economic and cultural benefits for its members places the DGB closer to trade unionism in the United States than to the labor movements in either Spain or France.

NOTES

Braunthal, G. 1978. *Socialist Labor and Politics in Weimar Germany: The General Federation of German Trade Unions.* Hamden, Conn.: Archon Books.

Cullingford, E. C. M. 1976. *Trade Unions in West Germany.* London: Wilton House.

DGB, 1981, The German Trade Union Federation, Cologne, Deutz.

Grebing, H. 1969. *The History of the German Labour Movement.* London: Oswald Wolff.

Lieberman, S. 1977. *The Growth of European Mixed Economies, 1945–1970.* Cambridge: Schenkman.

Moses, J. A. 1982. *Trade Unionism in Germany from Bismarck to Hitler.* Vol. II. Totowa, N.J.; Barnes & Noble.

Steenson, G. P., 1978. *Karl Kautsky, 1854–1938, Marxism in the Classical Years.* Pittsburgh: University of Pittsburgh Press.

BIBLIOGRAPHY

Bullock, A. *Hitler—A Study in Tyranny.* London, 1964.

Czichon, E. *Wer verhalf Hitler zur Macht?* Cologne, 1967.

Deppe, F., et al. *Kritik der Mitbestimmung, Partnerschaft oder Klassenkampf?* Frankfurt, 1972.

Edinger, L. *Social Democracy and National Socialism.* Los Angeles, 1956.

Erger, J. *Der Kapp-Luettwitz Putsch.* Düsseldorf, 1967.

Foster, W. Z. *History of the Three Internationals: The World Socialist and Communist Movements from 1848 to the Present.* New York, 1955.

Freyburg, J., et al. *Geschichte der deutschen Sozialdemokratie 1863–1975.* Cologne, 1975.

Haffner, S. *Failure of a Revolution: Germany 1918–19.* London, 1973.

Heer, H. *Burgfrieden oder Klassenkampf, zur Politik der sozial-demokratischen Gewerkschaften, 1930–1933.* Neuwied, 1971.

Hunt, R. N.: *German Social Democracy, 1918–1933.* New Haven, Conn., 1964.

Krause, H. *Zur Geschichte der Unabhaengigen Sozial Demokratischen Partei Deutschlands.* Frankfurt, 1975.

Limmer, H. *Die deutsche Gewerkschaftsbewegung.* Munich, 1980.

Morgan, D. W. *The Socialist Left and the German Revolution.* Ithaca, N.Y., 1975.

Schorkse, C. E. *German Social Democracy, 1905–1917.* New York, 1955.

Teuteberg, H. J. *Geschichte der industriellen Mitbestimmung in Deutschland.* Tübingen, 1961.

Vetter, H. O., ed. *Vom Sozialistengesetz zur Mitbestimmung.* Frankfurt, 1975.

6

The Evolution of the French Labor Movement Through Four Revolutions: From the First to the Third Republics

THE PRECURSORS OF THE MODERN FRENCH TRADE UNIONS

The earliest forms of workers' organizations in France were the *compagnonnages*, journeymen's associations that were established as early as the fifteenth century. These organizations duplicated in many ways the masters' guilds, or *corporations*, and, like the guilds, the *compagnonnages* did not pursue exclusively economic goals. The *compagnonnages* were secret fraternities of bachelor journeymen that developed at a time when most journeymen no longer lived in the household of the master and when most of these workers could no longer expect to join the ranks of the masters and the *maîtrises*, the masters' corporations. The *compagnonnage* allowed journeymen of the same trade to live together in one house, usually an inn kept by the "father" *(père)* or mother *(mère)* of the trade. Out-of-town journeymen of the same trade, visiting the particular town, could also eat and sleep in the same inn. If a *compagnon* married or became a master, he would have to leave the organization. Ceremonies and rituals were an important part of the *compagnonnage;* these journeymen's brotherhoods were often simply transforms of the masters' *corporations.*

Compagnonnages developed mainly in the sixteenth and seventeenth centuries, particularly in trades in which journeymen were required to perfect their skills by engaging in a *tour de France;* by the middle of the seventeenth century the *compagnonnage* started to take the form of a federation, which included a number of trades.

All of the French *compagnons* were divided into three clans called "duties," or the *devoirs.* Each *devoir* consisted of a number of trades and sometimes the same trade was divided among different *devoirs.* These *devoirs* included The Sons of Master Jack, The Sons of Solomon, and The Sons of Master Soubise. Membership lists in these *devoirs* were kept secret so as to avoid persecution by the authorities, the church, and the masters. Within the *devoir*, hierarchical distinctions were strongly observed, although there were frequent fights among members of various trades in a single *devoir*.

The economic aspects of the *compagnonnage* made it a precursor of the later *syndicat*. In a *compagnonnage*, the *rouleur* kept a list of members in need of a job and located work for them. This activity gave the *compagnonnage* control over the labor supply in a given market and the organization had the power to withhold labor from a master who did not comply with its demands. These organizations were able to call strikes and to boycott masters for extended periods of time. If a master failed to follow the accepted standards of the trade, the *compagnonnage* would declare him *mis à l'index* or *damné*, which would render that master unable to get skilled workers.

Although both masters and journeymen viewed their trade as an economic, social, and moral community, and although most of the masters in a trade had been *compagnons* at one time, relationships between the *corporations* of the masters and the brotherhoods of the journeymen were of persistent opposition. These brotherhoods attained a peak of development in the first quarter of the nineteenth century. Although illegal, they were tolerated by the government. They declined after 1830, not so much because of repression by the police, but because with changing times they became an obsolete form of labor organization. The coming of the factory and of machine work displaced many crafts; workers discovered that labor organizations based on a single craft or industry could operate more efficiently than the multitrade *compagnonnage*. With new means of transportation, journeymen abandoned the ancient tradition of the *tour de France*. The more materialistic-minded worker of the nineteenth century was not as much interested in the ceremonies and rites of the *compagnonnage* as his fifteenth- or sixteenth-centuries predecessors. A number of *compagnonnages* survived until the end of the nineteenth century, but after the Great Revolution, French workers started to prefer other forms of labor organization.

Mutualités, or benevolent societies, established by workers for mutual aid in sickness, accident, or death had existed in France before the French Revolution; they generally embraced one single trade and to some extent played the role of trade unions. *Sociétés de résistance* offered no or very limited mutual benefits to members but were created to influence conditions of employment. A famous resistance society was the Devoir Mutuel, established in 1823 by the weavers of Lyon; it had about 3,000 members in 1833 and directed a strike in 1834 (Levine 1970, p. 32).

The eighteenth-century French *philosophes* had opposed both the masters' corporations and the journeymen's brotherhoods because they believed that social order had to reflect the laws of nature and human reason and not hierarchical discipline. When Turgot, himself a *philosophe*, became prime minister (1774–76), he ordered the guilds abolished.

The ideas of the French Enlightenment influenced the revolutionaries of the 1790s. Mirabeau, Danton, Marat, Robespierre, Saint-Just—all of them shared the view that the revolution had to constitute the triumph of nature and of reason over privilege, tradition, despotism, and superstition. For them, all privileged organizations had to disappear, including the *corporations* and the workers' associations. French institutions had to be reformed in order to bring them closer to the natural order. Human inventiveness and enterprise had to be freed from traditional restrictive laws. Both Diderot and Adam Smith wanted production and exchange to be governed by "natural laws," and according to both of them, the wealth of a nation would be maximized if everyone would be allowed to produce, buy, and sell in markets free of any governmental regulations. Since the masters' corporations or guilds and the journeymen's brotherhoods impeded the free operation of markets, they had to be abolished, according to the *philosophes*.

The pamphlet "What Is the Third Estate?" of the Abbé Sieyes introduced the Great Revolution. Sieyes attacked not only the privileges of the clergy and of the nobility but also those of magistrates, chartered companies, guilds, and cities. The representatives of the Third Estate, which constituted themselves into a National Assembly, tried, during the night of August 4, 1789, to implement the program of Sieyes. The privileges of both the nobility and of the church and those of cities and provinces were abolished.

A law of March 17, 1791 abolished the guilds and declared that, from that day on, everyone was "free to do such business, exercise such profession, art or trade as he may choose" (Levine 1970, p. 19). Following the disappearance of the masters' organizations, journeymen in Paris assembled in large meetings to discuss wages and conditions of work. The carpenters, relying on a law of August 21, 1790, which gave all citizens "the right to assemble peacefully and to form among themselves free associations subject only to the laws which all citizens must obey" formed *L'Union fraternelle des ouvriers en l'art de la charpente*, a benevolent association in appearance, a true trade union in reality (Levine 1970, p. 20).

The masters of Paris complained to the municipal authorities that the journeymen were forming large and illegal coalitions and that their example was being followed in the provinces. The municipal authorities then urged the constituent assembly to pass legislation regulating associations of workers. The assembly enacted the Le Chapelier Law of June 1791. The law read in part: "The citizens of the same estate or trade, entrepreneurs, those who run a shop, workingmen in any trade whatsoever, shall not, when assembled together, nominate presidents, nor secretaries, nor syndics, shall not keep any records, shall not deliberate nor pass resolutions nor form any regulations with reference to their pretended common interests" (Levine 1970, p. 22).

The law further declared that acts in violation of it would be punished with fines of 500 *livres* and with the temporary suspension of rights of citizenship. The eighth clause of the law prohibited all "gatherings composed of artisans, or workingmen, of journeymen or of laborers, or instigated by them and directed against the free exercise of industry and work to which all sorts of persons have a right under all sorts of conditions agreed upon by private contract" (Levine 1970, p. 22).

The French Revolution of 1789–94 introduced in France a bourgeois and capitalist society. The revolution succeeded in unifying the country after it abolished the seignorial social system and the privileged feudal classes. The spectacular victory of the middle class was largely due to the intransigence of the aristocracy, which provoked the anger of the masses. Using as its weapon exasperated urban workers, the bourgeoisie had no other alternative than the destruction of feudal institutions. A new democratic political system was introduced under which all citizens were equal before the law. This equality was limited to the equality of rights; differences in the economic means of individuals continued to exist because the bourgeoisie viewed the right to own property as a "natural right."

The revolution changed the relations between employers and employees. In prerevolution times, journeymen owed obedience to their master, not because the master owned the means of production and not because of a contract of employment. Rather, in the days of the *corporations,* the journeyman obeyed his master because the latter was his "superior"; in the ancient guild system, the authority of the master over his journeymen extended beyond matters relating directly to employment; the master even had control over the private lives of the journeymen. On the other hand, the master was not free to give employment to any worker of his choice; he was restricted in his selection of journeymen to those who had completed their apprenticeship with success.

After the revolution, the authority of the master became limited to matters relating to employment; the master could, however, hire as a journeyman any person of his choice. If a worker had the means and the wish to do so, he or she could start a business without having to obtain first a *maîtrise* from a trade corporation. The ancient classification of masters, journeymen, and apprentices was replaced by a categorization of property-owning employers and propertyless wage earners. The importance attached to private property rights by the Thermidorians, the governments that succeeded each other between the fall of Robespierre in 1794 and Napoleon's coup in 1799, favored in France the growth of a propertied middle class that looked at workers as suppliers of human labor who could be hired and dismissed at will.

A view regarding property rights that was different from that developed by the *philosophes* of the French Enlightenment was developed by the *sans-culottes* of Paris. The *sans-culottes* did not constitute a single class and represented various social groups that included wage workers, petty proprietors, and low-ranking public officials.

Although the radicalism of the *sans-culottes* helped the coming to power of Robespierre and the spread of the "Reign of Terror", their economic views were still anchored to those of the petty bourgeoisie. They looked at themselves as *gens de métier*, artisans who worked with both their hands and their mind. Believing that they were the laborious backbone of France, they centered their attacks on the idle aristocrats, the *rentiers,* and the rich. For them, only those who worked hard for a living, who led a simple life, could be virtuous, patriotic citizens. The political moderates, the counterrevolutionaries, the rich, the idle, the capitalists, the Girondints, those who gambled and attended theaters, those who paid low wages to workers—all were seen as unpatriotic aristocrats. Those who powdered their hair or wore it long and those who were simply indifferent to politics were placed in the same group. In the words of a *sans-culotte,* "Aristocrats are all the rich, all the wealthy merchants, all the monopolists, the middlemen, the bankers, the brokers, quibbling lawyers and all those who own anything" (Sewell 1980, p. 111).

Still, the *sans-culottes* accepted the institution of private property as long as the latter was relatively small; influenced by the mentality of the artisan bourgeoisie, they accepted the right to private property of the craftsman, the shopkeeper, and the small peasant. Unlike the National Assembly of 1791, they did not view the right to private property as an unlimited natural right. The *sans-culottes* felt that it was indeed the duty of government to regulate and limit the amount or value of private property an individual could own. In order to achieve social and economic equality and a "one and indivisible republic," it was proper for government to limit the area of land a person could own or provide that one person could not own more than one workshop or store. Furthermore, the *sans-culottes* argued that rights of private ownership could not be absolute; owners were simply trustees, *dépositaires,* of assets that ultimately belonged to society and had to be managed for the public good. Public rights were superior to private rights. Therefore, private ownership rights could not be inconsistent with the needs of the republic and with those of its egalitarian society.

In their view, the maintenance of the republic was equivalent to the maintenance of the popular will. The individual will had to serve and be harmonious with the popular will. Individual or group interests could not differ from the popular interest. The importance the *sans-culottes* attached to the unified popular will induced them to reject any form of masters' associations or journeymen's brotherhoods. In the words of Sewell (1980):

> The notion that men who exercised the same trade should have a special sense of community among themselves and should be concerned with the well-being of their own particular trade—whether this notion be expressed in the corporate idiom of the old regime or in the new post-revolutionary idiom of philanthropic aid and association—was directly contrary to the sans-culottes' ideal of the perfect unity of all citizens. For citizens to organize themselves on the basis of particular trades would be to form partial wills that could only conflict with the general will and hence would be counterrevolutionary. (p. 103)

The Jacobins represented the interests of the middle bourgeoisie but also relied on the support of the masses. Danton and Marat condemned the abuses generated by the individual ownership of great wealth. Robespierre and Saint-Just advocated an egalitarian distribution of wealth and the enactment of laws that would favor the growth of a class of small proprietors whose wealth was largely obtained from personal labor. Whereas the *sans-culottes* wanted a limitation on all individual property, the Jacobins were only interested in regulating individual ownership of land. Land, of course, constituted at that time the principal form of wealth. The Jacobins' program called for a free market economy in which the state could intervene to prevent the development of monopolies and the rise of a propertyless proletariat. These views led to the enactment of a number of laws in 1793 and 1794 whose main goal was to ensure the fragmentation of large individual wealth and the egalitarian distribution of bequests. A law of June 3, 1793 provided for the public sale in small parts of property left by emigrants; a law of June 10 of the same year ordered that communal property be divided among all of the residents in that community; a law of November 22 provided for similar sales of national property.

The entire French Revolution was nourished by an egalitarian current, a current typical of a society made up largely of artisans, small peasants, and shopkeepers. Egalitarianism was also deeply embedded in the minds of the masses. It was also to be a very important concept in the thinking of Pierre Joseph Proudhon, whose proposals for social and economic reforms were to be accepted as gospel by French labor leaders during most of the nineteenth century.

The vision of an egalitarian society made up largely by small proprietors had a great appeal for both the *petite bourgeoisie* and the large numbers of artisans, craftsmen, shopkeepers, and peasants who constituted the bulk of French society in the days of the Revolution and the Empire. During the first half of the nineteenth century, artisans continued to be far more numerous than factory workers, and small-scale artisan industry continued to predominate in the French economy until well past the middle of that century. Most of these artisans owned small workshops producing goods that were sold in a very immediate and very small market, and the maintenance of private ownership rights was important to them. Their numbers remained large in the nineteenth century because the relative small rate of growth of population and the equally small growth of domestic demand tended to retard the process of modern industrialization in the country.

The appearance of factories did not necessarily displace artisan work; actually, with the building of these factories, the satisfaction of the needs of the workers tended very often to strengthen the demand for the services of artisans and craftsmen. As observed by Sewell (1980): "In numerical terms, at least, this was an era of rise, rather than of decline, for urban artisans. For the better part of the nineteenth century, artisans remained the dominant sector of the urban working class, numerically, politically, and culturally" (p. 157). In spite of legal prohibitions, these artisans retained the prerevolution tradition of forming *compagnonnages* and other forms of *corporations ouvrières*.

Compagnonnages flourished at the end of the Napoleonic period when thousands of young men were demobilized; the number of *compagnons* during the Restoration government probably exceeded that of the prior century, even though *compagnonnage* was still illegal. The *compagnonnage* was tolerated by the Restoration government because it constituted a center of opposition to revolutionary feelings and ideas. Occasionally, the police arrested a few *compagnons* because of violence during strikes or because of fights with members of a rival group. Otherwise, the *compagnonnages* were allowed to operate quite freely, and, what is quite interesting, they went on acting very much as they had done in the days of the *ancien régime*. They continued to belong to one of the three traditional groups, they continued to have their ritualistic initiations, processions, and banquets; and they retained the *tour de France*, the *"mère,"* and the "damnation" of uncooperative masters. Bloody battles between members of rival group were waged as they had been centuries earlier, but in the nineteenth century, they would cooperate in a number of instances in the organization of a strike.

The *compagnonnage* was occasionally combined with the legal mutual aid society. These *sociétés de secours mutuel* provided mutual insurance benefits that were financed through the payment of dues by members.

The societies could operate legally by submitting their statutes to the authorities and by accepting their regulations. Very often, the mutual aid society was simply a front for a broader workers' association operating as a trade union. This explains why mutual aid societies grew rapidly after the collapse of the Empire, well after the middle of the nineteenth century. By the 1840s, they already represented the prototype of workers' organizations in France.

The long economic crisis of 1826–31 intensified the misery of the workers. Rising unemployment increased popular discontent with the reign of Charles X and triggered the revolution of 1830. The crisis started with poor potato and wheat harvests, which reduced the income of peasants and increased the price of bread in the cities.

Taking 1825 as the base year, the average price of bread rose by 40 percent in 1828 and by 60 percent in 1829 (Bron 1968, p. 58). In order to maintain their food intake, urban and rural workers had to reduce their purchases of finished goods, particularly clothing. Industrial production declined and unemployment rose. Many unemployed in the provinces were induced to move to Paris in search of employment, making it more difficult for unemployed Parisians to find jobs. Those who were employed often worked for a wage that had been reduced by one-third or by one-fourth below its pre-1826 level.

The crisis led workers to engage in spontaneous acts of insurrection and pillage. They destroyed machines in their factories and workshops, while appealing at the same time for public help. Local strikes, though dealt with harshly by the authorities, spread everywhere. In August 1824, 800 textile workers of Houlme (Seine-Inférieure) went on strike to protest the reduction of their wages; the ensuing battle with security forces resulted in the imprisonment of a number of workers; at their trial, the court ordered the execution of one, hard labor for three, and long jail sentences for fourteen. These sentences did not discourage French workers, who continued to strike throughout the country.

Both the economic crisis and middle-class apprehension that it was being displaced by the nobility brought the revolutionary days of July 27–29, 1830. The workers of Paris ended the reign of Charles X and the bourgeoisie installed on the throne of France the "bourgeois king," Louis-Philippe I, of the d'Orléans family. At that time, employed workers labored between 13 and 14 hours a day. The workday was particularly exhausting because it did not provide for rest periods. By today's standards, the "shorter" workday the workers demanded was still very long. The machinists of Paris demanded a workday of 11 hours; the workers of Rouen demonstrated for 12 hours. In both cases, both the authorities and the employers rejected the workers' petitions. At Roubaix, Anzin, and Montreuil, workers demanded an increase in wages and the *tarif,* a minimum wage that would establish a floor for all wages in a given trade.

A major workers' insurrection was that of the *canuts*, the silk weavers, of Lyon in 1831. In order to oppose a wage reduction, the *canuts* demanded a *tarif*. After signing a contract with the workers, many of the employers chose to ignore the agreement. The weavers then decided to settle matters through their own efforts. On November 21, 1831, about 30,000 workers, some of them armed and others carrying black flags, took over the city of Lyon. Their victory was short-lived because the government in Paris reacted by sending to Lyon 26,000 troops under the command of Marshall Soult. The soldiers occupied the city without resistance; harsh punishment of the workers followed.

The *liberté* that the new government proclaimed in 1830 applied only to individual action; the authorities heard only protests and demands of individuals. Peaceful workers' meetings and demonstrations were interpreted by the government of Louis-Philippe as "acts of disorder" that the authorities had to suppress. Leaders of workers' organizations were arrested and charged with participation in illegal coalitions.

The only way the workers could take to inform the public about their views and desires was that of the press. By September 1830 a number of workers' newspapers appeared for a short time in Paris. These were *L'Artisan, journal de la classe ouvrière (The Artisan, Journal of the Working Class)*, *Le Journal des ouvriers (The Workers' Journal)*, and *Le Peuple, journal général des ouvriers, rédigé par eux-mêmes (The People, General Workers' Journal, Edited by Themselves)*.

Economic revival in 1831 facilitated the establishment of new workers' organizations; the lives of the latter, however, were rather short because they were soon subjected to fines by the authorities, fines that exhausted their financial resources. More important than the appearance of these organizations was the emergence of a workers' class consciousness, a perception that workers, regardless of their trade, shared a common fate with workers in different trades and a future that demanded solidarity in action by all workers.

The number of mutual aid societies grew rapidly during the July Monarchy; on the eve of the revolution of 1848, there were about 2,000 of them in France. Resistance societies, in the guise of philanthropic or fraternal associations, developed even faster. These associations operated in groups of 20 members in order to avoid possible prosecution under Article 291 of the Penal Code, which prohibited associations of more than 20 persons. These societies organized strikes, both for economic and political reasons. Work stoppages were often simply an act of protest against the regime of Louis-Philippe.

More important than the formation of new workers' associations were new ideas that appeared in pamphlets and newspapers written by workers. Not only did these writers embrace republicanism, they also demanded that the worker receive the full fruit of his labor and denounced the exploitation of the worker by the bourgeois employer, who often acted more selfishly than the pre-1789 aristocratic lord.

In 1833, Parisian workers were interested in various forms of joint action. Some joined the traditional workers' corporation that tried to control conditions of work in a single trade. Many jobless workers tried to be part of a producers' cooperative, which gained in popularity as a means to fight unemployment. In 1833, workers also became interested in forming a new type of workers' association that would join and protect workers regardless of their trade; this new organization was to unite various single-trade workers' societies in order to strengthen the bargaining power of workers in general. The appearance of this new concept gave evidence that French workers were developing a true class consciousness, that they supported the idea that all workers, regardless of their skill or trade, belonged to the *classe ouvrière.* The importance of this new concept is noticed by Sewell, (1980), who observed:

> The idea of a fraternal association of all trades seems obvious, but this is just a sign of the distance of today's world from that of the 1830s. For workers who developed it at the time, the idea was a revelation. The corporate idiom, as it existed under the Empire and the Restoration, was capable of creating durable bonds between workers of a given trade or between members of a sect of compagnonnage. But far from emphasizing the commonality of all workers, it emphasized the internal cohesion of the corporation or sect by differentiating it from other trades or other sects. Sometimes this led to open rivalries or hatreds, such as between neighboring masters' corporations under the old regime or between rival sects of compagnonnage or between trades within compagnonnage. . . . It was only in the early 1830s, and above all in 1833, that an active sense of the brotherhood of all workers developed. (p. 213)

The arrival of factory production in France was accompanied by the writings of the early French Socialists, or "utopian socialists," as Marxists like to call them. This was only natural, because the beginning of modern industry in France exhibited the same depressing social features that had been so visible in England a few decades earlier. Wherever it was located, the factory attracted peasants from surrounding areas in ever larger numbers, employed their wives and their children, forced them into crowded shantytowns, submitted them to frequent periods of unemployment, and locked them into a social class despised and feared by the rest of society.

The misery of the French workers in the days of the empire, the Restoration, and the July Monarchy was observed by men who were shocked by the poverty, the alienation, and the hostility suffered by the new proletariat. At the sight of the hunger, the vice, and the crime that plagued the factory workers, social critics proposed either a partial or a total change of the existing social system. Their writings were soon labeled "socialist," a designation that gave hope to some and fear to others.

Count Henri de Saint-Simon is frequently viewed as an early French Socialist writer, a classification that may be debatable. Indeed, some of his disciples became leading industrialists. Although Saint-Simon glorified the role of the great factory owners and of the bankers in the process of economic growth, he was also concerned with the social and economic improvement of the proletariat. For him, a government constituted by selfless industrialists would be able to have industrial progress benefit everyone. Industrial progress could serve the living conditions of the most numerous and poorest class. Saint-Simon never visualized or advocated a "socialist utopia." He limited his attacks to those he perceived as contributing nothing to the process of production: the large landowners living in idleness from their rents, the nobility, state and church officials, and the 10,000 wealthiest property owners in France whose sudden death would not adversely affect the productive capacity of the country.

Saint-Simon can hardly be classified as the "father" of French socialism, because, for him, the principal objective of social organization was not human freedom, nor social and economic equality, nor the people's sovereignty, nor order. For Saint-Simon the most important objective of any social system is the attainment of a maximum output of goods and services. Social improvement cannot be obtained from a simple redistribution of existing wealth; social improvement depends immediately on the rate of growth of aggregate output. This is why, in the view of Saint-Simon, government must be formed by leading "producers." For Saint-Simon, the *industriel*, the producer, is not only the factory owner, the businessman, and the banker but anyone who contributes to production; he viewed the peasant who planted crops and raised animals, the sailor on a merchant ship, the locksmith, the cabinetmaker, and the small-scale manufacturer of hats as *industriels*. Saint-Simon, just like Proudhon, recognized that the bulk of French production resulted from the efforts of small-scale manufacturers, artisans and craftsmen, and peasants who owned only a few *parcelles* of land.

Charles Fourier, like Saint-Simon, is generally considered to be a leading French utopian socialist. Unlike Saint-Simon, however, Fourier was a true Socialist critic who felt that the contemporary period of "great industry," a period he also called that of "civilization," was weakened by commercial parasitism and by the predominance of the institution of "simple property," that property over which its owner had absolute rights, independently of any social interests.

For Fourier, the contemporary "civilization" is inefficient and produces barely one-fourth of what could be produced in his ideal "associative society." In the existing society, the state serves the interests of a mercantile and financial aristocracy that exploits the masses. Fourier felt that no real freedom exists in society; the poor classes are totally deprived of any real political and social freedom. Fortunately, the existing "civilization" carries the seeds of the superior "associative society." In his *Theory of Association* and *Theory of the Four Movements* Fourier tried to diagnose the ills affecting the contemporary society. He noticed that competition brings about economic chaos, the steady fall of wages and salaries, the progressive impoverishment of workers. Only the privileged classes, which live from the labor of wage workers, become wealthier in the "civilization." For most, the existing social system means unemployment, proletarization, moral degradation, and misery.

Yet Fourier did not attack the institution of private property and he rejected egalitarian and communitarian social models. His concept of "association" accepts a hierarchical structure based on differences in aptitudes, talents, and knowledge of individuals. In his "phalanstery" of 1,620 persons, there are wealthy and poor associates, their remuneration depending on their quantitative and qualitative participation in the association. Remuneration of the individual associate is based on the extent of manual work, knowledge and skills, and the individual's contribution of capital. Work involves mainly agricultural and artisanal activities, industrial production being of secondary importance. Fourier's "utopia" bears the typical early nineteenth-century French bias favoring agricultural and artisanal work, which are ranked much higher than factory labor.

The revolution of 1830 strengthened the ties that united the French labor movement, which was slowly emerging from its prehistory and the social critics and early Socialist writers. The slow process of industrialization was creating a new proletariat whose sad living conditions caused new writers to protest the existing social inequities. Most of these writers were influenced by Saint-Simon and Fourier.

The progress of industrialization in the 1830s was impeded by poor domestic transportation, by a deficient credit system, and by a strong protectionism that discouraged technological advance; still, there was an acceleration in the pace of industrialization during the July Monarchy, especially from 1840 on. Though industrial growth was irregular, new machinery was introduced in the cotton industry. Coke slowly replaced charcoal in the blast furnaces, and the steam engine became more widespread. Technological advance was accompanied by industrial concentration. The Company of the Loire Mines, a true monopoly, was founded in 1845; in metallurgy, the Creusot group controlled coal and iron ore mines, blast furnaces, and refineries. Large enterprises, however, were still the exception, and in most industries the majority of output was still turned out by the traditional domestic industry.

The new factories hired a growing number of unskilled workers, women, and children. Factory labor had no apprentices, journeymen, or masters. Labor in the factory was made up of simple wage workers, and all of them were simple agents of production, undistinguishable from each other, working under the same conditions, and living in the same poor city districts. Their work and living conditions strengthened the development of class consciousness among them, merged individual discontent into group rebellion, and prepared fertile ground in which the seeds of socialism could take roots. This relatively small, but expanding, class of new proletarians could often be hardly distinguished from the masses of artisans and small shopkeepers. The reformist writers of the 1830s came out of this small bourgeoisie and most of them had to work to live. Philippe Buchez, Louis Blanc, Etienne Cabet, Victor Considérant, Pierre Leroux, and Pierre-Joseph Proudhon belonged to this world of artisans, craftsmen, small businessmen, and low-ranking civil servants.

Although Philippe Buchez rejected Communist solutions to social problems, he recognized that society was divided into two groups—one owning the means of production and the other working for the former. For Buchez, the capitalist entreprenuer was a parasite who lived from the work of those he exploited. His idea of the "associationist society" would eliminate the exploitation of man by man. Victor Considérant, Fourier's principal disciple, propagated the latter's ideas throughout the country in the journal *Le Phalanstère*, founded in 1832, and in the daily *La démocratie pacifique*, started two years later.

Louis Blanc affirmed that political change had to precede any significant social change. As an active journalist, he not only contributed to a number of journals such as the *Revue républicaine*, but in 1839 he founded the *Revue du progrès politique, social et littéraire* and the *Journal du peuple*; in that year he published in the *Revue du progrès* an article titled "The Organization of Labor." The article was then published in book form, which had great success and became one of the books most read by French workers.

For Blanc, economic competition becomes a "system of extermination"; for the bourgeoisie, it means impoverishment and ruin as monopolies tend to displace small and medium-sized commerce and industry. Competition must be destroyed by competition. Blanc's remedy to capitalist competition is the "social workshop" or the producers' and consumers' cooperative established with the help of the state.

For Blanc, producers' and consumers' cooperatives would eliminate any management-labor problems, since these organizations would be managed by the workers themselves. During a transition period, salaries paid by these organizations would differ to reflect the hierarchical standing of members, but in the long run, all salaries paid by a social workshop would be equal. Its profits would be divided in three parts: One part was to be divided equally between the members of the organization; a second part was to be used to support the old, the invalid, the sick, and to assist other similar organizations facing financial difficulties; the third was to finance the purchase of tools and machines for potential new members. Members contributing capital to the organization would earn interest on their contribution but would share in the profits only in their capacity as workers.

With the help of the state, capitalist competition would be replaced by the system of association. The establishment of social workshops would permit a better regulation of the economy, the elimination of unemployment, and the adoption of more efficient technology without harm to workers. The introduction of universal suffrage would eliminate peacefully the domination of the state by the bourgeoisie and allow the state to become the "banker of the poor." Many of Blanc's ideas were to be adopted by the French workers during the Revolution of 1848.

Proudhon met Karl Marx in Paris during the summer of 1844. Their conversation brought out their disagreement on the ways to achieve a social revolution both men wanted. Marx relied on political action to arrive at the social revolution that would be led and controlled by the dictatorship of the proletariat. Proudhon believed that political action would only be an obstacle in the attainment of the social revolution. Proudhon, like Blanc, believed that the capitalist system could only be overthrown through a peaceful, associationist movement of workers; because of their superiority over private enterprises, producers' cooperatives would triumph over capitalist competition and bring about the transformation of the economic system. Proudhon's publication of the *Système des Contradictions Economiques ou Philosophie de la Misère* in 1846 ended all possible cooperation between the two men. Proudhon's work infuriated Marx so much that Marx felt compelled to attack Proudhon with his book *Poverty of Philosophy*, written in French.

Proudhon abhorred any type of authority. He could never accept dictatorial rule, whether imposed by a dictator, a political or military body, or a church. Edward Hyams (1979) quotes Proudhon:

> With the advent of the factory and of machines, Divine Right, the principle of Authority, makes its entry into political economy. Capital, the Boss, Privilege, Monopoly, Limited Liability, Shareholding—in a word, Property, these are to economy what Office, Authority, Sovereignty, Stat-

ute Law, Revelation, Religion, in a word, God, cause and principle of
all our miseries and all our crimes are in the context of Political
Power....

Commenting on the quote, Hyams says

This is a characteristically Proudhonian intrusion of God into an argument about economics. The reason for it is clear—he was attacking the
whole principle of authority, by which the liberty, dignity and initiative
of the individual human being is degraded and denied.... The ancients,
says Proudhon, accused human nature of being guilty of all evil in the
world, and Christianity followed suit, damning our kind as criminal *ab
ovo*. The modern philosophers, beginning with Rousseau, repudiate the
charge: man is born good; society depraves him. A distinction without
a difference, says Proudhon: collective man becomes the criminal. The
socialist solution is to dethrone God and enthrone Man; that is, to replace Providence by Providence. The radicals may damn the Church and
the Pope, yet they fall over each other in their eagerness to proclaim belief in a divine providence, or to make a new one. What is the point of
dethroning God, if you then replace him by the state? (pp. 85, 88)

Opposed to both Fourier and Proudhon were the early French Communists, disciples of the revolutionary dissidents François Noel Babeuf,
better known as Gracchus Babeuf, and Philippe Buonarroti. Babeuf had
been executed in 1797 for his part in the "Conspiracy of the Equals." His
doctrines were published by Buonarroti in a book titled *The Conspiracy
of the Equals* and produced in Brussels in 1828. For Babeuf, two social
classes oppose each other in society, a minority of the people composed
by wealthy property owners and the mass of the poor. In order to do
away with this conflict, the state had to take control of both production
and distribution; a popular dictatorship had to introduce an egalitarian
Communist system under which labor would be mandatory for all, the
workday being limited to eight hours.

Under the influence of Buonarroti, a neo-Babouvian movement developed after the revolution of 1830. Secret revolutionary societies were
founded, one of the most important being the Society of the Seasons,
directed by Martin Bernard, a printer, and by the professional revolutionary Auguste Blanqui. These early Communists advocated two main ideas:
First, there could be no equality between people unless the institution
of private ownership was abolished; second, a dictatorship was necessary
to implement needed social transformations.

An important Communist current was that of "Cabetism." Etienne
Cabet's *Voyage to Icaria* (1840) was the work of a "utopian Communist."

He demanded peaceful change and insisted that his proposals should lead, not to armed conflict, but to discussion, meditation, public support, and popular approval. His scheme contemplated social change in two different phases. During an initial period of transition, the institution of private property would be maintained, but public policy would attempt to reduce economic inequality and military budgets. The prices of basic necessities would be regulated by the government and no tax would encumber their sale; on the other hand, progressive taxation would be imposed on private wealth and on inheritances. At least 45 percent of the government budget would have to be allocated to the creation of jobs, the building of low-cost homes, and the development of public education. During the second phase, the "construction phase," the institution of private ownership would be abolished. The means of production and the stocks of primary resources would be socialized. Workers would be remunerated "according to their needs." Commerce would disappear because people would be able to obtain from public stores all the goods they needed. Technological advance would assure to all the "equality of abundance."

Cabet's idea of a peaceful and gradual evolution to an egalitarian and communitarian society gave him great popularity among French workers. His *Voyage to Icaria* had five editions between 1840 and 1848. His daily, *Le Populaire*, was very successful, and his main work, *True Christianity After Jesus Christ*, published in 1846, was printed twice before 1850.

The other Communist current was formed by the neo-Babouvians who belonged to the revolutionary tradition. The principal writers in this group were Albert Laponneraye, an ardent "Robespierrist" who went to jail for publishing the sentence "the people only changed the tyrant"; Richard Lahautière, a disciple of Babeuf; Jean-Jacques Pillot, who, after having been ordained a priest, preached atheism and condemned religion; and Théodore Dézamy, who best expounded Communist theory in France at the time in his book *The Code of the Community*, published in 1842.

All of these writers did not carefully explain how the existing society would be transformed into a Communist society. The ways of this transformation greatly preoccupied Louis-Auguste Blanqui. Blanqui spent 36 years of his life in prison; when free, he engaged in secret political activity and plotted the overthrow of the government. During the July Monarchy he participated in a number of secret societies and prepared a coup against the regime of Louis-Phillippe; the coup failed, Blanqui was arrested and received a death sentence, which was later commuted to life imprisonment. Liberated by the Revolution of 1848, he was incarcerated again soon thereafter.

Like so many other leftist writers, Blanqui perceived society divided into two classes: a wealthy minority that held political power and a majority constituted by the poor and the ignorant. The origin of this class distinction was the individual and unjust appropriation of land by members of the minority group. This minority ended up owning not only all the land but also the existing capital in society. The propertyless masses had to work for the privileged minority; the latter appropriated most of the fruits of the workers' labor. Because of their conflicting interests, there could be no possible reconciliation between the two classes; the fight for equality was carried by the oppressed majority throughout history. For Blanqui, the conflict between the two social groups would only disappear when social inequality would cease to exist. The "reign of justice through equality" will only arrive when the institution of private ownership is abolished and when capitalism is replaced by associationism. For Blanqui, it was only through carefully planned insurrection that capitalism could be overthrown. This is why Blanqui dedicated his life to the formation of small, armed groups and to the preparation of rebellions that were doomed to failure.

In spite of the great variety in social thought, one can affirm the existence of a main current of Socialist thought in France before 1848. Social reform was widely discussed, and most of its advocates sympathized with both republican and Socialist ideas. Most of the French working class during the first half of the nineteenth century rejected Communist proposals because of their loyalty to republicanism; the latter advocated the adoption of universal suffrage, which would allow in turn the enactment of reformist measures to ameliorate the condition of workers. The republicans demanded simple reforms, such as the improvement of primary education, progressive taxation, freedom of association, and an end to the necessity of workers to carry with them a "work booklet." The republicans were not alone in demanding social reforms, but, supported by most workers, they were the largest reformist group.

Reform was in fashion, and members of many social groups advocated social reform. Prince Louis Napoleon published in 1839 his *Napoleonic Ideas* and in 1844 his *Extinction of Pauperism;* to eliminate poverty, Louis Napoleon advocated the establishment of farms managed by associations of workers, mere tenants at the beginning and proprietors in time. French literature was also dominated by reformist sentiments. Lamartine denounced the powerful monopolies, and Victor Hugo pleaded for a greater awareness of social problems. Eugene Sue, influenced by the ideas of Fourier, flirted with socialism in his *Les mystères de Paris* (1842) and *Le Juif errant* (1844). George Sand proclaimed herself a Socialist, and in her novels the worker acquired pride and dignity.

On the whole, pre-1848 French socialism was characterized by the domination of reformism. The mass of craftsmen, artisans, small businessmen, and professionals wanted to retain the institution of private ownership and demanded a redistribution of land, freedom of association and of coalition, and the survival of the *petit propriétaire*. The spirit of the *sans-culottes* of 1793 was still very much alive in the 1830s.

THE FIGHT FOR THE LEGAL RIGHT TO FORM TRADE UNIONS: 1848–84

There were repeated economic crises during the July Monarchy; the economic downturns of 1830–32, 1836–37, and 1846–48 had harsh effects on the workers. Wages were reduced and unemployment increased, and the number of children employed in industrial enterprises rose. At public hearings conducted to determine the impact of factory work on the health of child-workers, employers testified that the regulation of child labor or its prohibition would force them to abandon their operations. Nevertheless, a child labor law was enacted by the government on March 22, 1841. It did not provide, however, for any official inspectors to enforce it, and only on December 7, 1868, was legislation finally provided for children.

Until 1868, employers were free to ignore the child labor law. This law applied only to enterprises employing more than 20 workers; it prohibited the employment of children below the age of 8, fixed a maximum workday of 8 hours for children between the ages of 8 and 12, and of 12 hours for children between 12 and 16. Night work was prohibited for children under the age of 12, but nighttime was defined as extending from 9 P.M. to 5 A.M. This law was a beginning of state regulation of industry and marked an initial departure from the firmly established principle that in a free market economy government should not regulate economic activity.

Unemployment, poverty, strikes, and the appearance of many, generally short-lived, Socialist, republican, and workers' newspapers strengthened a spirit of solidarity among French workers in the 1830s and in the 1840s. Following the revolution of 1830, workers in Paris published *Le journal des ouvriers*, which sold 24 issues, *Le Peuple*, and *L'Artisan*. Babouvian workers produced two issues of *L'Humanitaire* and, with greater success, *La Fraternité*, which circulated until 1847.

The most influential workers' paper was *L'Atelier*, which was produced from 1840 to 1850. *L'Atelier* initially propagated ideas close to those of Buchez and gave great importance to workers' support of Christian morality; later the paper gave emphasis to the development of individual freedoms and strongly opposed Communist ideology. *L'Atelier* also echoed Fourier's ideas and favored the establishment of producers' cooperatives financed by the state. The newspaper eventually centered its demands on the formation of workers' cooperatives, its editors making it clear that these associations would not be incompatible with the institution of private ownership. The May 16, 1841 issue of *L'Atelier* tried to allay possible bourgeois fears by noting: *"L'Atelier* is before anything else reformist, it teaches the progressively realizable ways to organize labor, ways which cannot be confused in any way with the communitarian theory . . . . It is the enemy of any expropriation, of any violence, and it will never advocate force until it will have exhausted all conciliatory ways" (Bron 1968, p. 103).

Numerous strikes attempted to reduce the length of the workday to ten hours and to oppose wage cuts. In the coal basin of the Loire, 65 mining firms had amalgamated into a single enterprise, the General Society of the Reunited Mines. The new firm ordered the reduction of all wages to a common low level. The miners struck in 1844 to protest the reduction in their wages; the government used troops to put an end to the strike, and many miners were arrested. Two years later, a similar effort by the same miners resulted in a number of miners killed by soldiers.

The period 1846–48 brought particularly severe economic, social, and political difficulties to France. Food prices rose rapidly after 1845 because of deficient wheat and potato harvests. The farmers' income diminished in 1846 and in 1847 because the income effects of higher food prices were more than offset by the diminished quantities they could sell. For the workers, higher food prices meant that they had to spend virtually all of their wages on food to survive; consequently, their demand for industrial products diminished drastically. A stock market crisis added to the difficulties, largely by stopping new investment in railroad construction; the decline in railroad construction, in turn, had an adverse impact on other industrial activities. The ensuing slowing down in industrial activity brought further wage reductions and higher unemployment.

The economic and financial crises forced hunger and misery on workers during the winter of 1847-48. Hungry mobs resorted to pillage, and workers joined republicans and students in acts of insurrection. The fact that the July Monarchy had denied the right to vote to artisans and the lower stratum of the middle class added political fuel to the fire of discontent.

On February 23, 1848, people from the eastern districts of Paris resorted to armed insurrection. The insurrection spread to most of Paris. When, on the following day, National Guard detachments joined the rebels, the "Bourgeois King" decided to abandon his throne and a provisional government proclaimed a new republic.

Remembering how quickly they had been forgotten after the revolution of 1830, the workers kept their weapons and presented the new government endless petitions. On the twenty-fifth, the republic proclaimed the right of association and the people's right to work; the government undertook to guarantee work to all citizens. It ordered the establishment of "national workshops" to alleviate unemployment. Because the government failed to establish a Labor Ministry, a large manifestation of workers induced the provisional government to create a commission to study employment problems; the commission was established on the twenty-eighth and was to hold its sessions in the Palace of Luxembourg; Louis Blanc became its president, and a mechanic named Albert was its vice-president. Among its 200 members were Victor Considérant, Pierre Leroux, and Constantin Pecqueur, men who had been influenced by Saint-Simon, Fourier, and Proudhon.

A decree of March 2 reduced the workday to 10 hours in Paris and to 11 hours in the provinces, and another decree established universal suffrage. Freedom of assembly and freedom of the press were proclaimed on the fourth. On March 8, the National Guard, traditionally manned by members of the middle class, declared that its ranks were open to all social classes. A large number of newspapers appeared, most of them doomed to a short life. François Raspail, a reformist republican, published *L'Ami du Peuple;* Lammenais, the defender of the poor and a democratic "regenerationist," produced *Le Peuple Constituant;* and Proudhon's *Le Représentant du Peuple* was read and discussed in many newly opened workers' clubs and cafés. The associationist movement flourished in France.

Initially, the provisional government appeared to sympathize with the workers' demand for a democratic republic that would favor the development of workers' associations through credits and contracts. Even moderate republicans, such as Garnier-Pagès, Goudchaux, Carnot, Marie, and Marrast; supported associations that would allow the workers to retain the fruits of their labor. At the Palace of Luxembourg, the commission approved Blanc's project of nationalizing major industries and using their revenues to finance a general associative movement. A number of workers' associations were started with the help of the commission. Even after the dissolution of the latter in May, associative efforts were continued by its members. About 300 producers' cooperatives were organized in the hope that these would reduce unemployment and start a peaceful social transformation of society.

Meanwhile, depression continued to plague the economy. The middle class apprehended that the government would start regulating economic activity. It was fearful of the workers who remained armed behind their barricades in Paris and of the "Socialists" in the Luxembourg Palace. The Paris stock exchange, which had remained closed from February 24 to March 6, witnessed a collapse of the prices of securities when it reopened. The drastic fall in securities prices placed banks in difficulties and some of them became bankrupt. The financial crisis restricted credit, and many industrial firms had to suspend operations. This economic disorder convinced the bourgeoisie that government policies had to be changed. Many republican moderates, such as Lamartine, Ledru-Rollin, and Garnier-Pagès, felt that only political changes were called for. The moderates obtained a great victory at the elections of April 23. Socialists were removed from government. When on May 15 a demonstration in support of the Polish rebels was organized, its leaders, Blanqui, Raspail, and Albert, were arrested. On the following day, the government ordered the dissolution of the Luxembourg commission.

The Socialist and moderate members of the provisional government had taken the position that the function of the national workshops was to supply any unemployed citizen with work similar to that the particular individual had lost. The national workshops were to perform a valuable economic role. The conservative bourgeois majority in government felt, however, that the national workshops should be simple relief agencies. The latter's view prevailed. Workers enrolled in these national workshops were asked to engage in mostly unskilled labor tasks in and near Paris. For their efforts, they were paid 2 francs a day. This sum was more an alms donation than a true wage; nevertheless, it attracted thousands of provincial unemployed to Paris. The support of the national workshops soon rose to 170,000 francs a day. As of May 17, the government declared that it would no longer accept job applicants looking for work in the national workshops. On the thirtieth, it declared that all persons with less than three months of residence in Paris were to return to their orginal domicile in the provinces. The number of jobless workers in Paris continued to increase. The government tried to borrow funds from the Bank of France in order to finance new public works; the bank "studied" the government's requests but failed to respond.

The government now considered two possible solutions to the problem of unemployment in Paris. Both alternatives included the drafting of unemployed young men into the armed forces. The first plan was for France to declare a war on another European power in order to restore bourgeois order in Europe. The second plan contemplated the removal of the "red danger" in France by means of military force. The government chose the second alternative. The national workshops were closed, and on June 22, the government ordered the enlistment of all single male workers 18 to 25 years old in the army. All other unemployed workers were to be sent to the provinces to be used in public works.

On the following day, barricades were built by workers in various districts of Paris. The government ordered General Eugène Cavaignac to suppress the workers' insurrection; 50,000 soldie:s fought the insurgent workers until June 26. The repression that followed was very harsh. Fifteen thousand workers were arrested and more than 3,000 were deported from France. Once again, a French revolution had failed to benefit the workers. General Cavaignac, now head of the government, ensured the maintenance of "law and order." Workers' demonstrations were forbidden on July 28, and many newspapers were ordered to cease publication. The new constitution, which was proclaimed on November 12, did not grant French citizens the right to work. Its guarantee of "freedom of contract" rendered unconstitutional the decree of March 2, which had limited the daily hours of work workers could be asked to perform. A law of November 27, 1849 prohibited all coalitions. Only mutual aid societies were exempted from this prohibition.

In spite of the "June Days," the associative movement did not weaken. Workers, peasants, and the petty bourgeoisie continued to believe that producers' cooperatives were the answer to bourgeois greed. Workers, peasants, and the small proprietors went on demanding tax reforms, easier credit, land for landless peasants, and state support for workers' associations. The bourgeoisie, frightened by these demands, looked to Louis Napoleon for protection.

The middle class, the church, and the royalists united in a conservative party whose motto was "Order, Property, Family, Religion." It succeeded in the elections of December 20, 1848 to have its candidate, Louis Napoleon, elected president of the republic. While Napoleon obtained 75 percent of the votes, Cavaignac obtained only 20 percent.

The Napoleon government quickly limited or abandoned existing liberal legislation. A law of May 31, 1850 limited the right to vote to those who could prove by means of tax records that they had resided for three years in a given *canton*. The poor, who did not pay taxes, and a large number of workers who had to move in search of work were deprived of the right to vote. A law of July 16 limited freedom of the press. Newspapers such as *L'Atelier* disappeared because of their inability to report freely or because they lacked the financial resources needed to pay the newly imposed taxes.

By 1851, the conservative alliance had silenced the labor movement; its leaders were in prison or in exile. But the very success of the conservative forces made French workers realize that they were members of a social class that was oppressed by the propertied groups.

The coup that transformed the president of the Second Republic into the emperor of the Second Empire dealt a hard blow to the workers' associative movement. The emperor was initially fearful that groups of workers, joining under the cover of mutual aid societies or of workers' cooperatives, could plot to rise against his rule. Consequently, the police proceeded to arrest a large number of labor leaders and dissolved many workers' associations. The authorities tolerated the existence of the tradition-inspired *compagnonnages* and allowed them to exist. These workers' organizations having abandoned any Socialist ideas they had proclaimed in 1848, had decided to become simple commercial enterprises. Many also became apolitical in order to minimize the loss of members.

Workers had indeed become disenchanted with "utopian socialism," having been shocked by the fact that conservative, antiassociative forces had succeeded in preventing the transformation of society that they had been waiting for. Some workers embraced the collectivist socialism of Bakunin, which held the promise of a revolutionary effort to overthrow the imperial regime. Fewer identified with the thoughts of Marx and Engels, but Marxist influence in France was still very weak.

The associative movement remained dormant during the 1850s. Greater government toleration of workers' organizations as of 1859 allowed an increased number of such organizations to operate in the open in spite of their illegal status. Many new workers' cooperatives appeared in Paris and in the provincial cities. Most of these organizations made it a point to publicize their acceptance of the existing political system. Their apolitical stance attracted the support of reformist bourgeois, who saw in these organizations a way of consolidating the existing social order by helping workers become small proprietors. In the 1860s, this associative movement obtained the endorsement of various middle-class groups, republicans, Orléanists, and supporters of Napoleon III. Republican support allowed the creation of the Crédit au Travail, a cooperative bank that was to finance the formation of small workers' associations. These associations were expected to compete with privately owned firms by hiring experienced managers and, if needed, wage labor and were to operate without any help from the state. In the 1860s, Proudhonians, Fourierists, *Ateliéristes*, and radical republicans such as Elie Réclus supported this "practical" associative movement.

During the early 1860s, Napoleon III tried to build up workers' support for his regime. Having lost the backing of French protectionists because of his free trade policy, the emperor proceeded to pardon imprisoned workers and allowed a delegation of French workers to visit the London Exposition of 1862. The bronze worker Tolain led 200 workers' delegates from Paris and 140 provincial delegates to England. The outcome of this visit had not been entirely foreseen by the emperor's advisers.

In London, the French workers were impressed by the superior organization of the British labor movement; British wages were higher than theirs, and the working conditions in England had never been attained in France. French and English workers met again in 1863, the justification for this meeting being the joint support of Polish insurgents, the real reason being the preparation of an international workers' agreement. The objective of this agreement was achieved on September 29, 1864, when the International Workingmen's Association (IWA) was founded in London in the presence of three French workers, one of them being Tolain. The association's central committee was located in London. A French *bureau* was opened at Nr. 44, Rue des Gravilliers, in Paris. Sections of the IWA were later formed in a number of French cities.

In France, the IWA claimed to be only an organization that furthered workers' education and information. Indeed, it did not undertake or support any action in the 1860s that could have frightened French employers. Nevertheless, a court order of 1868 ordered the dissolution of the French sections of the IWA, the court having found that the French delegates at the IWA congress in Lausanne had participated in a meeting in which speakers were hostile to the Second Empire.

French workers also participated in a number of congresses of the IWA in the 1860s. The first congress, held September 3–8, 1866, in Geneva, witnessed French delegates standing strongly behind Proudhonian ideas. They condemned any type of social revolution based on violence and dictatorial rule and they opposed political action and the strike as means to attain a new social system. What they demanded was cooperation based on individual freedom, interest-free credit, and the free exchange of commodities between producers facilitated by "labor coupons" issued by "Banks of the People."

B. H. Moss has doubted their sincerity and remarked that "it became increasingly clear that Proudhonism was an ideological mask for a movement that actually supported strikes and political action and sought in association the collective emancipation of trades" (1980, p. 52). Moss's view may be questioned, given the still strong predominance of petty bourgeois mentality among French workers and their delegates at this time; the majority of the French workers in the 1860s were still craftsmen and artisans who identifed with a trade, were proud of their skills, and were not predisposed to abandon the right to individual freedom and the sanctity of the *petite propriété*.

It is true, nevertheless, that the strength of Proudhonian views started to weaken at the following congress of the IWA in Lausanne in September 1867. During the Brussels congress of September 1868, Marxist ideas received greater support than Proudhonian ideology. At that congress, the delegates declared themselves in favor of using the strike, even the general strike, in the pursuit of their cause. Marxism firmly dominated other forms of socialism at the Basel congress of 1869.

The repression that followed the defeat of the Commune of 1871 brought an end to the IWA in France. Elsewhere, external and internal developments contributed to the rapid disintegration of the First International. The British workers soon abandoned it, finding it too revolutionary. In Germany and in Italy, the achievement of national unity lessened the interest of workers for the international aspects of their labor movements. Also, internal factionalism hastened the end of the IWA. Disagreements between the followers of Marx, who stood for a strongly centralized organization, and those of Bakunin, who objected to the power of the organization's General Council, marked the center of discussions at the IWA's conference in London in 1871 and at the association's congress at The Hague in 1872. These disagreements split the organization into a Marxist International, which expired in Philadelphia in 1876, and into a Bakuninist counterpart, whose existence ended at La Chaux-de-Fonds in Switzerland in 1880.

The Second Empire was not entirely adverse to the workers' associative efforts. Napoleon III became more tolerant of the labor movement as the years of his reign passed by. As of March 1852, mutual aid societies had been allowed to function. A law of June 1, 1853 provided that an equal number of employers' and workers' representatives would sit in the *conseils de prudhommes,* conciliatory agencies in labor-management disputes. Prince Jérôme-Napoléon, the emperor's cousin, talked to workers and published their views in his newspaper, *L'Opinion Nationale.*

On February 17, 1864, this newspaper published a list of workers' demands, probably written by Tolain, titled the "Manifesto of the Sixty." Among these demands were the abrogation of the law prohibiting coalitions, the creation of "syndical chambers," the reform of apprenticeship, the regulation of female work, and free primary and professional education. The government reacted favorably by declaring on May 25 of that year that coalitions would no longer be prohibited. The government, however, declared that anyone attempting to cause a work stoppage whose purpose was to bring about a change in wages or salaries or to interfere with the free exercise of economic activity through the use of threats or violence would be guilty of a crime.

Workers' delegates at the Paris Exposition of 1867 had petitioned the government for its toleration of *chambres syndicales* or *syndicats.* These terms had been employed to denote employers' associations, and the workers now demanded to be treated by the government in the same way it treated the employers. These *syndicats* were to provide mutual insurance, plan trade emancipation through association, and seek immediate improvement in matters of wages, hours of work, and so on. A *chambre syndicale* was to cover all the workers in a single trade and combine trade unionism with projects of association. In March 1868, the government declared it would tolerate such *syndicats* as long as they registered with the police and accepted police surveillance.

Mutual aid societies and *syndicats* from the Paris area then formed a federation under the leadership of the bookbinder Eugène Varlin. A goal of this federation was to make workers owners of machinery so as to render them independent of employers (Moss, 1980, p. 54). Similar federations were established in Lyon, Marseille, and Rouen; they all embraced the use of strikes and cooperation in policies that were inconsistent with those advocated by Proudhon. Indeed, French labor leaders seemed to have forgotten Proudhon during the last years of the empire. Strikes developed everywhere. On June 11, 1869, 15,000 miners of the Loire Basin went on strike to obtain higher wages, fewer work hours, and retirement pay. The strike extended to textile workers in Rouen, Elboeuf, and the Champagne area. Outbursts of violence between strikers and soldiers at Saint-Etienne and Aubin caused the deaths of a number of strikers. Low wages and rapidly climbing prices caused strikes to spread all over France during 1870. Strikes also became political in character, workers asking for a Socialist republic.

The strikes and the workers' insurrections that multiplied during the last years of the Second Empire combined both a protest against low wages and opposition to Napoleon's regime. The workers' fight for higher wages was also a fight for the establishment of a republic. They felt no loyalty for an imperial government that favored the bourgeoisie at their expense. Out of the workers' protest, and encouraged by the Franco-Prussian War, emerged the Paris Commune of 1871.

Many pages have been written about the commune. Many writers saw in this short-lived rebellion of *le petit monde* of Paris an effort that could have produced a true social revolution in France. Writers have either supported the commune with passion or have condemned it with hate. Among the latter were such notable French authors as Edmond de Goncourt, Théophile Gautier, and Alphonse Daudet.

The empire collapsed at Sedan on September 2, 1870, and on the fourth the republic was proclaimed in Paris. A national defense government, presided by the defeatist General Trochu, attempted to contain both the Prussians and the revolutionary mood of the workers of Paris. Parisian workers, artisans, and members of the liberal professions were exasperated by the rapidly rising prices of foodstuffs and by the Prussian bombing, the siege of Paris having started on September 19. Gradually, the idea of establishing a militarily aggressive and social-minded Parisian municipal government gained favor among those the war hurt most. A popular manifestation in Paris on January 22, 1871 demanded a more effective pursuit of the war against Prussia and the establishment of a Paris commune, reminiscent of that of 1792.

The government decided, however, to sign an armistice on September 28. A peace treaty with Prussia was to follow. Bismarck made it clear, however, that he would sign such a treaty only with a duly established French government. Rapidly instituted elections brought Adolphe Thiers to power on February 12.

The French middle class remained apprehensive of the revolutionary mood of the Parisian workers. It succeeded in having the National Assembly suspend the daily pay of 1.50 francs given to National Guardsmen, many of whom were workers without any other means of livelihood. The assembly then abrogated on March 10 a moratorium on the payment of rent, placing thousands of Parisians in serious difficulty. On the same day, the assembly decided to move from Paris to Versailles, anticipating the outburst of a revolutionary movement in the capital city.

The Parisian workers had kept their weapons; they had also secured in various parts of the city 227 cannons to prevent their capture by the Prussians. Thiers and the commander of the army of Paris, General Vinoy, decided to have the soldiers appropriate the cannons during the early hours of March 18. This attempt failed, and the workers started building barricades in the city. The insurrection of the commune, which was to last until May 28, 1871, had begun.

The Paris Commune was not the creation of a Socialist movement. Even though Socialist clubs and newspapers had multiplied in Paris after the fall of the Second Empire, the commune never reflected a single political or economic ideology. It was, rather, the result of the dissatisfactions of Parisians—dissatisfaction with the weakness and the indecision of the government of national defense; dissatisfaction with the monarchist National Assembly, which had capitulated to Prussia and had tolerated the partial occupation of Paris by German troops; dissatisfaction with conditions of widespread unemployment and hunger; dissatisfaction with the suspension of the moratorium on rents and the abrogation of the pay of the members of the National Guard. When Thiers attempted to disarm Paris, he found that *le petit peuple* of Paris and the workers' manned National Guard were ready to oppose his troops.

The commune was republican and proletarian, Blanquist and Proudhonian. It never became the government of one party, of one school of thought. On March 26, the Central Committee of the revolutionary National Guard instituted elections for a General Council of the commune. Of its 81 members, 33 were workers and craftsmen; the rest was constituted by representatives of the low bourgeoisie of Paris, journalists, commercial employees, some lawyers, and a few physicians. Most of them viewed themselves as nineteenth-century Jacobins who believed that the Commune of 1871 was the continuation of that of 1793. They supported the old revolutionary tradition of a strong central government and created a Committee of Public Safety; they stood for the institution of private property, which they found indispensable for the maintenance of individual freedom. Close to them were the followers of Louis-Auguste Blanqui, interested above all in taking power and in imposing social change. Among the leading *Blanquistes* was Edouard Vaillant, a physician and an engineer and a member of the First International.

A minority in the General Council were influenced by the ideas of Proudhon and of Bakunin. They opposed centralization and dictatorship and favored instead the establishment of federations of autonomous communes and of free producers' cooperatives. One of their main representatives was the bookbinder Eugène Varlin, a member of the First International, who was executed by the Versailles forces on May 28; another was Benoît Malon, a dyer, also a member of the International. All of these men were very much concerned with the improvement of the social and economic lives of their compatriots.

Members of the First International represented a minority in the government of the commune, and even they never pressed for dramatic transformations in the relationships between capital and labor. The most drastic economic decrees of the commune prohibited nightwork in bakeries and instructed workers' syndical chambers that abandoned workshops could be operated by workers' associations; Proudhonians on the Labor, Industry and Trade Commission promptly added to the terms of the decree that juries would determine the final transfer of these workshops to labor groups and that this would be done after indemnification to the original owner. (Journal officiel, April 17, 1871). The leaders of the commune had little to say about a class struggle; neither did they identify with any given social class. S. Bernstein, quoting Louis Dubreuilh, notes that "the Commune said nothing about socialist ideals, because, as a socialist historian wrote, 'it had little or nothing to say.' It was, it must be repeated, an extremely mixed assembly in which the authoritarian Jacobin element elbowed the federalist and Proudhonian element of the International. . . ."(1965, p. 42). When Marx in his *Civil War in France* asserted that the commune was the expression of a fight against the bourgeoisie by a dictatorship of the proletariat, he presented a thesis with little historical foundation.

On April 19, the council published its "Declaration to the French People," essentially a Proudhonian document giving emphasis to the development of autonomous communes, as well as to the development of education, exchange, and credit. The moratorium on the payment of rents was restored and workers' associative efforts were encouraged.

What the commune failed to do was to plan an effective defense of Paris. The government in Versailles initiated its attack on Paris on April 2. When the government troops, under the command of Mac-Mahon, entered Paris on May 27 and 28, 1871, they did not take prisoners. The soldiers from Versailles promptly shot about 25,000 men, women, and children. Courts-martial ordered the summary execution of more than

300,000 people (Bron 1968, p. 233). Once again, as in 1830 and 1848, the bourgeoisie succeeded in establishing its harsh rule over the masses. The defeat of the commune dealt a hard blow to the ideals of peaceful associationism. After 1871, Proudhonian philosophy only influenced anarchists and syndicalists. Socialists embraced Marxism.

The conservative royalist deputies who constituted the majority of the assembly during the early years of the Third Republic had little understanding and interest in the economic difficulties of the masses. They refused to tolerate strikes, and miners' strikes in the north and in the Pas-de-Calais were harshly opposed by government forces in 1872. Bourgeois fears of the First International induced the assembly to enact the Dufaure Law of March 14, 1872, a law that made it a crime for anyone in France to affiliate with that organization. In November 1875, the Ducarre Commission resolved that it was the duty of government to preserve the system of liberal capitalism and the individual's "liberty to contract and to work" within that system.

French political economists advocated that the workers should be taught the principles of liberal political economy so that they would understand the errors of Socialist thought. Le Play appealed to the "beneficent capitalist" to give the example of hard work and saving to his workers and to instruct them that religion and property were the main pillars of Christian society. The Associations of Catholic Workingmen's Clubs of Count Albert de Mun also preached workers' respect for the faith and for the *patron*. These clubs, which offered their members cheap lodging, libraries, credit, and entertainment, also purported to "educate" them by trying to persuade them that capitalist profits and interest were necessary for the growth of the economy.

Bourgeois fears of workers' organizations explain why labor unions were not legalized, even though there was growing interest in the causes that induced labor unrest. Many "social-minded" members of the middle class tried to soothe the pain that the repression of the commune had imposed on workers by trying to convince the latter that hard work, saving, individual initiative, and dedication to family and faith alone could improve their economic and social status. To restore the workers' respect for the government, a modicum of new labor legislation was enacted. The law of 1841 had covered the employment of children in factories and in shops of more than 20 workers. The law of 1874 prohibited the employment of children under 10. The law limited the number of daily hours of work to 6 for children aged 10 to 12; children between the ages of 12 and 16 could not be forced to work for more than 12 hours. The law also prohibited underground work for women and children under 12. For the first time, the assembly allowed the appointment of inspectors to ensure the enforcement of the law.

The repression of the commune lowered the interest of workers in

Socialist and revolutionary doctrines. Once again, the workers of France tied their hopes to the cooperative movement. Cooperatives could best be formed by syndical chambers, and the main striving of skilled workers in the years that followed the commune was to organize such chambers. As noted by Bernstein (1965):

> Under such leaders as Chabert, Desmoulins, Barberet, Oudin, Portalis and Pauliat, the labor movement began to take new life. Jewelers, printers, lithographers, and masons were followed by glove makers, toolmakers, upholsterers, bookbinders, carpenters, saddlers, etc. in organizing syndical chambers. . . . In less than three months, a labor federation was formed under the innocuous title, Circle of Workers' Syndical Union. (p. 59)

The leader of this drive to form new syndical chambers was a journalist, Barberet, who strongly urged the workers to avoid strikes. He stressed that instead of wasting funds on useless strikes, workers should use their funds to finance the establishment of workers' cooperatives that would make them independent of capitalist employers and of the wage system. Even through the Circle of the Workers' Syndical Union was promptly closed by the authorities, syndical chambers and workers' cooperatives continued to increase in numbers.

The associationist movement received the support of the 104-member French workers' delegation that visited the Vienna Exposition in 1873. The reports these workers submitted upon their return indicated the importance they attached to the development of workers' cooperatives as a way to make workers independent of the wage system. The small firm being representative of the French industrial concern, the producers' cooperative appeared ideally suited to take the place of small private enterprises. These workers also asked for the right to create syndical chambers, indispensable for the creation of cooperatives; they claimed that these chambers would promote peaceful management-labor relations, would arbitrate disputes between workers and employers, would channel workers' savings into the creation of cooperative enterprises, and would facilitate the extension of credit to workers.

The republican victory at the elections of March 1876 encouraged workers to hold their first labor congress since the end of the commune. Three hundred and forty delegates met in Paris from October 2 to 10, 1876, representing more than 120 syndicates. Their demands were quite modest; they advocated a workday of eight hours for women, old age insurance, free professional education, and the freedom of workers to combine. The next workers' congress was held at Lyon from January 28 to February 8, 1878; 180 delegates still urged moderation in workers' demands. When in May of that year Jules Guesde attempted to organize an international congress of workers, he and his collaborators were arrested and placed in prison. It was in prison that Guesde wrote his "Program and Address of the French Revolutionary Socialists." Two months before the meetings in Lyon, the first Marxist journal *L'Egalité*, was published in France under the editorship of Guesde.

Marxist collectivism sounded a new note at the workers' congress at Marseille, which began on October 20, 1879. The delegates embraced a new ideological course, declaring themselves in favor of collectivism, internationalism, and the class struggle and opposed to the private ownership of the means of production. The cooperative effort was given secondary importance. This congress was the beginning of the first Marxist party in France. The *Fédération du Parti des Travailleurs Socialistes de France* (Federation of the Party of Socialist Workers of France) was created in 1879. This party was to change its name to *Parti Ouvrier Français* (French Workers' party) in 1882.

In 1879, the republicans obtained control of the Senate. Political power passed from the wealthy, financial bourgeoisie to a middle class represented mostly by members of the liberal professions—lawyers, professors, and journalists, desirous of counting on the workers' support. This new political majority voted on March 3, 1879 to free all those still in prison for their activities in the commune, and a general amnesty for all those involved in the commune was proclaimed in June 1880. The same majority enacted the Waldeck-Rousseau Law of March 21, 1884, which allowed the establishment of any association, including workers' associations; the law required, however, such associations to file with the authorities their statutes and the names of their members. Subject to this registration requirement, labor unions finally became open and legal organizations in France.

NOTES

Bernstein, S. 1965. *The Beginnings of Marxian Socialism in France*. New York: Russell & Russell.

Bron, J. 1968. *Histoire du Mouvement Ouvrier Français*. Vol. I. Paris: Les Editions Ouvrières.

Hyams, E. 1979. *Pierre-Joseph Proudhon: His Revolutionary Life, Mind, and Works*. London: John Murray.

Journal Officiel de la Commune, April 17, 1871.

Levine, L. 1970. *Syndicalism in France*. New York: AMS Press.

Moss, B. H. 1980. *The Origins of the French Labor Movement, 1830–1914*. Berkeley: University of California Press.

Sewell, W. H., Jr. 1980. *Work and Revolution in France: The Language of Labor from the Old Regime to 1848*. Cambridge: Cambridge University Press.

BIBLIOGRAPHY

Aguet, J. P. *Les grèves sous la monarchie de Juillet (1830–1847).* Geneva, 1954.

Benoist, L. *Le Compagnonnage et les métiers.* Paris, 1966.

Bezucha, R. J. *The Lyon Uprising of 1834: Social and Political Conflict in a Nineteenth-Century City.* Cambridge, 1974.

Caire, G. *Les Syndicats Ouvriers.* Paris, 1971.

Coonaert, E. *Les Corporations en France avant 1789.* Paris, 1941.

Decoufle, A. *La Commune de Paris.* Paris, 1969.

Dolleans, E. *Histoire du Mouvement Ouvrier.* 3 vols. Paris, 1953.

Dommanget, M. *Les idées politiques et sociales d'Auguste Blanqui.* New York, 1957.

Duveau, G. *La vie ouvrière en France sous le Second Empire.* Paris, 1946.

Jackson, J. H. *Marx, Proudhon and European Socialism.* New York, n.d.

Lefranc, G. *Le Syndicalisme en France.* Paris, 1953.

——. *Histoire du mouvement ouvrier en France des origines à nos jours.* Paris, 1947.

Lissagaray, P. O. *Histoire de la Commune de 1871.* 3 vols. Paris, 1967.

Lorwin, V. R. *The French Labor Movement.* Cambridge, 1954.

Soboul, A. *Les Sans-culottes parisiens en l'an II.* Paris, 1958.

Woodcock, G. *Pierre-Joseph Proudhon.* New York, 1956.

Zevaes, A. *Jules Guesde.* Paris, 1929.

7

The Impacts of Marxism and Revolutionary Syndicalism on the French Labor Movement in the Twentieth Century

THE DEVELOPMENT OF MARXIST DOCTRINE IN FRANCE

Marxist thought gained a foothold in France after the defeat of the Commune of Paris. Marx's ideas were propagated in France not by labor leaders in the country but by *communards* in exile. In London, Blanquists became acquainted with Marxist theory and incorporated into their teachings the concepts of the employers' appropriation of the surplus value and of the class struggle, as well as the Marxian goal of collective ownership of the means of production. Vaillant accepted the inevitability of the social revolution. Paul Brousse, initially a member of the Anarchist Federation of the Jura, a man who had condemned central authority and the state, abandoned anarchist ideology after meeting Marx in London in 1879.

Protesting the dictatorial ways of the General Council of the First International, as well as its strong adherence to Marxist views, French refugees in Switzerland supported the federalist democracy and the ideological pluralism allowed by the Jurassian Federation. Benoît Malon, Gustave Lefrançais, and Jules Guesde accused the General Council of trying to establish a strong hierarchical and authoritarian international labor organization, intolerant of any views inconsistent with Marxist thought.

Until his return to France in 1876, Guesde had remained much closer to anarchism than to Marxian socialism. In an article he published in *La Solidarité Révolutionnaire* of July 1, 1873, he maintained that the emancipation of the masses required the "abolition, the destruction of the state" (Bernstein 1965, p. 103). Guesde came very close to embracing anarchosyndicalism when, in his *Essai de catéchisme socialiste,* published in

1874, he advocated the formation of a society administered by a federation of workers' associations and characterized by the absence of a centralized state authority. What Guesde stood for when he returned to Paris from exile was not the centralized and unitary Marxist "dictatorship of the proletariat," but a federalist form of socialism based on collective ownership of land and capital by federations of trades, workers' associations, and communes. His views pleased French skilled workers and the *petits propriétaires*. When, after 1880, Guesde came closer to Marxism, he was repudiated by many French workers who rejected basic Marxist views. In 1876, Guesde's collectivism, however, opposed authority and the state. At that time, he advocated that collectively owned land and capital would be leased by independent communes to "free associations of producers" in return for "social rent." After deducting this "social rent" from their income, members of these producers' associations would be able to receive the full exchange value of their production. The commune would in turn utilize the rent it received to subsidize education and social welfare projects (Moss 1980, p. 83).

Collectivism was also supported in France by the Baron Hippolyte de Colins, who claimed that poverty was a direct result of the fact that land was privately owned. For the Colinsists, poverty was not the effect of the wage system, but, rather, due to the fact that landless workers were forced to sell their labor to the owners of land and capital; the competition for jobs by such workers forced the wage rate down to a subsistence level. If such workers could make a livelihood by working some land they would own, they would be freed of the necessity of selling their labor; they would only do it when the wage rate would be sufficiently high, when working for someone else would produce an income larger than that obtained from work on their own land.

For the Colinsists, as long as property rights remained unaltered, workers' cooperation, workers' representation in the legislature would be unable to change significantly the economic status of the working class.

In 1872, Benoît Malon published his *L'Internationale* in which he briefly presented Marx as one of the intellectual founders of the First International. In his *Exposé des écoles socialistes françaises*, published one year later, a brief explanation of Marx's theories was presented to show that Marx predicted that production would be based on collective ownership in the postrevolution era. Three years later, the first French translation of the first volume of *Das Kapital* appeared in France.

Marxist theories were discussed by students meeting in the Café Soufflet in Paris, a place often visited by Guesde. It was in this café that Guesde made the acquaintance of Karl Hirsch, a young German journalist who introduced Guesde to Marxian socialism. Hirsch's influence became manifest when *L'Egalité* became the first French newspaper to propagate and endorse Marx's "scientific socialism." Guesde, as chief editor of this organ, abandoned his earlier quasi-anarchist stance by advising workers to participate in the electoral struggle and to form their own political party "to assure the triumph of the social revolution" *(L'Egalité 1877)*. Although Guesde and his sympathizers did not believe that social change could be brought about by peaceful and lawful means, they felt that the formation of a workers' political party would arouse in the working class a strong feeling of class consciousness, a feeling that would eventually support the revolutionary effort.

Marxian socialism started to gain ground during the period between the workers' congress in Lyon and that in Marseille. After having defied the government's prohibition to hold an international workers' congress in Paris in September 1878, Guesde was imprisoned; the defense he presented in court was read by many French workers and permitted his views to be disseminated throughout France. Back in prison, Guesde and his colleagues wrote a manifesto, the "Program and Address of French Social Revolutionaries." This document demanded freedom of the press, freedom of assembly and of combination, and the social ownership of land and of the means of production. This statement, together with his court defense, allowed Guesde to obtain greater notoriety in France. This does not mean that the majority of France's workers started to embrace Guesde's views. Many *petits propriétaires*—and France's working class was still composed chiefly by these in the 1870s—distrusted Guesde's collectivism.

The workers' congress at Marseille in 1879 strengthened the position of the collectivists. The delegates indeed resolved that under a system in which private ownership prevailed, workers would always receive a small part of the product of their labor. Given the Lassallean "iron law of wages," workers in the capitalist system would have to remain poor. Only through the collective ownership of the means of production could workers escape subsistence wages. In order to achieve the collectivization of land and capital, workers had to form a political party that would operate independently and separately of any bourgeois influence.

Thus, rejecting cooperation, the Marseille congress opted for the formation of a new Socialist party. This party was initially named the Federation of the Party of Socialist Workingmen of France, later changed to the Workers' party. The country was divided into six different regions, each of which was to organize its own party federation and hold its own regional party congresses. An annual national party congress was to elect the party's national executive committee. The various regions were those of the center (Paris), the east (Lyon), the south (Marseille), the west (Bordeaux), the north (Lille), and Algeria (Algiers).

The political views of the party's membership differed sharply from region to region. The federations of the center and of the east supported revolutionary collectivism, whereas the federation of the south was strongly influenced by anarchism and declared that it would not participate in elections. The federation of the west was inclined toward peaceful reformism and followed the views of the first two labor congresses; that of the north rejected the socialization of the means of production and supported cooperativism. Most party leaders appeared to favor the development of a federalist socialism led by federations of trades and communes rather than a centralist approach to socialism. Both Malon and Brousse supported the federalist trade socialism that appealed to the skilled workers.

As of 1880, Guesde, under the influence of Karl Marx and of Paul Lafargue, dedicated his efforts to attacking the federalist tradition and establishing a strongly centralized workers' party presenting a uniform revolutionary Marxist program that would be backed by the unskilled factory workers. In May of that year, Guesde visited Marx and Engels in London and obtained Marx's help in the formulation of a party program.

The program enumerated a number of political and economic demands. Among the former were freedom of the press, of assembly and of coalition, the abolition of the mandatory workers' *livret*, the nationalization of the property of the religious orders, the arming of the people, and the abrogation of the law that prohibited the establishment of French sections of the International. The list of economic demands included an eight-hour workday for adults, a work week of six days, the prohibition of labor for children under the age of 14, a six-hour workday for children of 14 to 18 years of age, a minimum wage law, equal wages for equal work, free public education, employers' responsibility for on-the-job accidents, the control of mines and railroads by workers, the abolition of indirect taxes, and the imposition of progressive income and inheritance taxes (Moss 1980 p. 107).

In order to minimize the effects of workers' hostility to Marx and to Marxism, Guesde asked Malon to present this "minimum program" as his own, and Malon agreed to introduce the program in France as the work of several French labor leaders. Because the program supported workers' participation in the electoral process, it was opposed by the anarchists. The program, however, was accepted by the party's federation of the center in July 1880 and by the collectivist delegates at the party's fourth national congress at Le Havre in the same year. At that congress, the majority of the delegates were, however, reformists, who, after expelling the collectivists from the Cercle Franklin meeting hall, proceeded to condemn collectivism and to support moderate demands that conformed with the views adopted by the first two labor congresses, those of Paris and Lyon.

These "revolutionary reformists" grouped around Malon, Brousse, and the journal *Le Prolétaire*. Although they accepted some Marxist beliefs, such as the polarization of classes, the conquest of political power by a workers' political party, and the social revolution, they rejected Guesde's attempts to centralize the party's organization. They were above all federalists who could not accept authoritarian rule. Both Malon and Brousse had embraced a federalist socialism whose establishment would be facilitated by a broadly based Socialist party that would accommodate people with very different views, from anarchists on the extreme left to radical republicans on the far right.

At the party's congress in Reims in November 1881, the Broussists attacked Guesde's minimum program and claimed that Guesde was the main cause of the party's poor showing at the legislative elections of 1881. Brousse, following the tactics of "all possibilities," intended to expand the base of the Parti Ouvrier by welcoming to its ranks all workers who wished to fight for the abolition of the wage system and for immediate reforms. His followers became known as the "possibilists." They were opposed by those of Guesde who condemned the federalist tradition of the French labor movement. The Guesdists, claiming that all federalism was bourgeois, decided to aim their propaganda at industrial factory workers and to ignore the country's urban skilled workers, who, they claimed, had become part of the petty bourgeoisie. The Guesdists proceeded to organize workers in the country's industrial centers, especially in the north, around Lille and Roubaix, and in the east, particularly in the area of Lyon. The Broussists, claiming that their rivals wanted to introduce into the labor movement the dictatorship of Jules Guesde and to force all workers to accept Marxist dogma, were very successful in Paris and in the provinces, attracting to their ranks both reformists and anarchists.

The Broussists greatly outnumbered the Guesdists at the third congress of the Parti Ouvrier, held at Saint-Etienne in 1882. Outnumbered, the Guesdists walked out of the Saint-Etienne congress and met separately in Roanne. The Guesdists accused the delegates in Saint-Etienne of being reformists. In fact, doctrinal differences between Broussists and Guesdists were minimal; their principal disagreement centered on how the party should be organized, the Broussists preferring a loose federalist organization, while the Guesdists strove for a party united under a centralized direction. The delegates in Saint-Etienne considered themselves as revolutionary as the Guesdists. The title they gave to their party, the *Parti Ouvrier Socialiste Révolutionnaire Français*, or the Socialist Revolutionary French Workers' party, revealed that the Broussists, just like the Guesdists, thought themselves revolutionary collectivists. Their insistence on party democracy and on independence of Marxist doctrine separated them, however, from the followers of Guesde.

After the Saint-Etienne episode, Guesde decided to abandon trade socialism and to establish a new workers' party with a centralized organization and a uniform program that would appeal to France's unskilled industrial labor. This party, the *Parti Ouvrier Français*, or the French Workers' party, was to become the first workers' party in France to reject the federalist tradition of the French labor movement; its members were the poor, unskilled industrial workers of the Allier Basin, the north, the Pas-de-Calais, and the Rhône Valley.

Brousse tried to expand the base of his party by appealing to all workers, and soon had its name changed to the more neutral *Fédération des Travailleurs Socialistes de France*, the Federation of the Socialist Workers of France. The party leadership stressed obtaining reforms through workers' participation in the electoral process and the avoidance of illegal or violent action. Though Brousse and Malon retained a revolutionary rhetoric, in fact they supported alliances with the radical republicans and placed great reliance on the trade unions as agents of reform; party members had to belong to a trade union, and trade union members formed the bulk of the party. Brousse's possibilists were mostly Parisian skilled workers. The Broussists were not strong in the provinces. The federation of the north had joined the Guesdists; in the south, labor leaders maintained an apolitical stance, while in the east, Broussists were opposed by anarchists, Blanquists, and Guesdists. The federation of the west remained loyal to cooperativism. Old *communards* returning to France formed a reformist and cooperativist Socialist Republican Alliance in 1880 and did not join the possibilists of Brousse.

In 1890, Brousse entered into an alliance with the radicals, hoping that this move would strengthen the influence of the party and gain votes for it. The rank and file of Parisian workers rebelled against this move and, under the leadership of Jean Allemane, called for a workers' assembly in Paris to give the party a new direction. Having been expelled by the Broussists at the party's congress at Châtellerault in October 1890, the Allemanists in turn forced the Broussists to leave the Paris assembly. The Allemanists, claiming that Brousse's followers were opportunists too absorbed with elections, proclaimed that they would restore the revolutionary spirit of the party.

Instead of stressing political action, the Allemanists gave emphasis to economic action through the trade unions, or *syndicats*. For them, the trade unions were necessarily the revolutionary agencies capable of transforming society by means of the general strike. Loyal to French labor tradition and without abandoning Marxist doctrine, Allemanists advocated a federalist Socialist system administered by federations of trade unions and of workers' communes. They were active in the *bourses du travail* movement and participated in the organization of a National federation of *bourses*. Their belief in subordinating the party to the trade unions induced them to become part of the growing syndicalist movement. After 1897, they ceased holding congresses, and most Allemanists became simple trade union leaders. By 1900, most Allemanists had joined the Parti Socialiste Français of Jean Jaurès.

The idea of establishing centers where workers of different skills could meet and discuss employment contracts and conditions of work was developed as early as 1790. It surfaced again after the defeat of the commune and was implemented in 1887, when the municipal government of Paris donated a house, Rue du Château-d'Eau, to help in the formation of the first *bourse*. Other *bourses* were founded in Marseille, Nîmes, Bourges, Saint-Etienne, Alais, Toulouse, and elsewhere. A constituent congress of the National Federation of the Bourses du Travail of France was held at Saint-Etienne on February 8, 1892. The guiding spirit of the national Federation was the young Fernand Pelloutier, a man who believed that the general strike was labor's ultimate weapon but that workers' education was just as important.

New *bourses* were created at Nancy, Nantes, Nice, Dijon, and Roanne. There were 23 of them in 1893, 69 in 1900, and 140 in 1911 (Bron 1970, vol. II, p. 59). These *bourses* became concerned with locating jobs for their members, with housing transient workers, with educational activities, and with helping in the development of mutual aid societies and of workers' cooperatives; in these various activities they resembled the old *compagnonnages*.

During the last years of the nineteenth century, an anarchist movement, inspired by Proudhon and Bakunin, developed separately from the workers' groups influenced by the views of Marx and Engels. Supporters of the general strike and of "propaganda by the deed," anarchists made their presence felt in the early 1890s through demonstrations and individual acts of terror. Acting in small independent groups, anarchists were most numerous among the craftsmen of Dijon, Lyon, Saint-Etienne, Grenoble, Valence, and Marseille. Their propaganda was disseminated by a press appearing irregularly, newspapers such as *Le Revolté* of Jean Grave and *Le Père Peinard* of Emile Pouget. Writers such as Jean Richepin, Paul Valéry, Henri de Régnier, Stéphane Mallarmé, Elie and Elisée Réclus, and Tristan Bernard contributed to their journals, *Les Temps Nouveaux*, *Le Libertaire*, and *La Sociale*.

THE CONFÉDÉRATION GÉNÉRALE DU TRAVAIL AND REVOLUTIONARY SYNDICALISM

Peter Stearns (1971) has defined syndicalism in terms of three main characteristics: "complete hostility to the existing system; a belief that the only way to attack this system was by economic rather than political means, notably a great general strike; and a vague indication that the future society would be organized without a central political structure, on the basis of local economic units directed by the producers themselves'' (p. 9). In France, the cause of syndicalism was advanced by revolutionary trade unionists dissatisfied with the moderation of the political Socialists. The first national federation of trade unions, the *Fédération des Syndicats et Groupes Corporatifs de France*, was established in 1886 and was soon controlled by the Guesdists.

The Guesdists wanted to use this federation as a school of indoctrination that would provide members for their party. The Guesdists, believing that the party and not the trade unions should be the decision-making power in the event of a revolution, opposed the use of the general strike as a revolutionary weapon out of fear that it could place the unions in the seat of command. Their view that the party and not the unions should direct the revolution separated them from the Allemanists, anarchists, and Blanquists, who supported revolutionary trade union leadership.

In the 1890s, the Guesdists were left out of a labor movement that developed around the *bourses du travail* and supported the use of the general strike. This movement, led by the Allemanists, embraced independent revolutionary trade unionism or syndicalism. The Allemanists supported the idea that the class struggle should be fought on the economic front by trade unions operating independently of any political party. The goal was a federalist socialism to be organized on the basis of trade federations. Supported by anarchists and Blanquists, the Allemanists organized the *Fédération Nationale des Bourses du Travail* in 1892. This federation was to organize all workers independently of the various Socialist political factions. The Allemanists then invited all of the trade unions in the nation to participate in a congress in Paris in 1893. Anticipating worker agitation, the government closed the *bourse* in Paris. Nevertheless, the congress met, and the delegates gave their support to the use of the insurrectionary general strike. Moreover, they proposed that the two labor federations should join.

In 1895, 75 delegates representing 18 *bourses*, 126 unions, and 28 trade federations met at Limoges and established the *Confédération Générale du Travail* (CGT), an organization then opposed by both the Guesdists and the Fédération Nationale des Bourses du Travail. Although it acknowledged its revolutionary purpose, the CGT imposed political neutrality on its member unions. Most of these unions were Parisian unions under the control of Allemanists who supported both collectivism and the strategy of the general strike.

The CGT started as a relatively small labor organization with about

400,000 members. It had to face the competition of both the Fédération Nationale des Syndicats, a federation that continued to exist until 1898, and the federation of the *bourses.* During the first years after its formation, the CGT stagnated. The *bourses,* on the other hand, expanded under the leadership of Fernand Pelloutier. The predominance of anarchosyndicalist thought among the leaders of both the CGT and the *bourses,* as well as the *affaire Millerand,* were to facilitate the union of both organizations in 1902.

As of 1901, the secretary of the CGT was Victor Griffuelhes, a shoemaker from Nérac, a Blanquist whose views came very close to those of anarchism. The secretary of the *Fédération Nationale des Bourses du Travail* was Georges Yvetot, an anarchist. Both men supported similar policies and goals. Both were federalist collectivists who approved the use of the general strike as a means to overthrow the capitalist system.

The "Millerand question" further united revolutionary trade union leaders. The Socialist Alexandre Millerand, a parliamentarian deputy for Paris, accepted a seat in the bourgeois government of Waldeck-Rousseau and entered that government with General Gallifet, who had led the repression against the *communards.* Allemanists, Guesdists, Blanquists, and anarchists joined in protesting the participation of a "political" Socialist in a bourgeois government.

Millerand, as minister in the Waldeck-Rousseau cabinet, succeeded in having the government enact a number of decrees that shortened the workday for adults and provided for old age benefits. Labor leaders felt, however, that the government was attempting to weaken the trade union movement; their opposition to "political" socialism strengthened their enthusiasm for revolutionary syndicalism. Many of these leaders were anarchists who had entered the unions to avoid government prosecution; their antipolitical stance and their support of the strategy of the general strike gave a stronger mandate to the anarchosyndicalists in the CGT.

During the first decade of the twentieth century, the CGT gave more importance to the encouragement of partial strikes than to the broadening of its membership base. During the period 1904–06, the CGT pursued the policy of agitating in favor of the eight-hour workday; although such a workday had been obtained in the United States by the American Federation of Labor, in France, where the average workday still lasted 12 hours, the demand for the shorter day was interpreted by employers as an exceedingly radical demand. The French government decided to silence the CGT by arresting some of its leaders, by drafting strikers into the army, and by having troops put down strikes. The impact of these acts of repression soon became obvious. Griffuelhes was replaced by Louis Niel as secretary of the CGT in 1909. Both Niel and his successor, Léon Jouhaux, were former anarchists, but they changed the strategy of the CGT by giving greater importance to the improvement of the labor organization, the pursuit of new labor legislation, and reformist action.

It should be noted that as late as 1906, 72 percent of all French workers were employed in small workshops of less than 20 workers, and 20 percent of all French workers still labored in their own homes, maintaining a traditional domestic system of production (Bron 1970, vol. II, p. 96). The preponderance of small firms in French industry was in keeping with the prevailing ideology of French workers during the first decade of the twentieth century. The structure of France's secondary sector explains why most French workers preferred anarchosyndicalism to Marxism.

A simplified version of Marxist doctrine was propagated by political groupings of Guesdists and of Blanquists. A *Parti Socialiste de France* was organized in 1901 to advocate Marxist doctrine. A more moderate *Parti Socialiste Français*, under the leadership of Aristide Briand and of Jean Jaurès, was established one year later. Jaurès, a man who did not reject a possible participation of Socialists in a bourgeois government if such participation was deemed necessary to safeguard the republic, gave emphasis to immediate economic reforms, which he considered to be initial steps leading to the social revolution, to the nationalization of key industries, and to the separation of church and state. Frightened by his powerful rhetoric, the bourgeoisie reacted by having Jaurès murdered in 1914.

The 1904 Amsterdam congress of the Second International had resolved that there should be only one Socialist party in each country. In order to conform to this resolution, France's Socialist parties united into a *Parti Socialiste Unifié* in April 1905, better known as the SFIO, the *Section Française de l'Internationale Ouvrière*. The new unified party was to adhere to Marxist principles, although in practice it was to follow a compromise between Guesdist centralism and Jauresian federalism.

The Guesdists still claimed that trade union organizations were unable to carry out successfully the revolution and to manage a Socialist economy. They insisted on the establishment of formal relationships between the party and the labor organization that would ensure the political primacy of the party. Most trade union leaders, however, distrusted the policies of a Socialist party that had civil servants, members of the liberal professions, and businessmen as members.

The opposing views of Guesdists and of trade unionists surfaced at the CGT congress, held at Amiens from October 8 to 14, 1906. Victor Renard, secretary of the Textile Federation and a member of the *Parti Ouvrier* Français of Guesde, asked for a close collaboration between the CGT and the SFIO. His resolution was defeated by a large majority. Instead, the delegates approved a resolution on October 13, commonly known as the Charter of Amiens. The charter defined the CGT as an independent revolutionary labor movement trying to achieve the collectivization of the means of production through economic action. It stood for trade socialism and was independent of any political party. Although it embraced revolutionary syndicalism, it did not order its unions to ignore politics. Rather, it emphasized the fact that the labor organization would not be subservient to the Socialist political party. It split the French labor movement into two separate and independent groups, one being the political party and the other the trade unions.

During the decade that preceded the beginning of World War I, the SFIO's views started to resemble those of the German Social Democratic party. Although Guesdists in the French Socialist party still talked about the revolution, their belief in the coming of this revolution in the near future weakened. Party officials became less and less interested in deepening their understanding of Marxist doctrine, and even though they still affirmed that their goal was a social revolution achieved by means of the class struggle, they identified with the belief of Jaurès that a complete transformation of society could be achieved by peaceful and progressive evolution.

The party's reformism was backed by many new members in the party, people who did not belong to the industrial proletariat. These were small landowners and businessmen who were more concerned with the obtention of immediate regional or professional benefits than with the overthrow of the capitalist system. Under their influence, the party gradually abandoned revolutionary views for the more conformist tactics of social democracy.

The CGT itself was divided by factionalist strife. A number of member unions started questioning the desirability of the general strike as a revolutionary weapon. Pressurized by reformists, Griffuelhes resigned in February 1909. His successor seldom spoke about taking action to destroy the state; his policies centered, rather, on achieving immediate economic goals in such matters as wages and conditions of work. Niel was replaced by Léon Jouhaux on May 28, 1909, the son of a *communard* who initially sympathized with revolutionary syndicalism. Jouhaux soon became a prudent labor leader who attached more importance to the organization of the masses than to the revolutionary efforts of a few, and even though the government was taking harsh measures to suppress strikes and workers' demonstrations, Jouhaux nevertheless rejected the general strike as a workers' weapon.

Under Niel and Jouhaux, the CGT ceased to be the bastion of revolutionary syndicalism.

The Charter of Amiens had revealed the ideal of a majority within the CGT that society should be reorganized on the basis of the syndical organization so that the political state could disappear. For the syndicalists there should be no national borders; borders only satisfied the selfish interests of the national bourgeoisie.

Syndicalists distrusted and opposed the government and believed that legislation favorable to workers was only passed to encourage the syndicates to register with the authorities and to reveal the identity of their officers and members. That the government used troops against the strikers during 1906–10 and drafted striking workers into the army strengthened the syndicalists' distrust for government.

These views had their roots in anarchism and anarchosyndicalism. Another such view favored by the revolutionary syndicalists was the importance of "direct action" by workers, the benefits of such action being determined by the "educational potential" of such action on workers rather than by the economic benefits it could bring them. Syndicalists encouraged strikes, not so much because they could raise wages or shorten hours of work, but because they provided the training that workers had to acquire in order to be able to engage in the class struggle. The revolutionary syndicalists borrowed the belief from the anarchists that in this struggle it was the small, autonomous group of workers that knew best how to further the interests of its members.

Hoping to be able to destroy the state, the revolutionary syndicalists rejected as useless any participation of workers or of trade unions in political life. At least until 1909, the syndicalists were also strong antimilitarists, feeling that the army had always been used by the government to defend the interests of the middle class.

Between 1906 and 1914, the SFIO and the CGT pretended to be able alone to bring about the social revolution. In the case of the CGT, an organization that shortly before the outbreak of World War I counted perhaps only 6,000 members, this claim did not appear to be realistic. The relative weakness of the CGT was well perceived by Léon Jouhaux and by Alphonse Merrheim, the latter being the leader of the Union of Metallurgical Workers. Both men wanted the CGT to be built on a wider membership base and to rely on a stronger organization; attempts to centralize such organization were, however, resisted by the dogmatic revolutionary syndicalists.

A minority within the CGT backed a more conciliatory policy. Although it, too, was revolutionary, it felt that the capitalist system was not about to collapse and that some cooperation was more beneficial than all-out opposition. The secretary of the Printers' Union and the leader of the "reformist" minority within the CGT, Auguste Keufer, declared that "on the question of Direct Action, I am compelled to declare that from the workers' point of view, we regard it as highly dangerous. . . . The method of revolutionary action will inevitably produce reprisals of which the workers will be the victims" (Saposs 1931, p. 22). As 1914 approached, this minority also took a strong stand against the antimilitarism of the majority.

The reality of war drastically changed the policy orientation of the majority in the CGT. At the burial of Jean Jaurès, Léon Jouhaux noted that "it is not we who have willed this war; and the despots who have loosed it shall be chastised. Emperors of Germany and Austria, lordlings of Prussia, who have desired the war out of hatred for democracy, we pledge ourselves to sound the knell of your reign. We will be the soldiers of liberty" (Saposs 1931, p. 26). The CGT majority applauded these words. Gone were the antimilitaristic feelings; gone was the advocacy of a general strike to oppose the war. The CGT's abandonment of its antimilitarist position was followed by the renouncement of its entire ideology. In its enthusiasm to defend France against foreign aggression, it accepted cooperation with all social classes that pursued the same objective; this meant that the war induced it to forsake class struggle and "direct action."

Even before France entered the war, the CGT had modified its Amiens policy by joining the SFIO in an "Action Committee" whose task was to improve cooperation between labor and the public authorities. As Jaurès had predicted, a "sacred union" was formed among the government, the bourgeoisie, and labor to organize the defense of the endangered homeland. In the face of the conciliatory position of the CGT, the ministries of war and of the interior, which had prepared a list of all "dangerous" pacifists who were to be incarcerated upon the outbreak of war, the famous "Carnet B," left people on that list unmolested. The government even expressed its indignation at the murder of Jaurès. In turn, Jouhaux and other labor leaders showed their willingness to participate in government-appointed commissions together with representatives of the middle class. The CGT no longer insisted that work had to stop on May 1 and that workers had to demonstrate in support of the eight-hour workday.

A reaction against the cooperation of the CGT leadership with the government started as early as 1915. The Union of Metalworkers refused to "place the moral authority of the CGT at the disposal of the Government for the intensification of the carnage and ruin provoked by the war" (Saposs 1931, p. 35). Little attention was paid to this reaction by the majority of the CGT and by most French workers. Many labor leaders felt, however, that a renewal of international labor contacts could help in a more rapid reestablishment of peace. The Swiss Socialist Robert Grimm contacted in January 1915 the opposition elements in the CGT and in the SFIO. A conference was organized at Zimmerwald, Switzerland, and labor representatives from both the Allied and the Central Powers nations participated during September 5 to 8. Merrheim and

Bourderon represented the CGT and the SFIO. The French and German representatives agreed that there should be a "peace without victors and without vanquished," and a majority of the attendants rejected Lenin and Trotsky's program calling for immediate insurrection. In France, the Union of Metalworkers continued to attack Jouhaux for having participated in government-appointed commissions and for agreeing to cooperate with employers' associations.

At the CGT Conference at Clermont-Ferrand of December 23–25, 1917, an effort was made to reconcile the views of the majority and the minority in the CGT. It was resolved that the CGT would support the peace proposals made by U.S. President Woodrow Wilson and would press the French government to reveal its conditions for peace. An extremist minority, encouraged by the Russian Revolution, felt that the continuing support on the part of the majority for the *Union Sacrée* made their cooperation with the CGT majority impossible. They were already talking about forming a new CGT.

The government did not publish its conditions for peace. In May 1918, young French workers were conscripted in large numbers and were replaced by American workers. The war continued. Spontaneous strikes ensued in Paris, Lyon, and Saint-Etienne; 100,000 workers stopped work in the Paris region. The government reacted by making numerous arrests, claiming that the strikes had been instigated by German agents. The CGT minority then held a congress at Saint-Etienne; the delegates of some 200 syndicates resolved that although they opposed a split, they would assume the leadership of the trade union movement if the majority in the CGT continued to act in an "irresponsible" way.

A CGT congress in Paris followed in July 1918. The CGT minority divided into two factions. The moderates rejected the willingness of the minority extremists to abandon the CGT. The extremists criticized the majority for having entered into an alliance with the government and with the bourgeoisie. The entire minority was disappointed by the "reformist" speech of Jouhaux, whose principal message was that the prewar ideology of revolutionary syndicalism had to be abandoned by the CGT. Jouhaux was reelected secretary of the organization by a large majority vote. The delegates were all aware that a schism threatened the CGT.

The CGT membership had increased dramatically; by the end of the war it had attained 2.5 million. The CGT leadership, supported by a large majority, continued to pursue the policies it had adopted during the years of war. The minimum program it published in December 1918 was reformist in nature. Jouhaux accepted being part of the French delegation to the Peace Conference, and the CGT formed its own "economic council" in which were employed a number of bourgeois technicians. The CGT majority continued to be opposed by a minority composed of anarchists,

Communists, and syndicalists that accused the CGT leadership of having embraced reformist "Gompersism" and of ignoring the Charter of Amiens. The minority's protest was strengthened by the events in Germany and Russia, and many minority members believed that the collapse of capitalism was imminent.

June 1919 witnessed a series of major strikes throughout France, largely for economic reasons, although the CGT minority tried to take advantage of them for their own political ends. The miners were successful in obtaining an eight-hour workday; but the strike of the Parisian metalworkers ended in defeat for the union, and this defeat was presented by the CGT minority as being due to the policy of class cooperation followed by the CGT leadership.

At the CGT congress at Lyon in September 1919, the minority tried again to oust Jouhaux by denouncing his "reformist" and "class cooperation" policies. The minority condemned his presence at the Peace Conference, the participation of CGT leaders in various government commissions, and the use of bourgeois technicians in the CGT's Economic Council. Nevertheless, an enormous majority of the delegates supported Jouhaux and inflicted a severe defeat on the minority.

1920 brought a rapidly rising cost of living while the rise of wages lagged behind price inflation; this caused an outburst of new strikes. What started as a local strike by employees of the Paris-Lyon-Mediterranean Railway in the Paris region, a strike started without the approval of the CGT, rapidly became a general railroad workers' strike. The Railroad Workers' Federation was controlled by members of the CGT's extremist minority. On April 30, the federation called for a general strike. The CGT decided to support the federation and requested miners, dockers, and seamen to strengthen the railroad workers' stand with sympathy strikes. On May 3, the government placed the entire executive committee of the Railroad Workers' Federation under arrest, together with a number of men belonging to the CGT minority. The strike ended in disaster for both the railroad workers and the CGT. Twenty-two thousand railroad workers were dismissed from their jobs. The CGT, accused of having pursued a political revolution, was ordered dissolved by a court. Disappointed, masses of workers deserted the CGT, and by June, its membership was down to a prewar number of about 600,000.

The court order was not executed. The CGT was able to convene a congress at Orléans in September 1920. At this congress, the minority continued to attack the majority for its class cooperation. The minority also demanded the immediate adherence of the CGT to the Red International of Labor Unions (RILU), an organization closely connected to the Communist International with headquarters in Moscow. Minority delegates denounced the Second International and its International Federation of Trade Unions, usually known as the Amsterdam International, an organization in which Jouhaux was a vice-president. The majority remained loyal to its established policy; it expressed sympathy for the Russian Revolution but rejected foreign political influence. The final vote once again gave victory to the majority position.

The minority then assembled in a separate conference, approved what the majority had rejected, and decided to place within the trade unions "syndicalist revolutionary committees" that would try to convert union members to the minority views. The CGT leadership reacted by announcing that all syndicates maintaining such committees could face expulsion from the CGT.

As tension between the two factions grew, Jouhaux decided to make a last effort to keep the CGT from being divided. A congress was to be held at Lille on July 25, 1921. The two factions were unable to agree. The minority convened its own congress in Paris on Christmas Day, 1921, a congress that established a new labor organization, the *Confédération du Travail Unitaire* (CGTU).

POST-WORLD WAR I LABOR IDEOLOGIES

Two opposing factions soon developed within the CGTU. The anarchists, joined by revolutionary syndicalists, felt that Bolshevism led to the formation of a government that was not too different from government in the bourgeois state. They pointed out that the Soviet government exercised a tyrannical authority over individuals and that it kept the RILU subservient to the Communist party. The Communists, on the other hand, demanded the speedy attachment of the CGTU to the Communist International. At the CGTU congress at Saint-Etienne in June 1922, Monmousseau, a strong Communist, was elected chief executive of the CGTU. Anarchists and Communists clashed at Saint-Etienne. The former felt that the CGTU leadership followed policies that were as foreign to the ideals of the Charter of Amiens as those supported by the CGT. Indeed, the French Communist party followed the old Guesdist view that trade unions should be subservient to a political party and tried to propagandize trade unions by establishing in them "syndical commissions" whose task was to indoctrinate workers in Communist ideas.

The Building Federation and some other labor organizations having threatened to abandon the CGTU, the latter held a congress at Bourges in November 1923. At this congress, anarchist and syndicalist delegates insisted that the trade union movement had to remain independent of any political party. They argued that the movement could not become subservient to an International committed to the acceptance of a political doctrine. The majority of the delegates, however, voted in favor of the Communist position. The Building Federation then withdrew from the CGTU. The CGTU minority decided in November 1924 to form a new labor organization dedicated to the principles of the Charter of Amiens. This new organization, which never achieved great success, was initially known as the *Union Fédérative des Syndicats Autonomes* (UFSA) and was renamed in 1926 the *Confédération Générale du Travail Syndicaliste-Révolutionnaire"* (CGTSR).

Another syndicalist group, led by Monatte, formed an independent Ligue Syndicaliste, whose objective was to unify the French labor movement under the principles of the Charter of Amiens.

Freed of anarchist and syndicalist opposition, the CGTU declared its attachment to the Communist International and abandoned the principles of the Charter of Amiens. Its leaders followed Communist ideology as dictated by the RILU. In their view, trade unions were no longer the foremost instruments of revolution and were subordinate to the dictate of the Communist party. The CGTU advocated revolution, a revolution to be achieved through the mobilization of the masses of workers. Unlike the syndicalists, who tended to rely on active minorities to launch the revolution, the CGTU leaders preferred to count on large numbers of followers of uncertain dedication. In order to appeal to the masses, the CGTU favored the support of all strikes. Like the old revolutionary syndicalists, it considered new legislation beneficial to workers as having been enacted by a hostile government in order to weaken the labor movement. Unlike the syndicalists, the CGTU did not attach great importance to the general strike, believing that civil war would be the best way of achieving the revolution.

In spite of its antibourgeois rhetoric, and after having criticized the CGT for its participation in public commissions, the CGTU started presenting candidates for election to the *conseils de prudhommes;* the justification for this apparently inconsistent behavior was that in order to appeal to the masses it had to show an interest in their daily problems and that its presence on such councils would help it in the preparation of the revolution.

While the CGTU turned more and more to Russian communism, the CGT reacted with increased strength against it. The CGT's position was summarized by Merrheim in these words: "What is this Communist dictatorship of the proletariat? It is a dictatorship exercised, not *by* the proletariat, but by a party *on* the proletariat" (Saposs 1931, p. 74). The CGT leadership promptly abandoned Marxism and embracd Proudhonian thought. It decided to achieve three goals: the immediate improvement of working conditions in France, the education of the working class, and the development of plans of social reorganization based on the socialization of economic activity and on the administration of such activity by workers.

A *Confédération Française des Travailleurs Chrétiens* (CFTC) was founded in 1919 to coordinate the activities of Christian trade unions and to compete with the radical labor organizations. Strongest in the north, it never achieved the size of the two major CGTs. In 1923 its membership amounted to about 125,000 people, most of them white-collar and female workers.

The 1920s did not witness conflict between left-wing ideology alone. Mussolinian Fascism had an impact in France, an impact that would strengthen with the deterioration of the economy in the early 1930s. The French economy was affected relatively late by the Great Depression. France's foreign economic sector was the first to feel its constricting effects as protectionism increased in the world and as the United Kingdom devalued the pound sterling in 1931, turning the French franc into an overvalued currency. French industrial production fell with French exports. French steel production declined by 40 percent between 1930 and 1935.

A deteriorating economy and the Italian and German "demonstration effects" combined to encourage the formation of strongly nationalistic, right-wing "leagues." One of the oldest of such organizations was *L'Action Française*, under the leadership of Charles Maurras, who wanted to return to a hierarchical, nondemocratic society dedicated to the national interest and to the support of the church. Maurras never hesitated to use force, blackmail, and anti-Semitism to achieve his goals. *Le Francisme* of Marcel Bucard and *la Solidarité Française* of Jean Renaud were other right-wing groups founded in 1933 that embraced the cult of violence and Italian Fascism. Both organizations were financed by the perfume manufacturer François Coty. The most important quasi-Fascist group was the *Croix-de-Feu*, the Crosses of Fire, a group also financed by Coty. It purported to oppose both socialism and communism, was hostile to the trade unions, and supported the establishment of an authoritarian government able to "unify" all Frenchmen. By 1934, with Hitler in power for a full year, the activities of these groups represented a serious threat for the various political, syndical, and social organizations that adhered to France's democratic and parliamentarian political system.

On February 6, 1934, various right-wing groups demonstrated in front of the Palais-Bourbon in Paris, calling for a conservative government. Fights broke out when the police intervened, and a number of people were killed. On the following day, the CGT decided to call a 24-hour general strike to take place on the twelfth "against the threats of Fascism and for the defense of political liberties" (Bron 1970, vol. II, p. 208). On the same day, the CGT asked the SFIO, the League of the Rights of Man, and other Socialist groups to support it. The CGT did not invite the Communist party, the CGTU, the CFTC or the radicals to join the strike. The Communists, defying a government prohibition, demonstrated on the ninth; a number of people were killed when the demonstrators clashed with the police. On the tenth, the Communist party and the CGTU decided to participate in the general strike on the twelfth.

In the words of Lorwin (1954):

> February twelfth remains one of the great days in the history of French labor. It saw its first successful general strike.... The aims were not those of a single class, but of all democratically-minded Frenchmen, "the defense of the republic, but not of shady republican politicians. With the strength of deep purpose, with no appeal to violence, over a million men and women stopped work in the capital...." Curious paradox: the economic strike is hardly possible but the political strike succeeds. (p. 69)

The strike united in common action the CGT and the CGTU. There was talk of unification between the two labor organizations. Unification was favored by the Communist party, which, under directives from Moscow, favored the formation of a leftist United Front to oppose Fascism more effectively. In July 1934, the French Communist and Socialist parties entered into a Unity of Action Pact in order to combine efforts to oppose the right-wing leagues and war and to protect democratic institutions. The Communist party invited the labor organizations and even the liberal bourgeoisie to participate in such effort. The Communist Maurice Thorez spoke about the formation of a "Popular Front" and of a "Popular Assembly" by all anti-Fascist forces. The awareness of the growing strength of the *Croix-de-Feu* in 1935 caused the Left to assemble in Paris to hear speakers belonging to the SFIO, the Communist party, the CGT, the CGTU, the League of the Rights of Man, anti-Fascist intellectuals, and radicals. The leaders of the Fascist leagues responded with anti-Semitic speeches and ugly attacks on Socialist leader Léon Blum.

On June 17, 1935, representatives of various leftist groups formed a Committee for Popular Assembly whose task was to prepare a large left-wing demonstration on July 14. Following massive demonstrations of the Left on the national holiday, the SFIO agreed to take part in a National Committee for Popular Assembly representing various leftist political and labor organizations, in order to prepare for the elections of 1936. This National Committee published its program on January 10, 1936, which called for a united fight against Fascism and against the Fascist leagues and for the support of the trade unions and secular education. Its economic policy aimed to reduce unemployment in the country and to increase the purchasing power of the masses. In this regard, it demanded a shorter work week without a decrease in pay, improved old age pensions, unemployment insurance, and public works to reduce unemployment. Nothing was said about the nationalization of industries. The program was limited to economic reforms whose enactment would not change significantly the existing economic system. It was not the intention of the Left to frighten the bourgeoisie.

The CGTU, which had experienced for some time a loss of membership, was interested in uniting with the CGT. The latter organization, faithful to the Charter of Amiens, continued to reject the Communist International and dependence on any political party. It demanded, therefore, that the CGTU merge into the CGT. Reunification procedures were finally agreed to by both labor organizations in September 1935. Fusion was to start at the local union level according to the wishes of the CGT, which counted on its more numerous membership to have its principles maintained by the new, combined organization.

At the first congress of the new CGT, held at Toulouse in March 1936, the majority of the delegates indeed adhered to the CGT's traditional federalist structure and retained the CGT's membership in the Amsterdam International. They reaffirmed the 1906 resolution that the labor organization should remain independent of any political party, although they agreed that the CGT would be able to enter into temporary alliances with political parties to oppose threats to democratic freedoms. The delegates also demanded unemployment insurance, paid vacations, a 40-hour work week, the nationalization of key industries and of the Bank of France, national economic planning, and large-scale public works.

The Popular Front, a temporary alliance of Socialists, radicals, Communists, the CGT and other leftist groups, was successful at the national elections of May 1936. Léon Blum became the first French Socialist prime minister. Blum believed in legal reforms and in a democratic system. He invited both the Communists and the CGT to take part in his cabinet. Both refused.

Unemployment and low wages continued to plague the workers. In May and June, French workers expressed their discontent by means of the sit-down strike. Workers "occupied" the factories, stopping any activity in them. Sit-down strikes developed at Le Havre, Toulouse, and in the metallurgical enterprises of the Paris region. The strike then extended to the chemical industry, the textile industry, large retail stores, and the postal service. Eager to terminate this strike wave, the employers' federation, the Confédération Générale de la Production Française" (CGPF), asked the government to arrange a meeting with the CGT. Blum agreed, and representatives of the employers' and the workers' federations met at the Hôtel Matignon in Paris on June 7, 1936.

The famous "Matignon Agreement" was signed the same evening. This agreement constituted a major victory for French labor. Employers agreed to participate in collective bargaining and recognized the right of workers to organize; they agreed to cease discriminating against union members in hiring and firing and consented to the election of shop stewards. Wages were to be raised by an average of 12 percent, and the employers promised not to retaliate against workers who had participated in strikes. Also in June, the government enacted a number of new labor laws. A collective bargaining law implemented the Matignon Agreement; another law provided for vacations with pay for workers who had spent at least one year on a job; and a third law provided for the 40-hour work week.

The signing of the Matignon Agreement boosted the CGT's membership. It attained 4 million in June 1937 (Bron 1970, vol. II, p. 230). Most of the new members were unskilled or semiskilled workers who readily accepted Communist indoctrination and leadership. The CFTC also expanded, its membership growing from about 150,000 members in 1936 to 500,000 one year later. Its members were mostly bank and insurance company clerks, as well as textile workers from Alsace. The Communist party also witnessed a marked growth in membership. Its militants, usually young and well-trained men, were very active in the strike movement of 1936. Counting about 55,000 members in 1934, the party grew to about 340,000 by the end of 1937. The SFIO also increased, but much less than the Communist party.

The economic policy of the Popular Front rested on the main idea that wage increases and the 40-hour work week would generate increased purchasing power and reduce unemployment; higher sales would offset the adverse effect of higher labor cost. Employers, instead of using the 40-hour work week as a base, limited plant operations to 40 hours per week and did not hire additional labor. Also, unlike the American "New Deal" administration, the Popular Front did not rely on deficit financing of new sources of economic activity. In France, higher wages and shorter hours of work proved to be weak stimulants of economic growth. Price increases generally wiped out the consumption effects of wage increases, and, in the rare case when the worker was able to buy more, he bought more foodstuffs rather than more manufactured goods.

Having adopted the new title of *Confédération Générale du Patronat Français*, and having replaced its leadership with more intransigent men, the employers' federation started to abandon the ideas of the Matignon Agreement and ignored demands of the CGT for further negotiations. Employers were inflexible in their rejection of trade union proposals for codetermination in the decision-making process.

The French economy was stagnating for a number of reasons. The

French entrepreneurial class appeared to have lost any interest in industrial modernization and in productivity increases; in order to raise profits, it increased prices. Domestic investment was also weakened by continuous flight of capital. The government refused to devalue the franc until October 1, 1936, and the overvaluation of the French currency burdened French exports. While in France, hatred and distrust separated the political Right and the political Left, Communists and Socialists, and the bourgeoisie and the Blum government, these divisions paralyzing the economy, German industry and military power expanded under Nazi rule. Conscious of French economic weakness, Hitler marched into the demilitarized Rhineland in March 1936 in violation of the Treaty of Versailles.

During the first half of 1937, French industrial production continued to fall, unemployment rose, and capital flight continued. Unable to achieve economic recovery, Blum resigned on June 21, 1937. With Blum's resignation, the Popular Front collapsed. Under the ministries of Chautemps and Daladier, France moved to the right. An attempt by the CGT to prevent the government from modifying the 40-hour work week law through a one-day general strike in 1938 ended in failure; employers retaliated by firing large numbers of strikers and union representatives. Management-labor cooperation had ended and government-labor relations had deteriorated. Disappointed, about 2 million workers gave up their membership in the CGT. The outbreak of war and mobilization further depleted the ranks of the labor organization.

WORLD WAR II AND THE FRENCH LABOR MOVEMENT SINCE 1945

The signing of the Soviet-German Pact of August 23, 1939 strengthened factionalism within the French working class. The CGT was divided into a group hostile to Nazi Germany and a group that supported the Soviet Union and its treaty with Germany. On September 2, the SFIO voted in favor of military credits, and on the following day France entered the war. The entry of Russian troops in Poland on September 17 induced the CGT leadership to declare that it could no longer cooperate with those who supported the Soviet Union. On September 26, the government ordered the dissolution of the Communist party and Communist senators and deputies were expelled from Parliament.

On June 16, 1940, Marshall Henri Pétain became head of the French government; on the eighteenth, General Charles de Gaulle called on all French citizens to resist the enemy. The Vichy government, heading a new "French State," proceeded to outlaw all employers' and workers' organizations by a law of August 16, 1940. The CGT and the CFTC were dissolved, and the labor movement leadership was soon dispersed, as some leaders quietly accepted these events and others hid or ended in prison. For more than a year, the government had no definite plan for the organization of labor. Strikes and lockouts were prohibited and the Vichy government opposed the concept of the class struggle. It was only in October 1941 that the government produced a Labor Charter (*Chartre du Travail*), which purported to establish cooperation between the social classes. In each type of economic activity, employers, technicians, foremen, and workers were mandated to join a *syndicat unique*, a single syndicate. Voluntary, pluralist unions were forbidden. The *syndicat unique* was to have no political or religious interests. These syndicates were to unite in regional and national federations.

At the enterprise, local, regional, and national levels, mixed commissions, the *comités sociaux*, dealt with social welfare questions; the government followed the "leadership principle," which vested in employers almost total authority in the direction of their business. For each industry, an all-employers committee, *comités d'organisation*, had the power to allocate raw materials, set prices, and regulate production and distribution.

After 1943, the Vichy government abandoned any interest in the well-being of French labor. In June 1942, it announced that 250,000 French workers would be sent to Germany in exchange for the liberation of French prisoners held by the Germans. On September 4, 1942 and on February 16, 1943, the Vichy authorities registered men between the ages of 20 and 50 for possible work abroad. The main concern of Marcel Déat, Pétain's last labor minister and a strong Nazi sympathizer, was to supply the Germans with French forced labor.

When German forces attacked the Soviet Union on June 22, 1941, internal resistance to the Vichy government strengthened as Socialists, Communists, and syndicalists found it easier to cooperate. In April 1943, the reformist Jouhaux wing and the Communist wing of the CGT agreed to unite and act jointly; the CGT and the CFTC agreed to cooperate, and both organizations had representatives in the national Council of the Resistance, established in May 1943. In Algiers, de Gaulle's Consultative Assembly, whose president was the reformist CGT leader Georges Buisson, decreed the reestablishment of syndical freedom in France on July 27, 1944, and abrogated the Vichy labor laws and the Labor Charter. As German armies in France started withdrawing, the CGT and the CFTC ordered all railroad workers to strike on August 17, 1944 and called for a general strike on the eighteenth to impede the movement of German troops.

Liberation did not unify the labor movement nor the political Left. Negotiations were started to unite the CGT and the CFTC but were not successful, largely because the CFTC refused to merge with an organization whose members adhered to Socialist or Communist ideology. The Communist party's claim that it should be fused with the SFIO into a single workers' party was rejected by the Socialists, who condemned the Communists' loyalty to the government of the Soviet Union, their doctrinal inflexibility, and their desire to control political life in France.

After liberation, the trade unions proceeded rapidly to build up their strength. The CGT counted more than 5 million members by September 1945, and the CFTC increased its membership to 350,000 in the same year.

Between 1944 and 1946, the government agreed to implement in part the program of social and economic reforms that had been developed by the wartime Resistance. In conformity with this program, the coal mines, the production and distribution of natural gas and of electricity, the four largest deposit banks, the Bank of France, and 34 insurance companies were nationalized, compensation being paid to the former owners. Because Louis Renault died while waiting trial on charges of collaboration with the enemy, the Renault automobile works was nationalized without compensation.

A law was enacted providing that in enterprises of 50 or more workers, plant committees, *comités d'entreprise*, formed by representatives of employees, would regulate social welfare programs in the firm and would have advisory power in matters relating to economic and technical considerations. The status of labor was enhanced by the establishment of a National Economic Council, whose task was to advise the government on economic and social legislation. Léon Jouhaux became its president. Labor also benefited from a revised and extended social security system that increased old age, disability, health, and maternity benefits.

The constitution of the Fourth Republic, adopted in October 1946, was favorable to organized labor. It guaranteed workers the right to join a trade union of their choice, the right to strike, and the right to elect representatives who could engage in collective bargaining and join the management of an enterprise.

The postwar partition of a large part of the world into capitalist and Communist camps had deep repercussions in France. In order to obtain economic aid, the French government decided to side with the Western democracies. This meant that the French government became hostile to Communist participation. When Communist ministers abstained from voting on military credits for French operations in Indochina, the Socialist prime minister, Paul Ramadier, promptly dismissed them in May 1947. The wartime political alliance between Socialists and Communists came to an end.

This rupture was also to affect the CGT. As soon as the trade unions had been reconstituted after liberation, the Communists made a major effort to obtain key positions in them. To achieve their goals, they used both legal and illegal means. They posed as the great heroes of the Resistance and as great patriots who had suffered large casualties and who never collaborated with the enemy. They claimed to be best organized to protect French workers against food shortages, high prices, and unfair taxes. They did not hesitate to get rid of opponents through character or even physical assassination. By the end of 1945, the Communists had succeeded in obtaining control of the CGT, and it became an arm of the Communist party.

Suffering most severely from inflation and food shortages, workers soon felt that liberation had failed to introduce a better society in France. Workers' discontent was to factionalize the CGT. The first manifestation of discontent became apparent in 1946, when an anarchosyndicalist group withdrew from the CGT. These dissenters formed the Confédération Nationale du Travail (CNT). Communications workers staged a major strike in the summer of 1946 and also left the CGT. More important, a group made up of Socialists and syndicalists started to oppose Communist rule in the CGT. This reformist group became known as Force Ouvrière and was loyal only to Jouhaux. It threatened to produce a new major schism in the CGT.

Jouhaux, who had been secretary of the CGT for nearly 40 years, tried to prevent a division. Supporters of Force Ouvrière met, however, on December 18, 1947 and decided to abandon the CGT. They established a new labor federation on April 12–13, 1948, the CGT-FO, an organization that demanded national economic planning, true syndical freedom, and opposition to both Communism and Gaullism. The CGT-FO appealed mostly to salaried employees and to public servants; the federation remained closely tied to the SFIO and was supportive of negotiation with employers and with government. For a while, it appeared that the CGT-FO leadership hoped for a fusion with the Christian CFTC and with the anarchist CNT. Fusion never occurred. The French labor movement was more fragmented in 1947 and in 1948 than ever before.

THE DIVIDED FRENCH LABOR MOVEMENT IN 1950–58

The armed intervention of the United States in Korea in the summer of 1950 turned the cold war, which had developed between the free and the Communist countries since 1948, into a hot war, a war that was to ramify into the four-year-old colonial struggle of France in Indochina. It became impossible for the French labor organizations to ignore these wars. While the Force Ouvrière took a strong anti-Communist position, the CGT openly sided with the East.

In 1950, the CGT remained the country's strongest labor organization, counting about 2.4 million members, compared with about 833,000 for the CGT-FO and 1.1 million for the CFTC (Lefranc 1984, p. 102). In conformance with its goal of ending the capitalist system of production, the CGT adopted in 1953 an economic program that contemplated new nationalizations. The CGT did not demand the nationalization of industries operating at a loss; it wanted the nationalization of all monopolies that dominated the economic and political life of the country. The CGT also advocated national economic planning in which workers and their labor organizations would participate.

The Force Ouvriére, hostile to communism and to Communist influence in the CGT, refused to have any contact with the latter. While supporting a gradual improvement of the capitalist system at home, the FO generally supported the foreign and colonial policies of the Fourth Republic. The FO followed the American example of trade unions, limiting themselves to negotiations with employers and occasionally using the strike as a means to exert pressure.

The Catholic hierarchy within the CFTC remained hostile to Marxist ideology and tried to maintain its members loyal to the papal directives. The majority's attachment to the church was opposed by a minority within the CFTC that would have liked to attract into the organization both believers and nonbelievers.

The labor organizations disagreed on many developments. The Schuman Plan for the establishment of a multinational European Coal and Steel Community was strongly supported by both the FO and the CFTC. These labor organizations welcomed the creation of an international agency that would diminish ill feelings between the former enemy countries, France and Germany, and that would unite them in the building of defenses against the threat of world communism. The European Coal and Steel Community was strongly opposed by the CGT, which protested the use of the Ruhr-Lorraine resources to strengthen an anti-Soviet Union coalition that included a still non-"denazified" West Germany.

Both employers and the government took advantage of the division in the ranks of French labor. The government identifying with the West, proceeded to arrest a number of CGT leaders on the charge that they threatened the security of the state. Intersyndical disagreement and factionalism within the labor organizations weakened the strike efforts of 1953. Internal factionalism within the CGT became apparent at the organization's congress of June 1955, when a number of delegates demanded that the CGT limit itself to a program of immediately obtainable economic reforms. This proposal was rejected.

The end of the Korean War on July 27, 1953, and the Geneva Conference on Indochina of April 26, 1954, lessened the discord among the various labor organizations. The new conflict in Algeria, unlike the Koreañ War, was not an armed struggle between Communist and non-Communist forces and did not divide the labor movement as did the Korean War.

1955 was marked by a revival of economic strikes. Workers wanted wage increases that would offset the effects of price inflation. There were violent confrontations between strikers and security forces at Saint-Nazaire and Nantes. There were strikes by miners, and construction, metallurgical, textile, railroad, and shipyard workers. The intensification of labor unrest and the Algerian conflict brought de Gaulle back to power on June 1, 1958 and caused the end of the Fourth Republic.

LABOR AND THE FIFTH REPUBLIC

The new regime of de Gaulle was supported by 79.2 percent of the French electorate, in spite of the opposition to it by leftist parties, the CGT, and a minority of the CFTC. The new government was committed to a new economic policy. It understood that, with the end of the colonial era, French manufacturing had to turn from the protected home and colonial markets and face the more competitive international market. If France was to be able to compete with success within the European Economic Community (EEC), it had to restructure its industry into larger, more efficient units, and this had to be done through relocation, modernization, reorganization, and powerful government interventions.

The government decided to help those industries that showed the greatest likelihood of being able to compete in the international market. De Gaulle's interest in the EEC was not purely economic. By having France participate in the EEC, de Gaulle hoped to weaken the economic influence and the political power of the United States in Europe. De Gaulle's economic and political ambitions were to have serious effects on French unions and on French workers. As noted by Peter Lange et al. (1982):

> To the extent that industrial structures and their markets changed, dislocations in the lives of workers were inevitable. Certain backward and inefficient industries might go under, while others prospered. Entire regions were likely to decline or grow in accordance with the effectiveness of their economic base and their position in the new market flows...the regime chose to ignore the problem and to leave French workers, together with their unions, to react to the labor market effects of extensive economic change according to their own lights. Gaullism was afflicted with a powerful belief that intermediary social groups such as unions were nuisances to be disregarded and isolated through

magisterial claims, delivered by the General himself, that the regime stood above all sectoral conflicts and reflected the national interest. Gaullist governments may also have been convinced of the then current economic myth that steady economic growth in itself would be a powerful enough solvent for popular discontents to render them unimportant. (pp. 25, 26)

When the coal mines at Decazeville became unprofitable enterprises in the EEC, their owners ordered the relocation of a number of workers. Because relocated workers faced early retirement, reduced wages, and the loss of many social security benefits, the miners resisted, and on December 19, 1961 stopped all work and occupied the mines. The strike lasted until February 23, 1962, and ended in failure, largely because the government ignored the protesting miners. Coal mining was a declining industry in France and therefore did not attract the interest of the government. Strikes extended to iron ore and potassium mines on March 1, 1963. The government responded by threatening to draft all miners into the armed forces. An agreement was finally signed on April 3 that allowed miners' wages to be immediately raised by 6.5 percent.

The economic policy of the government elicited different responses on the part of the labor organizations. The CGT, following the lead of the Communist party, which once again favored a United Front, started looking for allies in the labor movement. It announced its willingness to engage in common action with other labor federations on issues of common concern. The Force Ouvrière refused to respond to the CGT's proposals of cooperation, maintaining its strong anti-Communist stance. The CFTC underwent a major change in its social and economic orientations in 1964, a change that facilitated cooperation with the CGT.

On November 7, 1964, an extraordinary congress of the CFTC changed both the name and the statutes of the organization. The CFTC became the *Confédération Française Démocratique du Travail* CFDT, the French Democratic Confederation of Labor. A minority of the delegates who continued to embrace the early ideals of the organization formed a separate federation that retained the name of CFTC, also known as the CFTC *Maintenue*. The CFDT abandoned any attachment to church doctrine, opened its membership to both believers and nonbelievers, and rejected its former belief in class harmony for the participation in the class struggle.

The leaders of the CFDT also strove to obtain the cooperation of other labor federations. Having been rejected in such efforts by the FO, they turned to the CGT. The latter organization had apprehended a possible alliance between the FO and the CFDT and, in order to prevent the formation of a large non-Communist labor block, quickly agreed on joint action with the CFDT. The CGT-CFDT agreement of January 10, 1966 stipulated that both labor organizations would cooperate in the pursuit of higher purchasing power for workers, the improvement of their working and living conditions, the right to work, and the revision of tax laws in favor of workers.

Cooperation between the CGT and the CFDT was soon put to a test on the occasion of a strike at the chemical works Rhodiaceta in Besançon in February 1967. The CGT demanded wage increases; the CFDT emphasized job security. The strike ended in March with a partial victory for the workers; they received an average wage increase of 4.5 percent and the right to a four-month notice before dismissal.

In March, 3,200 shipyard workers of the shipbuilding works Penhoët at Saint-Nazaire initiated a strike that soon extended to all industrial activity in the region around the city. The strike ended in May, when the workers accepted wage increases averaging 7 percent.

Rising unemployment and employers' intransigence kept workers' discontent high. Toulon experienced a general strike in April 1968. Early in May of that year, strikes multiplied in nine western departments in protest against the level of unemployment.

The protest of workers was echoed by the voice of university students who wanted changes in the antiquated system of higher education and were infuriated by the lack of jobs available at the end of their studies. The student organizations *Union Nationale des Etudiants de France* (UNEF) and the *Fédération de l'Education Nationale* (FEN) and the CGT and the CFDT agreed to organize, on May 13, 1968, large protest demonstrations and a 24-hour general strike. The FO decided to join this strike; the CFTC refused to participate. The demonstrations on May 13 were joined by lycée students and by different youth organizations. During the following days, millions of workers participated in sit-down strikes throughout the country. The workers demanded higher wages, increased trade union privileges in the enterprise, and, in some cases, workers' codetermination in management.

On May 24, a demonstration of the UNEF, which threatened to approach the Hôtel de Ville in Paris, was dispersed by the police. Young people then proceeded to set up barricades in the Latin Quarter and set automobiles afire. It is probable that the students, as well as certain leftist political groups, believed that the time had come to carry out a social revolution.

The Communist party and the CGT were much more cautious and advocated moderation and reform. Negotiations for the cessation of strike activity in France were started on May 25 at the Labor Ministry, located in the Rue De Grenelle in Paris, among government officials, the employers' federation, the CGT, and the CFDT. An agreement, known as the De Grenelle Agreement, was concluded two days later. The employers agreed to raise wages by 7 percent on June 1 and by a further 3 percent on October 1. The process of collective bargaining was to be improved through the establishment of "parity commissions" in which representatives of employers and of workers would sit in equal numbers. The government promised to improve the social security system, to provide, through new legislation, more union power in the enterprise, and to maintain more carefully workers' purchasing power.

Following the events of May 1968, the government decided to take "innovative steps" in the field of labor-management relations. On September 16, 1969, Jacques Chaban-Delmas proposed in the National Assembly the formulation of "progress contracts" in the public sector of the economy. The management of public enterprises and the pertinent trade unions were to enter into pluri-annual wage and salary agreements that were to provide for the participation of workers in the profits of the enterprise, a gradual shortening of the work week, and improved working conditions. The *contrats de progrès* were to do away with the motivation for wildcat strikes that had multiplied after 1968. The government hoped that these long-term contracts would render the neocapitalist system acceptable to the workers.

The first *contrat de progrès* was signed on October 11, 1969 by several labor organizations representing workers in the public sector, with the exception of the CGT. The contract provided for yearly salary and wage increases up to 1974 and required that within this four-year period workers covered by the agreement were not to strike for wage increases. Another *contrat* was signed on December 10, providing for salary and wage increases to be tied to increases in prices and in production. The CGT condemned these agreements on the basis that they represented class collaboration and an abandonment by organized labor of its right to strike.

To be successful, the *contrat de progrès* had to be supported by relative price stability. Inflation in the 1970s became the strongest limitation on the effectiveness of these long-term contracts. The rate of inflation increased in the early 1970s in response to the international raw materials crisis that preceded the energy crisis. Whereas consumer prices rose by 4.8 percent in 1970, they rose by 7.3 percent in 1973. The rate of inflation exceeded 13 percent in 1974.

Inflation was not the only economic factor that adversely affected the French economy in the early 1970s. Unemployment rose with inflation. A rising balance of payments deficit forced the government to adopt an anti-inflationary program during the fall of 1974, a program that reduced the rate of inflation to 11.8 percent in 1975 and improved France's exterior position. However, it also caused the rate of unemployment to double and reduced to zero the growth rate of the gross national product.

Government efforts to stimulate the economy in 1976 caused the growth rate to rise to 5 percent, but inflation remained at nearly 10 percent and unemployment went on increasing; in the same year, the country's balance of payments registered one of the highest deficits experienced since 1945. The restrictive Barre Plan of late 1976 succeeded in reducing the balance of payments deficit, but the rate of inflation remained high and unemployment continued to grow (Lange et al. 1982, p. 36).

Whatever "stop-go" measures were taken by the government, the rate of inflation appeared to be anchored to a 10 percent rate and unemployment kept worsening. In order to avoid rapidly increasing balance of payments deficits, the government tried to keep the economy tied to a slow pace of growth. The former Gaullist policy that pursued high growth at all costs had become a matter of the past. The government's strategy in the 1960s had extended protective measures to firms unable to compete in the international markets and to firms producing exportables for which world demand was declining. In the 1970s, the government gave emphasis to the policy of "industrial redeployment." Peter Lange et al. (1982) describe the government's new industrial policy as follows:

> Gaullist-style protection of lame ducks had to be ended. More generally, various governmental programs of subsidization and market regulation had to be dismantled to allow prices and costs to settle at their true market levels. Secondly, the state had to structure its fiscal and monetary activities to promote profitability and, by inference, investment, while simultaneously increasng its selective intervention to promote industrial activities which had a clearly promising international future. (p. 38)

Opposing the government's economic policy was the 1972 program of the United Left, known as the Common Program. This program reflected to a large extent the views of the Communist party, which urged that economic reform be based on nationalizations and on "democratic planning." The Communist party and the CGT subscribed to the Marxist view that capital had overaccumulated during the postwar boom and that, given the rising organic composition of capital, the rate of profit was bound to fall. They also asserted that in order to partially counteract the effects of a declining rate of profit at home, capitalist countries would intensify efforts to widen their share of the international market. In the struggle for a larger share of international markets, France was at a disadvantage in the competition with high-technology nations such as West

Germany, the United States, and Japan. Chances were that, in the future, France would see its share in the world market decline.

Whereas the Gaullists had pushed for stronger export performance, the Communists and the CGT demanded the development of the domestic market. Economic policy should not favor the development of French multinationals able to compete with foreign conglomerates in international markets; this would only favor the growth of cooperation between the state and monopoly capitalism, to the detriment of the French consumer and the French worker. The French Communist party and the CGT proposed, instead, the creation of a new public sector that would make the French economy more independent of international markets and better equipped to raise domestic demand for French products. The nationalized enterprises would be managed by representatives of consumers, workers, and the government. These three groups would also participate in democratic economic planning.

The CFDT also supported policies designed to favor the development of import-replacing domestic industries. Instead of nationalizations, it advocated the gradual transformation of the economic system into "self-managed socialism," *socialisme autogestionnaire.* Labor should take advantage of the existing economic crisis to initiate the transformation of French capitalism into the new Socialist system. Echoing old syndicalist ideas, the CFDT proposed that the agencies best suited to undertake this social change were the trade unions. Little was said about how this transformation should proceed.

Believing that the existing economic crisis could produce major social innovations, the CGT and the CFDT decided to renew their unity-in-action agreement in the spring of 1974. Meanwhile, workers were becoming aware that the French economy was not experiencing merely short-term "stagflation" problems and that under conditions of long-term crisis local strikes could not benefit them. The CGT and the CFDT, too, became less interested in organizing individual strikes; instead, they turned their attention to planning mass demonstrations against government policy. The *journées d'action* of October 7, 1976 and May 24, 1977 became the largest demonstrations against the government since the days of May 1968. By the mid-1970s, the immediate goals of the CGT were to provide the United Left with the strongest popular political support.

The defeat of the United Left in May 1978 brought to an end the partnership between the CGT and the CFDT.

1978 brought a drastic reversal in CFDT policy. The confederation's leadership recognized that its subordination of labor market activity to politics during 1974–78 had been a mistake. The new policy orientation emphasized collective bargaining without any demands for social change.

Negotiation with employers and with government officials was to take the place of "self-management rhetoric." This change in policy, described by the CFDT as *recentrage* ("recentering"), was essentially a return to the confederation's position in the early 1960s.

The political defeat of the Left brought a sharp division within the CGT leadership. Two factions disagreed on the strategy the trade unions should follow. The "proposition" faction argued that the CGT should react to the crisis by proposing to all Frenchmen new industrial solutions that would also facilitate the way for social transformation. The confederation was not to be concerned exclusively with wages and conditions of work; its leadership should be able to point out new ways of solving the economic crisis through action originating in the trade unions. The views of the "propositionists" were those of a new syndicalism.

The "oppositionists," on the other hand, remained loyal to the Marxist view that the Communist party should lead the workers in the political arena. They supported the party's argument that the crisis was due above all to the "industrial redeployment" policy of the government, a policy that was designed to benefit monopoly capitalism at the cost of the workers. After the elections of 1978, the Communists claimed that the Socialists had cooperated with the government's strategy. The "opposition" group urged the CGT to oppose the government's industrial policy and to cooperate with the Communist party. It was critical of the Socialists and of the CFDT for being "reformists" and "class collaborators."

These different views were clearly manifested during the metallurgical industry crises of 1978 and 1979. The large metallurgical enterprises Usinor and Sacilor, the French government, and the EEC's Davignon Plan contemplated the restructuring of the entire French metallurgical industry, a development that threatened to bring unemployment to about 50,000 workers. The workers protested through strikes that extended from the north and from Lorraine to Brest, Rennes, and other cities. On February 16, 1979, a general strike paralyzed the entire metallurgical industry. The CGT Metalworkers Federation countered the government's "redeployment plans" with a different plan; it purported to modernize the industry and to minimize job losses. This plan urged the government to invest in French steel and to invigorate its domestic consumption in order to maintain for the future the country's capacity to produce the steel it needed. This action was clearly "propositionist" in nature. The "opposition" forces, however, had their day on March 23, when they organized a "March on Paris" of more than 100,000 persons to protest the closing down of French metallurgical works.

A political Right-Center, adverse to labor, had dominated French political life for more than two decades. A sudden change took place on May

10, 1981, when the Socialist François Mitterand was elected president of the Fifth Republic. The 1981 elections gave the Socialist party an absolute majority in Parliament and it gave French labor a supportive government.

CONCLUSION

At the beginning of the 1980s, the French labor movement remained fragmented, not only in terms of a number of independent labor organizations, but also in terms of the policies these organizations advocated. The CGT remained closely tied to the French Communist party and to its policy. This party still clung to the Marxist concept that social transformation could only begin with the "seizure of power" by the political party of the proletariat. "Seizure of power" did not necessarily mean an act of violent revolution. For the Communists in the early 1980s, the term meant carrying out a wave of significant reforms, all of them designed to weaken the power of monopoly capital. For the CGT, therefore, labor market use of trade union activity was subordinated to its political use. The CGT also embraced the old Bolshevik idea that social change is essentially a political affair best left to politicians. The CGT leadership thus felt that it was not for the trade unions to try to achieve major economic reforms. The "proposition" group within the CGT took exception to this conclusion, but it appeared that, by the start of the 1980s, the "oppositionists" represented the majority of the CGT's leadership.

The CFDT and the Force Ouvrière decided, on the other hand, to limit their activities to strict labor market functions. Accepting the disunity of the French labor movement, both organizations seemed to believe that their apolitical stance would eventually strengthen them at the expense of the CGT.

The French labor movement faced the serious economic crises of the 1980s divided and with inconsistent goals. In this, it resembled the Spanish labor movement. Both in France and in Spain, labor organizations subordinated the achievement of obtainable, limited economic objectives to the pursuit of long-term political goals—a characteristic not found in either the German or the American labor movements.

NOTES

Bernstein, S. 1965. *The Beginnings of Marxian Socialism in France.* New York: Russell & Russell.

Bron, J. 1970. *Histoire du Mouvement Ouvrier Français.* Vols. II and III. Paris: Les Editions Ouvrières.

Lange, P., et al. 1982. *Unions, Change and Crisis: French and Italian Union Strategy and the Political Economy, 1945–1980.* London: Allen & Unwin.

L'Egalité. 1877. November 18.

Lefranc, G. 1984. *Le Syndicalisme en France.* Paris: Presses Universitaires de France.

Lorwin, V. R. 1954. *The French Labor Movement.* Cambridge, Mass.: Harvard University Press.

Moss, B. H. 1980. *The Origins of the French Labor Movement, 1830–1914.* Berkeley: University of California Press.

Saposs, D. J. 1931. *The Labor Movement in Post-War France.* New York: Columbia University Press.

Stearns, P. 1971. *Revolutionary Syndicalism and French Labor.* New Brunswick, N.J.: Rutgers University Press.

BIBLIOGRAPHY

Branciard, M. *Société française et luttes de classes.* Vols. II and III. Lyon, 1977.

Dolleans, E. *Histoire du mouvement ouvrier.* 2 vols. Paris, 1947–48.

Jouhaux, L. *Le Syndicalisme et la C.G.T.* Paris, 1920.

———*La C.G.T., ce qu'elle est, ce qu'elle veut.* Paris, 1937.

Lefranc, G. *Histoire du mouvement ouvrier en France des origines à nos jours.* Paris 1947.

Reberioux, M. Jaurès et la classe ouvrière. Paris, 1981.

Rosmer, A. *Le mouvement ouvrier pendant la guerre: de l'union sacrée à Zimmerwald.* Paris, 1936.

8

The American Labor Movement in the Light of European Thought

BRITISH, FRENCH, AND GERMAN INFLUENCES ON AMERICAN LABOR BEFORE THE CIVIL WAR

From its very beginning, and unlike the case in European countries, American society lacked a social stratification inherited from a feudal past; native Americans as well as immigrants did not cling to a tradition that induced them to accept the social class in which they were born. Class struggle, therefore, became more brutal in America than in Europe. The promise of socialism appeared to be great in the United States, where capitalism exhibited its most crass abuses; the social soil of America seemed well suited for the growth of a Socialist movement. In fact, socialism did not flourish in the United States.

Various reasons may be cited to explain the weakness of socialism in America. In the first place, some of the major objectives for which socialism fought in Europe, for example, universal suffrage and freedom of the press, quickly became part of American political democracy. It was also difficult for Socialist ideas to take strong roots in a society in which the working class was divided into hostile factions. Diversity in ethnic, linguistic, and religious background kept the American working class fragmented into distinct socioeconomic groups whose antipathies for each other retarded the development of a proletarian class consciousness. The native, white American worker drew a social line between himself and the recent immigrant and between himself and the native worker of a different color. The skilled, native, white American worker soon became part of a workers' "aristocracy" that did not identify with immigrants and with black or Hispanic workers.

The great majority of the immigrants to the United States came to escape poverty and debt at home. They generally belonged to the poorest social strata in their homelands and left behind them friends and relatives for the economic promise of the New World. For these people, the United States was the country of "unlimited opportunities" where economic, social, and geographic mobility remained free of any feudalistic class barriers. Even though many of these immigrants were to end their days in the ugly ghettos of the industrial cities of the East, they remained confident that the American politicoeconomic system would allow their children or grandchildren to "succeed" and to attain a higher material standard of living. This hope made them accept a system that often forced them into the misery of the sweatshops.

Socialism in the United States was further weakened by the eagerness of many immigrants to become independent landowners. The appeal of the frontier was still strong in pre–Civil War days. While Irish immigrants tended to remain in the eastern cities, where they formed a cheap industrial labor force, German immigrants remained in the factories only long enough to accumulate the financial resources needed to allow them to move westward in search of a farm.

During the first decades of the nineteenth century, the American economy was still largely agrarian and mercantile. The Northeast had developed an industrial sector based on the production of textiles, small firearms, furniture, tools, and small-scale metallurgy. The development of a capitalist system, and the economic booms of 1800–19 and 1824–37 induced the trade societies of the late eighteenth century, which until then had been essentially mutual aid societies, to become interested in the wages paid to and the conditions of work of their journeymen members.

In 1794, the shoemakers of Philadelphia organized the Federal Society of Journeymen Cordwainers, probably the first trade union in the United States, an organization that picketed the masters' shops in 1799, engaged in a strike, and survived for 12 years. Soon after, the printers and the cabinetmakers of the city of New York also established unions whose main efforts centered on the maintenance of wages and the attainment of a ten-hour workday.

With prices rising faster than wages, skilled workers in Albany, Baltimore, Boston, New York, Philadelphia, Pittsburgh, Washington, and elsewhere tried to protect their standard of living by forming local craft unions, organizations whose membership was small. These organizations were formed by cabinetmakers, carpenters, coopers, cordwainers, printers, shipwrights, tailors, and weavers. These early unions attempted to resist the employers' attempts to reduce their payroll by hiring cheap, poorly trained workers, such as immigrants, women, and children. Hence their effort to establish the closed-shop system. And, like modern trade unions, they strove to obtain higher wages, shorter hours to work, and better working conditions.

In 1827, an association of various unions was established in Philadelphia; the Mechanics' Union of Trade Associations was the first labor organization in the United States that united unions of different crafts into a citywide workers' association. The leaders of the Mechanics' Union embraced an early form of the labor theory of value and claimed that labor produced all value, labor being therefore superior to capital. They were concerned not only with the economic well-being of their members but also with their social status, and called for the nomination of candidates for political office who represented the interests of the workers.

As the economic gap separating the capitalists from the skilled workers expanded in the 1820s, the latter became more interested in ideas and proposals touching the distribution of wealth in a democratic society. This explains the growing interest in America for the ideas of the European utopian socialists, such as Owen, Fourier, and Cabet. Owen's vision of a communitarian life based on education, reason, and science was not acclaimed by many American workers, who felt that such life would promote atheism and immorality. After an initial period of expansion in the 1820s, the Owenist movement was weakened by a surge in trade union organization, which characterized the period 1828-37.

The years of depression from 1837 to 1845, the expansion of the factory system, and massive immigration slowed down trade union expansion in the first half of the 1840s. During those years, skilled workers and the liberal middle class again became interested in social reform. This period witnessed a renewal of religious and social interest, and much was discussed about the evils of slavery, the rights of women, and the need of public education for the poor. It was during these years of religious and intellectual ferment that Fourierism was introduced in the United States.

Albert Brisbane, a journalist and writer, published in 1840 *The Social Destiny of Man, or Association and Reorganization of Industry,* a book that contained translated excerpts from the writings of Fourier. Brisbane also obtained the cooperation of Horace Greeley, the editor in chief of the *New York Tribune,* in the dissemination of Fourier's ideas through that newspaper. These ideas were well received by the educated bourgeoisie of New England, who felt that they facilitated friendly relationships between capitalists and workers and permitted a more efficient organization of industry. Communitarian Christian groups gave their own religious interpretation to Fourier's ideas and supported more than 30 Fourierist communities in the United States.

Owenists and Fourierists condemned labor action directed at obtain-

ing immediate economic objectives and rejected strikes because they deep-
ened class antagonism. Instead, they offered workers "solutions" that
were to help them become independent of the wage system. They advocated agrarian reform and the creation of consumers' and producers'
cooperatives.

The high inflation of the 1830s and the invariable lag of wage increases behind price increases induced workers to form new trade societies. Blacksmiths, bricklayers, cigar makers, comb makers, hatters, lock-
smiths, piano makers, plumbers, and saddlers formed unions to resist the
efforts of employers to keep wages down in times of rising prices. Unskilled and semiskilled workers in the cotton factories and in metallurgy
became interested in forming their own unions. Women workers founded
their own organizations, such as the United Seamstresses Society in Baltimore and the Ladies Shoebinders in New York City (Dulles and
Dubofsky 1984, p. 54). In a number of cities, "trades' unions," that is,
associations of various trade unions in a given city, were formed to give
workers greater bargaining power in the pursuit of economic objectives.
Their formation largely reflected workers' disenchantment with the politically oriented workingmen's parties. A National Trades' Union was organized in 1834 to represent all of organized labor in the country. Its goals
were purely economic.

The depression that started in 1837 weakened organized labor much
more than the action of hostile employers' associations or courts. The failure of Fourierist "phalanxes" and of both consumers' and producers'
cooperatives showed that the social reformers of the time—men such as
Albert Brisbane, Horace Greeley, George Ripley, Wendell Phillips, William Lloyd Garrison, Charles A. Dana, and William H. Channing—were
unable to offer solutions to the problems of skilled and unskilled workers in the new industrial society.

The heavy German immigration of the early 1850s brought to the
United States the first German Socialists. At the time, German immigrants
constituted the second largest ethnic group within the American
proletariat. The Irish still represented the majority of the industrial workers in America. Of the 200,000 German immigrants who entered the
United States every year, many were skilled workers who found jobs in
small industries where employers were not strong enough to oppose the
formation of trade unions. Wherever Germans represented a majority of
the workers, labor soon organized. Many of these German immigrants
had been members of the League of the Just and had been influenced by
its leader, Wilhelm Weitling.

The most influential German Socialist in the United States in the
1850s was Wilhelm Weitling. He arrived for the first time in the United
States in 1847 and quickly contacted Brisbane and other American dis-

ciples of Fourier. He also organized a secret society in America, the League of Deliverance, or *Befreiungsbund*, a society that reached German communities in Texas. Weitling returned to Germany in 1848, but was back in the United States in the following year. Upon his return, he proceeded to establish "exchange banks," stores of raw materials and manufactured products. Workers were to deposit their products in these "banks" and were to receive from them whatever they needed that was of equal value, value being measured by the quantity of human labor embodied in the goods. This project received the support of American workers who founded a General Workingmen's League to implement Weitling's plan. The league helped in the creation of a Communist colony in Wisconsin, the "Communia."

A number of cooperative enterprises were started on the basis of Weitling's ideas in the New York City area in 1850. Weitling also founded the Central Committee of the United Trades, an organization representing a number of cooperative and exchange associations. All of these projects had failed by 1854, largely because they were unable to enroll a sufficient number of members and because they lacked sufficient capital.

The poor success of the cooperativist movement induced German labor leaders in the United States to embrace more radical ideas. By the mid-1850s, a number of German immigrants, mostly political refugees and intellectuals, tried to convince the trade union leadership to combine the pursuit of economic objectives with political action. This happened at a time when American trade unions, disappointed with the outcome of reformist ideas, sought above all to maximize the economic benefits of their own members.

Joseph Weydemeyer was one of the early German immigrants who tried to disseminate Marxist socialism in the United States. In order to combine the economic and political struggle of workers, he founded a revolutionary organization, the *Proletenbund*, and published two dailies, both of them titled *Revolution*. Both the organization and the newspapers had a very short-lived existence. Weydemeyer organized a general assembly of all German labor organizations in the United States, which met in New York City in 1853. This assembly founded a new labor organization, the *Allgemeiner Arbeiterbund*, renamed later the *Amerikanischer Arbeiterbund*; this organization welcomed into its ranks all workers without regard to ethnic or religious identity and grouped them in "clubs." The organization demanded the ten-hour workday, the abolition of child labor, and free education for all children. During 1853 it published a revolutionary newspaper, *Die Reform*.

By 1855, the number of German Socialists in the United States had diminished considerably. Weydemeyer had left New York City for Milwaukee. Many of his disciples joined the Republican party, established in 1854. The depression of 1857 ended most of the Socialist clubs.

In spite of some limited attempts to introduce Marxist doctrine in the United States, the Socialist movement in America before 1860 took essentially a utopian character. The communities that were founded on the basis of Owen's or Fourier's visions were part of an old tradition that had favored the development of religious communities in America since the earliest days of the nation. The masses of American workers showed little interest if any in these communities and in the ideas of their founders. The trade unions formed in the pre–Civil War period emphasized the pursuit of realizable, limited economic objectives, and their leaders in general remained indifferent to the teachings of Owen, Fourier, and Marx.

THE "SECOND INDUSTRIAL REVOLUTION," THE NATIONAL LABOR UNION, AND THE FIRST INTERNATIONAL IN THE UNITED STATES

The social and economic transformations that occurred in the United States after the Civil War were of such magnitude that many historians have referred to the 1865–95 period as a time of a "second Industrial Revolution." The outcome of the Civil War meant the triumph of industrial and financial capitalism in America. The war effort and the rapid expansion of the railway network after the war stimulated the growth of large-scale, nationwide industry. The new means of transportation opened the national market to any manufactured product and encouraged industrial firms to expand the scale of their operations.

Few trade unions had survived the economic crisis of 1857. The economy remained depressed until 1862, when currency inflation and military production started stimulating industry and changed the economic downturn into years of prosperity, 1863 and 1864, a prosperity that culminated in the boom year of 1865. With the return to conditions of full employment and with rapidly rising prices, labor activity revived. New local trade unions and city trades' assemblies were formed. Labor leaders embraced the idea that American labor should have a national organization, especially at a time when industry was acquiring nationwide scale. The masses of workers did not share the enthusiasm of their leaders for the idea. Skilled workers remained indifferent to it. Massive immigration and the increasing entry of women into the labor force hindered the formation of a proletarian strategy. Many European immigrants had received some political formation in their home countries, but British Chartists, Germans escaping Prussian conscription, the men of the Paris Commune, Russian nihilists, and Marxist Socialists did not share similar views.

The first National Labor Congress was organized in Baltimore in 1866 and was attended by 77 delegates representing local trade unions, trades' assemblies, and national unions. This congress established a National Labor Union that was to represent skilled and unskilled workers in America, as well as farmers. It purported to join trade unionists and social reformers in a political program whose goals were to reform society and abolish the wage system. It advocated the enactment of laws to establish the eight-hour workday in every state of the Union; it demanded the abolition of convict labor, the restriction of immigration, the sale of public lands only to actual settlers, and the creation of a U.S. Department of Labor. It became interested in currency and in banking reform in order to facilitate the availability of capital to consumers' and to producers' cooperatives. William H. Sylvis, a man very much devoted to the cause of American labor, became the president of the National Labor Union in 1868, but died suddenly one year later. His successor, Richard F. Trevellick, converted the National Labor Union into the National Labor Reform Party. This organization collapsed in 1872.

The history of the National Labor Union is not only interesting because it illustrates the ephemeral existence of a politically oriented labor organization in America but also because the union was linked to the development of Socialist thought in the United States after the Civil War. This development originated from two different sources. It was nourished by German immigrants who had been influenced by Ferdinand Lassalle. It was also promoted by the First International, founded in London in 1864. Until 1870, the International did not have sections in the United States. It attempted to influence the American working class through the National Labor Union. After 1870, the International established its own sections in most major American cities.

A German immigrant, Friedrich Sorge, had founded a Communist club in New York City in 1857. This club, which never developed a relationship with workers, declared itself to be a section of the International in 1867. In 1865, German workers in the United States, most of them disciples of Lassalle, founded a General German Workingmen's Union, which became the first official section of the International in America in 1869 (Droz 1979, p. 474). Many German members of the National Labor Union were also members of the International. The latter, already on the decline, joined the International in 1870 but never joined the International in common action.

By 1872, the International counted about 30 sections in the United States with a membership of about 5,000. There were sections in Chicago, Newark, New Orleans, New York, San Francisco, and Washington. In New York City the International had a French, a Czech, two American, and four German sections. Friedrich Sorge became the secretary of the

Central Committee of the International in the United States. Many trade unions, however, refused to join the International in America. Its expansion was also restricted by internal factionalism among Marxists and Lassalleans, German Socialists, and American radicals. American radicals had been influenced by Fourier and by Swedenborg, and instead of revolution, they supported cooperativism.

Sorge, realizing that the American working class had not yet developed a strong class feeling advised American workers to fight for the passage of laws that would allow the immediate implementation of limited social and economic reforms, such as the abolition of child labor in factories, the responsibility of employers for injuries suffered by workers in the course of their duties, the abolition of indirect taxes, and so on. Even such a nonrevolutionary program failed to attract the interest of most trade unions.

The First International held its last congress in Philadelphia in July 1876. Earlier, Lassallean workers in the United States had organized two Socialist parties. One was the eastern Social Democratic Party of North America and the other the Labor Party of Illinois, based in Chicago. A few days after the International held its last congress, a new workers' party was formed. This was the Workingmen's Party of the United States, whose membership included members of the expired International and those of the two Lassallean parties. This new party borrowed the principles of the International, but announced that it would only be a national organization whose goals were dictated by Lassalleans. The latter succeeded in quickly controlling this party, which, in 1877, changed its name to the Socialist Labor party, a party that was to be dominated by a new generation of German immigrants who tried to follow the strategy of German social democracy.

The founding of the Socialist Labor party coincided with a period of great labor turmoil in the United States. The depression and the rising unemployment of the 1870s induced jobless workers to demonstrate and to strike, often marked by violence and bloodshed. The despair of the workers was intensified by the indifference with which the authorities viewed the problems of those whose wages had been cut or those who had no employment at all. The conservative bourgeoisie reacted by claiming that the cause of labor unrest was the spread of Communist and anarchist thought in America. In fact, the battles between the miners and the "police" hired by the coal mine operators of eastern Pennsylvania in 1875 and the rioting by railroad workers in 1877 that resulted in the intervention of federal troops were generally spontaneous manifestations of protest against reduced wages, unemployment, and hunger and were not influenced by any political ideology.

The Socialist Labor party was weakened by internal division. Its

Marxist faction gave priority to the encouragement of trade unionism as a way of preparing the workers for the eventual revolutionary struggle. Its Lassalleans advocated direct political activity and gave little importance to the role of unions. A third group within the party was becoming interested in the anarchism preached by Johann Most, a German immigrant who had arrived in the United States in 1882. Most advocated acts of violence as "propaganda by the deed." He was instrumental in the organization of an assembly of revolutionary Socialists that met in Pittsburgh on October 14, 1883. Of the 26 attending delegates, 24 of them were German, and speeches were given in both German and English. The delegates founded an International Working People's Association and called for the establishment of a society based on cooperative production and the "free exchange of equivalent products by and between the productive organizations without commerce and profit mongering" (Taft 1964, p. 130).

This anarchist organization was largely based in Chicago; it published in that city German-language newspapers such as the *Arbeiter Zeitung*, the *Vorbote*, and the *Fackel*; it also published a newspaper in English, the *Alarm*. The radical workers in Chicago formed a small minority within the total labor force of that city, but they nevertheless established their Central Labor Union, a labor organization composed mostly of German trade unions.

THE HAYMARKET SQUARE TRIAL AND ITS REPERCUSSIONS ON THE KNIGHTS OF LABOR AND THE AMERICAN FEDERATION OF LABOR

In the new industrial economy that developed after the Civil War, the wage earner had to compete with an unlimited number of other workers for often scarce jobs and with a powerful corporate employer for the division of business profits. In this type of competition, the worker was at a disadvantage. As noted by Judge Rogers of the Rhode Island Supreme Court in 1892: "While corporations are the richest and strongest bodies, as a rule, in this state, their employees are often the weakest and the least able to protect themselves, frequently being dependent upon their current wage for their daily bread" (Kirkland 1951, p. 496).

Workers sought to strengthen their bargaining position by forming trade unions, but the depression of 1873 –77 caused most of these to disappear. The few that survived had no control over most of the industries of the new industrial state. In anthracite coal mining, trade unionism was identified by the employers with acts of terrorism attributed to a secret workers' organization, the Molly Maguires. In bituminous coal mining, the arrest of trade union leaders eradicated unionism from the industry. In the basic iron and steel industry, only the Sons of Vulcan, the puddlers' union, showed significant membership. The Amalgamated Association of Iron and Steel Workers, founded in 1876 by skilled workers, remained weak.

In December 1869, nine Philadelphia tailors organized the first local assembly of the Noble and Holy Order of the Knights of Labor. Their leader was a former Baptist minister, Uriah S. Stephens, a man dedicated to building a secret, international labor organization whose members' solidarity would be strengthened by a religious ritual.

The Knights adopted a platform and a constitution at Reading, Pennsylvania, in 1878. The platform called for equal pay for equal work for both sexes, the payment of wages in money once a week, the prohibition of work in factories, mines, and workshops by children under the age of 14, the substitution of arbitration for strikes, the reservation of public lands for actual settlers, and the development of consumers' and of producers' cooperatives. The platform did not embrace a Socialist program; it did not call for the overthrow of the existing economic system. The constitution provided for the establishment of local assemblies, district assemblies, and a general assembly; it created a General Executive Board and the office of General Master Workman.

The local assemblies of the Knights were generally constituted by a single craft, but there were locals representing an industrial plant, and in small cities, "mixed locals" represented a variety of trades. Many district assemblies were also practically made up by a single trade. The Knights welcomed to their ranks anyone who worked or had worked for wages; it accepted as members merchants and farmers, women, blacks, and foreigners, and skilled an unskilled workers. It did not accept physicians, lawyers, bankers, or liquor dealers.

In 1879, Stephens was succeeded as General Master Workman by Terence V. Powderly, an Irish machinist, a man who was opposed to the secret and ritualistic features of the order and who furthered the secularization of the organization. Under his leadership, and probably in spite of it, the Knights experienced a rapid expansion of their membership. By 1881, the Knights counted about 200,000 members; five years later, the organization had registered 702,924 members and had become the largest labor organization in American history (Kirkland 1951, p. 501).

It had become evident in the early 1880s that the political efforts of organized labor had ended in failure. The trade unions had appeared to many workers to be the best means to achieve economic improvement. The unions, however, had rejected the foreigner and the nonwhite and had achieved little for their members. The secret and fraternal Order of the Knights of Labor appealed in the late 1870s and in the early 1880s to thousands of workers. Many immigrant workers joined the Knights but were soon disappointed by Powderly's dislike of strikes and by his belief that the reduction of the length of the workday to eight hours should be secured through legislation and not through labor protest. Powderly's cautious and uncertain policies induced many foreign workers to listen to the voice of American anarchism.

Much to the regret of Powderly, the General Assembly of the Knights of Labor introduced in 1884 a new article in the preamble of the Knights' constitution; Article XXI, in effect, resolved "to shorten the hours of labor by a general refusal to work for more than eight hours (Ware 1929, p. 301). In October of the same year, the Federation of Organized Trades and Labor Unions, the future American Federation of Labor, passed a resolution to the effect that "eight hours shall constitute a legal day's work from and after May 1, 1886" (Ware 1929, p. 301). The federation called for an eight-hour strike on May 1, 1886, in order to obtain its demand. Various local assemblies of the Knights voted in favor of joining this strike, but on March 13 1886, Powderly issued a secret circular that warned the order against participating in strikes and in the May 1 demonstration. It read: "No assembly must strike for the eight-hour system on May lst under the impression they are obeying orders from headquarters, for such an order was not and will not be given (Ware 1929, p. 312).

The eight-hour strike of May 1 was a failure, except perhaps in Chicago, where 80,000 workers stopped working. The lumber shovelers at the McCormick Reaper plant in Chicago had struck on February 11 of that year to obtain reduced hours of work and highter wages. The strike appeared to be settled in April but resumed when the company insisted in retaining in its employ strikebreakers who had been used during the strike. On May 3, the workers of the McCormick plant held a meeting near the plant, and August Spies, the editor of the anarchist *Arbeiter Zeitung* and a member of the Central Labor Union, spoke to them. The meeting was peaceful at first, but toward its end, a fight developed between workers and strikebreakers. The police intervened and shots were fired at the workers; a number of these were killed and wounded.

Furious, Spies wrote a "Revenge Circular" in which he called for workers' armed resistance. Workers were called to meet at Haymarket Square in Chicago in the evening of May 4 to protest the shooting at the workers' gathering near the McCormick plant. Anticipating trouble, the authorities dispatched that evening a police detachment of 180 men that was positioned near the square. Spies addressed the crowd and introduced the next speaker, Albert Parsons, the editor of *Alarm*. Parsons was followed by Samuel Fielden, a member of the English-speaking anarchist group of Chicago. Most of the assembled workers then started leaving; at that time, a policeman, Captain William Ward, approached Fielden and ordered the rest of the crowd to disperse. Fielden protested, and as he spoke, someone threw a bomb into the group of policemen. One policeman was instantly killed, and six others died later from their wounds.

This act of violence led to a roundup of known anarchists by the police. Among those arrested and indicted for murder were Albert Parsons, August Spies, Adolph Fischer, Michael Schwab, Samuel Fielden, Oscar Neebe, George Engel, and Louis Lingg. These eight men were found guilty of murder, and Engel, Fischer, Parsons, and Spies were hanged on November 11, 1886. Lingg committed suicide in prison, and the state governor eventually spared the lives of Fielden and of Schwab. Organized labor, and particularly the Knights of Labor, went on record as rejecting any sympathy for the indicted anarchists; indeed, the Chicago organ of the Knights proclaimed: "Let it be understood by all the world that the Knights of Labor have no affiliation, association, sympathy or respect for the band of cowardly murderers, cut-throats and robbers, known as anarchists" (Dulles and Dubofsky 1984, p. 119).

Conservatives outside the labor movement, however, blamed the Knights for the Haymarket Square bombing and preached that organized labor was influenced by anarchism and tainted by violence. The labor movement lost popularity throughout the nation; the Haymarket Square trial was followed by antilabor legislation enacted in most states and by the private and public harassment of labor leaders. Some historians have referred to the period 1887–93 as a time when the American labor movement was "liquidated." In fact, many of the local assemblies of the Knights disappeared during these years and by 1893 the membership of the Noble and Holy Order had fallen to 75,000 (Dulles and Dubofsky 1984, p. 139). In that year, James R. Sovereign replaced Powderly as Grand Master Workman and dedicated himself primarily to reform politics. His efforts only precipitated the fall in the numbers of the Knights. Noneconomic action had brought failure to both the Anarchists and the Knights in the United States.

In 1892, the Amalgamated Association of Iron and Steel Workers was dissolved by court order, a result of a battle between striking steelworkers and Pinkerton detectives at the Carnegie Homestead Works, near Pittsburgh. Two years later, President Grover Cleveland sent federal troops to Chicago to oppose striking railroad workers, and the American Railway Union of Eugene V. Debs was broken up. By the mid-1890s, the American labor movement was no stronger than it had been in the 1870s. The power of the large corporations, however, was stronger than ever before.

The might of corporate management over labor was backed by the attorney general of the United States and by the courts; both embraced the view that the first article of the Sherman Antitrust Act prohibited trade union activity. Judges even barred threatened trade union activity by means of writs of injunction, issued on the theory that courts had the duty to prevent possible damage to property rights. Violators of an injunction prohibiting a strike were prosecuted, not for the perpetration of a crime, but for being in contempt of court. By the mid-1890s, the employers' strong belief that they could dictate terms of employment to workers was well illustrated by this remark of Jay Gould: "I can hire one half of the working class to kill the other half" (Kirkland 1951, p. 507).

The rise of the giant corporation, the emergence of the "pool" and the "trust," and the appearance on the economic stage of the unscrupulous and greedy "captain of industry" multiplied the foes of trade unions. The leaders of the new corporate empires regarded labor as simply another factor of production and were determined to prevent trade unions from gaining any influence in their business "estates."

The Knights of Labor also became an opponent of the trade unions. The leadership of the Knights and that of the trade unions followed opposing policies and held inconsistent views over what action should be pursued by workers. The local assemblies of the Knights often ignored wage scales on which trade unions relied, and members of the assemblies agreed to work for lower wages than those demanded by the trade unions. The willingness of the Knights to form local assemblies composed by former trade union dissidents and by nonunion workers embittered trade union leaders. Mark L. Crawford, president of the International Typographical Union, complained in 1884 that assemblies of the Knights "admit as members men who have not served sufficient apprenticeship, as well as men who have "ratted" in our own organization..." (Taft 1964, p. 108).

Trade union leaders were also more supportive of the strike than the Knights leadership. Peter J. McGuire of the Carpenters' Union, testifying before a Senate committee in 1883, declared:

> No strike is a loss or a failure to the workers, even if the point sought is not gained for the time being. If naught else, they at least teach the capitalists that they are expensive luxuries to be indulged in. Consequently, we find it proven by facts that in trades where strikes have been most prevalent in the past, the employers are now more ready to listen to the demands of their employees. Very few employers who have passed through the agonies of one or two strikes ever care to enter into any further struggle, and this is a warning to employers generally....
> (Taft 1964, p. 110)

In the early 1880s, many trade union leaders had given up their faith in cooperative action; they also opposed political activity and considered only the attainment of immediate, limited objectives by means of economic pressure tactics. The testimony of Adolph Strasser of the Cigar Makers Union, presented to a Senate committee in 1883, best illustrates the philosophy of the trade union leadership:

> *Chairman*: I was only asking you in regard to your ultimate ends.
>
> *Witness* [Strasser]: We have no ultimate ends. We are going on from day to day. We are fighting only for immediate objects—objects that can be realized in a few years.
>
> *Mr. Call*: You want something better to eat and to wear, and better houses to live in?
>
> *Witness*: Yes, we want to dress better and to live better, and become better citizens generally.
>
> *Chairman*: I see you are a little sensitive lest it be thought that you are a mere theorizer. I do not look upon you in that light at all.
>
> *Witness*: Well, we say in our constitution that we are opposed to theorists, and I have to represent the organization here. We are all practical men. (Kirkland 1951, pp. 507, 508)

Trade union leaders such as Peter J. McGuire, Adolph Strasser, Ferdinand Laurrell, and Samuel Gompers remained interested in the eventual transformation of their society and they did not reject basic Socialist ideology. As "practical men" however, they centered their efforts on obtaining immediate economic benefits for union members and left for an undeterminate future the radical transformation of the existing society.

Representatives of the Knights of Labor and of the trade unions met in Pittsburgh in 1881 in an effort to cooperate. The outcome of this conference was the establishment of the Federation of Organized Trades and Labor Unions. Disagreements between the leaders of the Knights of Labor and those of the trade unions limited the activity of this federation and condemned it to a short existence. Its major decision was to promote the idea of an eight-hour strike on May 1, 1886.

In December 1886, representatives of a number of national trade unions and those of the nearly extinct federation met in Columbus, Ohio, with the purpose of founding a new labor organization that would work exclusively to promote the economic interests of the craft unions it represented. The American Federation of Labor, with Samuel Gompers as its first president, was thus founded on December 8, 1886. Among the national unions participating in this organization were the Brotherhood of Carpenters and Joiners, the Cigar Makers, the Granite Cutters, the Furniture Workers, the Iron Molders, the Journeymen Bakers, the Journeymen Tailors, the Metalworkers, the Miners and Mine Laborers, and the Typographers. The railway brotherhoods did not affiliate. As of 1886, the American Federation of Labor had a membership of about 150,000; by

1892, the number had risen to 250,000 (Dulles and Dubofsy 1984, pp. 152, 154).

The Haymarket Square trials had succeeded in spreading fear of radicalism, not only among the middle class, but also among the members of the trade unions. It was not by sheer historical coincidence that the American Federation of Labor was founded in the same year the Chicago anarchists Engel, Fischer, Parsons, and Spies were hanged. The American Federation of Labor went immediately on record as rejecting all political action, as accepting the capitalist system, and as pursuing only limited economic objectives. The weakness of the radical voice in 1886 is best shown by the creation and the rapid disappearance of the United Labor party, a party organized by radicals, reformers, and Socialists who campaigned in favor of the election of Henry George, a radical economist, as mayor of New York City. George was not elected, and the United Labor party promptly vanished from the political arena.

As mentioned above, a national convention of all Socialist groups in the country, groups mostly formed by German-Americans upholding radical or Socialist ideologies, had met in Philadelphia in July 1876. Among the delegates to this convention were Peter J. McGuire and Adolph Strasser, the future architects of the American Federation of Labor, as well as Otto Wedemeyer and Friedrich Sorge. This convention established a Workingmen's party of the United States, renamed the Socialist Labor party (SLP) in the following year.

After the founding of the American Federation of Labor, the Socialist Labor party attempted to infiltrate its leadership. When this strategy failed, the SLP leader, Daniel De Leon, an immigrant from the island of Curaçao, tried to develop a labor organization to compete with the American Federation of Labor. The Socialist Trade and Labor Alliance was founded in December 1895 on the basis of about 15,000 members. The goal of the alliance was to organize Socialist trade unions. What it achieved in fact was a widening ideological gap between Socialists and trade unionists.

SOCIALIST THOUGHT AT THE TURN OF THE CENTURY AND WORKERS' OPPOSITION TO THE AMERICAN FEDERATION OF LABOR

It was not through the efforts of De Leon that millions of Americans became acquainted with Socialist ideas at the end of the century. Anticapitalist ideology was propagated by the Protestant Social Gospel movement in the years 1880 to 1890; its evangelists were influenced by the British Christian Socialists, the Fabians, and the social critique of John

Ruskin. In fact, these preachers were only nominal Socialists; they rejected all attacks on individualism, they did not believe in class conflict, and they distrusted any concentration of power. Indigenous anticapitalist thought was also advocated by a rural grass-roots socialism that represented a mixture of populism, utopian socialism, and Marxism; its most distinguished representative was J. A. Wayland, who denounced the evils of capitalism, coalitions of businessmen and politicians, and the corrupt officials of the American Federation of Labor in his weekly *The Appeal to Reason*. Finally, Edward Bellamy's novel *Looking Backward* presented to its readers the picture of an ideal American society in which all production and distribution had come under the control of the state.

Former leaders of the American Railway Union formed in Chicago in 1897 a group named Social Democracy whose goals were to found cooperative communities in the American West, to campaign for the nationalization of certain industries and a shorter workday, and to obtain the enactment of laws by means of the referendum. This group attracted many dissident members of the Socialist Labor party, who, after joining Social Democracy, started opposing the founding of cooperative communities in the West. Unable to form a majority within Social Democracy, the opponents to colonization plans formed in 1898 the Social Democratic party, which called itself a "revolutionary class organization."

The Social Democratic party disappeared in 1901, when a reorganization of all Socialist groups in America led to the creation of the Socialist Party of America. The new Socialist party was to be a nationwide party, although until 1916 the major strength of the party was found in states west of the Mississippi, mostly states where miners, lumbermen, and small farmers constituted a large part of the labor force. By 1914, the states with the largest Socialist groups were Oklahoma, Nevada, Montana, Washington, California, Idaho, Wisconsin, and Texas. The mass of party members was made up by small farmers living west of the Mississippi. In the cities, Socialists were mostly skilled workers, immigrants, and intellectuals. The percentage of foreigners in the party rose steadily. In 1912, foreigners represented one-sixth of the party's membership of 118,000; in 1917, they represented 32,894 members out of a total membership of 80,126 (Droz 1979, p. 493).

The party itself tolerated different views. It did not publish an organ representing the official party line. During the first decade of the twentieth century, the party factionalized into various groups. The conservative wing of the party was best represented by Victor Berger, a German immigrant who had been a printer, a teacher, and a journalist, a man who felt that socialism had to deal with the concrete problems of American workers and who believed that the party should make every effort to gain the adherence of the American Federation of Labor. A more centrist position was taken by Morris Hillquit, a Russian immigrant who stood for orthodox Marxist ideology. The radical wing was led by such men as Eugene V. Debs and William "Big Bill" Haywood. Debs represented the amalgamation of radical ideologies that opposed capitalism. Haywood, an official of the Western Federation of Miners, was interested in organizing unskilled workers.

The control of the Socialist Party of America remained in the hands of the rightist and of the centrist elements in the party. In spite of this, most American trade unions remained opposed to socialism. The ideology of the majority of American organized labor was procapitalist, and most American labor leaders continued to advocate class cooperation.

Some of the leaders of the Socialist Party of America proposed that Socialists should infiltrate the leadership of the American Federation of Labor and influence its policies from within. Others proposed the creation of a Socialist labor federation. A third group felt that American workers needed a new type of labor federation. During the summer of 1904, Debs, Haywood, and De Leon argued that a labor federation based on industrial trade unions would be more effective in achieving a transformation of society than the American Federation of Labor. In the United States, the voice demanding industrial trade unionism came from the West.

Western miners were accustomed to settle differences with the mine owners by acts of violence and had no great sympathy for the conservative and cautious ways of eastern labor leaders. Delegates of a number of unions of metalliferous miners met in Butte, Montana, on May 15, 1893 and founded the Western Federation of Miners. This federation affiliated with the American Federation of Labor in 1896, but its delegates became disappointed with the AF of L leadership at the Cincinnati convention of the AF of L in the same year. The leaders of the Western Federation of Miners then developed a plan to organize all western workers in a new labor federation. This plan was approved at a congress held in Salt Lake City on May 10, 1898, and a Western Labor Union was founded to implement the plan. This organization changed its name to the American Labor Union in 1902 in order to become a more effective opponent of the AF of L. Like De Leon's Socialist Trade and Labor Alliance, the American Labor Union never became sufficiently powerful to challenge seriously the hegemony of the AF of L. "Dual unionism" had failed to weaken the federation's policy of apolitical, conservative trade unionism.

Six persons met in Chicago in the autumn of 1904 to study the possible formation of a new labor federation. These men had been active in both labor and Socialist groups in America. They were William E. Trautman, editor of the Brauer Zeitung, official organ of the United Brewery Workmen; George Estes, president of the United Brotherhood of Railway

Employees, and W. L. Hall, its secretary; Isaac Cowan, representative of the Amalgamated Society of Engineers; Clarence Smith, general secretary of the American Labor Union; and Thomas J. Haggerty, editor of the *Voice of Labor*, the official organ of the American Labor Union. Eugene V. Debs, a long-time supporter of industrial unionism, and Charles 0. Sherman, secretary of the United Metal Workers, although involved in the discussions, were unable to attend.

The six men sent out invitations to a larger group to meet in Chicago on January 2, 1905, in order to organize a new labor federation, "builded as the structure of a socialist society, embracing within itself the working class in approximately the same groups and departments and industries that the workers would assume in the working class administration of the Co-operative Commonwealth" (Taft 1964, p. 289). Twenty persons attended the secret meeting on January 2. They issued a manifesto and prepared plans for the establishment of a new labor federation. The manifesto called for a labor movement consisting "of one great industrial union embracing all industries, providing for craft autonomy locally, industrial autonomy internationally and working class unity generally" (Taft 1964, p. 290).

The first industrial union congress met in Chicago on June 27, 1905. The most important labor union represented at this congress was the Western Federation of Miners. The congress represented 43 labor organizations and its delegates represented about 50,000 workers. The leading figures of this congress were William D. Haywood, Eugene V. Debs, Daniel De Leon, and Thomas J. Haggerty. Haggerty was the principal author of the constitution of the Industrial Workers of the World (IWW), a new federation that organized workers into industries and industries into departments. The preamble to the constitution supported both political and industrial workers' action and declared that "the working class and the employing class have nothing in common." Charles 0. Sherman was elected president of the IWW and W. E. Trautman became its secretary-treasurer.

Factionalism soon divided the IWW leadership. At the organization's 1908 convention, reformist supporters of Sherman clashed with the advocates of "direct action," followers of Trautman and of a metal miner, Vincent St. John. St. John obtained the presidency, having been backed by IWW members who were mostly migrant workers employed in the mining, lumber, and sea-products industries. The factional strife led to the withdrawal of the Western Federation of Miners from the IWW. De Leon and his followers also withdrew, claiming that the IWW had fallen into the hands of anarchists. De Leon then formed a Detroit IWW, which, in 1915, changed its name to the Workers' International Industrial Union, an organization of minor importance.

The IWW represented the unskilled workers in a number of strikes, the most spectacular of which was that of the textile workers at Lawrence, Massachusetts, in 1912. On that occasion, although thousands of workers were involved in the strike, no permanent local IWW organization had been established when the strike ended. IWW leaders were indeed more interested in engaging in "propaganda by the deed" activity than in organizing trade unions. James P. Thompson, a founding IWW member, regarded the strike as "one big propaganda meeting" (Taft 1964, p. 294).

As of 1914, a major effort was made to organize migratory harvest workers in the grain belt of the Middle West. Autonomous IWW industrial locals were also successful in enrolling large numbers of unskilled and semiskilled industrial workers. It appeared that by 1916 the IWW had become a major labor federation that attracted the unskilled workers, the migratory and seasonal laborers, and the exploited foreigners.

On the eve of America's entry into World War I, the American Federation of Labor proclaimed its loyalty to the Wilson administration and to its war program. A patriotic Samuel Gompers pledged the support of his unions to the government and demanded government help in the implementation of the AF of L's programs. Following the country's entry into the war, the federal government in effect decided that in all of its contracts, the standards set by the AF of L would be enforced. Gompers became a member of the Advisory Committee of the National Council of Defense.

Government's courting of the American Federation of Labor was not duplicated in the case of the IWW. The pacifism and the anarchosyndicalist views of many IWW leaders irritated government officials and increased the adverse feelings of the masses for the labor organization. Rising prices without corresponding wage increases brought a large wave of strikes in 1917, many of them organized by the IWW. Employers found no great difficulty in convincing the public that the "Wobblies" were unpatriotic. While Gompers continued to support the government's war effort and to denounce all pacifist groups, court prosecutions and lynchings forced the IWW to fade from the American labor stage.

EMPLOYERS' ATTACKS ON ORGANIZED LABOR IN THE 1920s

A large wave of strikes broke out in 1919 in response to continuing wartime price increases and to the employers' withdrawals of concessions they had extended to workers during the years of war. Angered by the refusal of their employers to negotiate with trade union officials, more than 4 million workers participated in more than 3,500 strikes in 1919 (Dulles and Dubofsky 1984, p. 221). When steelworkers went out on strike because of the refusal of the chairman of United States Steel Corporation, Elbert Gary, to bargain with a committee representing 24 unions, local and state police were used to break up strike meetings. The steelworkers lost their strike. The federal government remained silent while the steel companies tried to convince the American public through an advertisement barrage that the strike was a Soviet plot and that Americans would "never stand for the 'red' rule of Bolshevism, I.W.W. ism or any other 'ism' that seeks to tear down the Constitution" (Dulles and Dubofsky 1984, p. 226). In the same year, an effort of the United Mine Workers to obtain wage increases was stopped by a court injunction secured by the federal government.

The inflationary postwar boom turned into a major depression in 1920. Prices fell drastically, and thousands of business failures brought unemployment to 5 million workers by mid-1921. The number of wage earners in manufacturing fell by almost one-fourth between 1919 and 1921—and this at a time of no government unemployment insurance. Employers took advantage of the depression and tried to crush trade union activity; and their offensive against organized labor was supported by the courts.

In 1917, the U.S. Supreme Court had upheld in *Hitchman Coal and Coke Company* v. *Mitchell* the legality of the so-called "yellow-dog contract." The contract between Hitchman and its workers provided that the latter would not join a labor organization during their period of employment. When the United Mine Workers tried to organize these workers, the company sought to stop the union's organizing efforts through a court-issued injunction. Ignoring the fact that workers had signed the yellow-dog contract under duress, the Supreme Court held that "the inducing of employees to unite with the union in an effort to subvert the system of employment at the mine by concerted breaches of the contracts of employment known to be in force . . . (was an) unlawful and malicious method. . ." (Taft 1964, p. 362). This decision allowed employers to use the yellow-dog contract as a means to hinder the unions in their organization efforts.

In *Duplex* v. *Deering* and in *Truax* v. *Corrigan* the Supreme Court upheld in 1921 the powers of federal and state courts to restrict union activity under the theory that the courts could do so to prevent irreparable injury to a property right. In *Truax* v. *Corrigan* the Supreme Court held that a state could not prohibit the issuance of injunctions in labor disputes because such prohibition could amount to a denial of protection of property by the state.

A First Industrial Conference had been organized by President

Woodrow Wilson for the furthering of industrial peace. The conference was to be attended by representatives of labor, management, farmers, and the public in general. The conference opened its meetings on October 6, 1919 with Elbert Gary and John D. Rockefeller, Jr., acting as representatives of the public. Gary strongly supported the "Open Shop American Plan" and held that, in the case of the steel strike, organized labor had no right to negotiate on behalf of the steelworkers. When employers refused to recognize the right of workers to bargain collectively through union officials of their choice, the labor delegates withdrew and the conference ended.

The employers' offensive against organized labor continued. A conference of state manufacturers' associations, meeting in Chicago on January 21, 1921, recommended that industrialists should not negotiate with unions. A. M. Glossbrenner of the Indiana Manufacturers Association claimed that "we will not employ an individual in any part of the plant that does not sign an individual contract in which it is expressed that he is not and will not become a member of a labor organization while in our employ" (Taft 964, p. 364). Employers advocated the "American Plan of Employment," also called the "Open-Shop Plan," which in effect asserted that they were "masters in their own house" and under no duty to negotiate with union officials about terms of employment. The employers' open-shop campaign was indeed an effort on their part to annul the gains obtained by organized labor during the years of World War I. Their strategy proved to be effective. Organized labor, which in 1920 still counted 5 million members, had only 3.5 million three years later (Dulles and Dubofsky 1984, p. 232).

More effective than the open-shop campaign, the yellow-dog contracts, and the writs of injunction in checking the expansion of the labor movement was the employers' resort to "welfare capitalism." In the prosperous 1920s, employers tried to dissuade workers from joining a union by providing them with favorable conditions of work. Firms established group insurance policies for their employees whose benefits were forfeited by any employee leaving his or her job. By 1926, about 5 million industrial workers were covered by such insurance programs. Employers also provided employees with free health clinics, old age pension programs, profit-sharing schemes, bonuses in the form of shares of company stock, and various forms of recreational facilities. The corporations that offered the most generous workers' welfare programs were also the ones that opposed most vigorously the trade unions. They were also the ones that established the employer-dominated company unions, which, in 1926, had a membership of about 1.4 million workers.

Both company unions and workers' welfare programs were under exclusive employer control. Employers were willing to maintain the welfare schemes as long as business was good; these programs promptly disappeared after the stock market crash of 1929. By that time, trade union membership in the country amounted to only 3.4 million workers, less than the membership in any previous year since 1917 (Dulles and Dubofsky 1984, p. 236).

The presidential campaign of 1924 induced the American Federation of Labor to depart temporarily from its traditional noninvolvement in politics and to support a third party in the elections. Following the electoral defeat of that party, the American Federation of Labor promptly abandoned the idea of supporting an independent labor party and reverted to nonpolitical action.

Representatives of farm, labor, and various liberal groups had formed in 1922 a Conference for Progressive Political Action. This organization protested the influence private monopolies had on government and on the entire economy. Socialists and representatives of farmer-labor groups in the conference favored the formation of an independent labor party. Leaders of the large trade unions opposed the establishment of such a party. The majority in the organization decided, however, to form a new political party that would participate in the presidential elections. This decision revealed the disenchantment of most workers with President Calvin Coolidge, the Republican presidential candidate, and with John W. Davis, a corporation lawyer, the Democrats' candidate. The conference entered the presidential campaign with Senator Robert M. La Follette as its candidate for president, and with Burton K. Wheeler, a progressive Democrat, as its candidate for vice-president. Its platform called for a fight against monopoly, for the enactment of excess profit taxes and of progressive taxes, for the lowering of the tariff, and for the abolition of the injunction in labor disputes.

The executive committee of the American Federation of Labor, feeling that neither major political party was supportive of organized labor, decided to enter politics and support the La Follette-Wheeler candidacies. This decision, which was opposed by William Green of the Mine Workers, was later found unwise by the American Federation of Labor leadership, and the federation promptly returned to its earlier nonpolitical course of action. At a time of intense hostility to organized labor as manifested by industrialists, corporation lawyers, government officials, and judges, labor leaders offered to cooperate with the capitalist magnates and tried to obtain their toleration by convincing them that the unions could offer labor discipline, greater efficiency in production, and more business stability. Most of the leaders of the American Federation of Labor remained indifferent to the fate of unskilled labor and uninterested in organizing along industrial lines.

The mass unemployment that followed the stock market crash of

1929 ousted the Republicans and brought in the New Deal administration. The Democrats opened up a new chapter in the history of the American labor movement.

THE GREAT DEPRESSION, GOVERNMENT, AND LABOR

The stock market crash of October 1929 initiated a fall in business activity and in employment that the country had never experienced before. Gross national product fell from $104 billion just before the events of October 1929 to $56 billion in 1933. Neither government nor the labor movement were prepared to cope with rapidly rising unemployment. The American Federation of Labor advocated a reduction of the work week and the creation of new public works, although most of its leaders opposed the establishment of government unemployment insurance. On March 23, 1932, President Herbert Hoover signed the Anti-Injunction Act, better known as the Norris-La Guardia Act, which regulated the issuance of injunction writs by federal courts in labor disputes. The law limited the use of injunctions by such courts, prohibited their use against certain labor activities, and granted a jury trial to defendants in contempt cases committed outside the courtroom. It gave organized labor a great victory by declaring that the yellow-dog contract was contrary to public policy and therefore unenforceable in the courts.

The first Franklin D. Roosevelt administration gave organized labor even greater advantages. The main goal of the National Industrial Recovery Act, as it was finally passed by Congress in June 1933, was to boost employment. Section 7(a) of the act gave workers the right to organize and to bargain collectively through representatives of their own choice and required that "no employee and no one seeking employment shall be required as a condition of employment to join any company union or to refrain from joining a labor organization of his own choosing." The act also provided for a federally financed program of public works and allowed industries to set up "fair competition" codes that would be exempt from the application of the federal antitrust laws. Every code had to include a statement recognizing the right of employees to bargain collectively through representatives of their own choice and to be free of employers' influence in the selection of such representatives. The codes were also to state that employers would comply with maximum hours of work, minimum wages, and other conditions of work as prescribed by the president of the United States.

The first industrywide code, the Cotton Textile Code, was approved by the administrator of the National Industrial Recovery Act on July 9, 1933. This official was to approve 557 other codes before the act was declared unconstitutional by the Supreme Court in May 1935. Under most codes, labor boards constituted by the administrator and by representatives of the employers and of the workers were set up to enforce the provisions of the particular code.

The enactment of the National Industrial Recovery Act launched a major organizational campaign by labor. Between June and October 1933 the American Federation of Labor gained some 800,000 new members. Employers did not remain idle. They gave new vitality to nearly extinct company unions and created new ones. In some industries, employers persisted in refusing to negotiate with representatives of their employees who were "outsiders." Disputes between employees and managers increased. In order to facilitate the mediation and the conciliation of such disputes, President Roosevelt established a National Labor Board on August 5, 1933, an agency headed by Senator Robert Wagner, who was assisted by six additional members, three representing labor and three representing management.

In its holding in the case of *A. I. Schlechter Poultry Corporation* v. *United States*, the Supreme Court found that the National Industrial Recovery Act was repugnant to the Constitution of the United States. This holding struck down the first federal law that gave labor the right to organize.

Section 7(a) of the National Industrial Recovery Act had granted labor the right to organize and to bargain collectively through freely chosen representatives with the employer. The section was mute, however, regarding the enforcement of its provisions. In many instances, employers continued to refuse to recognize union officials as representatives of their employees. This state of affairs was noted by Senator Wagner, who recognized that there were "some large employers who ignore public sentiment, who flaunt the clear intent of Congress and who are a law unto themselves" (Taft 1964, p. 451).

On February 29, 1934, Senator Wagner introduced a Labor Disputes Bill that required employers to engage in collective bargaining and barred employers from giving recognition to company unions. While this bill was pending in the Senate, Senator Joseph Robinson and Congressman Joseph Byrnes introduced Public Resolution 44, which was quickly accepted by Congress. Public Resolution 44 gave the president of the United States the power to establish boards to ascertain facts pertaining to disputes involving Section 7(a). These boards were authorized to conduct elections to determine the proper employees' bargaining representative, but they could not issue cease and desist orders; they could, however, refer cases involving violations of Section 7(a) to the Department of Justice.

In order to provide organized labor with more protective legislation, Senator Wagner introduced, on February 21, 1935, a National Labor Relations Bill that purported to vest in a permanent agency the power to enforce the provisions of Section 7(a) of the National Industrial Recovery Act. This bill, which on July 27 became the National Labor Relations Act more commonly known as the Wagner Act, not only recognized the right of workers to organize into unions of their own and to bargain with employers through representatives of their own choosing but also declared that it was the official policy of the United States to encourage both practices. The act took an unprecedented position; it listed unfair labor practices on the part of the employer. Employers were barred from directing, influencing, or interfering with labor organizations; they were not allowed to discriminate against union members in hiring, firing, or regarding conditions of employment; they were also compelled to bargain with the representatives of their employees. A National Labor Relations Board of three members was to supervise workers' elections and to determine in case of dispute the appropriate bargaining unit representing the employees; it was to hear complaints alleging violations of the terms of the act.

Employers and judges doubted at first the constitutionality of the act, and federal district courts went as far as issuing injunctions prohibiting hearings and other activities conducted by the board. The Supreme Court, in a split decision in *National Labor Relations Board* v. *Jones and Laughlin Steel Corporation*, upheld the constitutionality of the act in 1937. Once the constitutionality of the act was established, the National Labor Relations Board made a major effort to enforce the provisions of the Wagner Act. Between 1935 and 1945, the board heard 36,000 cases involving charges of unfair labor practices. It condemned not only the employers' use of yellow-dog contracts and the blacklisting of employees who were union members, it also prohibited employers from engaging in antiunion propaganda and ordered the dissolution of company unions; it barred employers from interfering with peaceful picketing by employees, and upheld the union-shop and closed-shop hiring practices.

The New Deal helped labor with other legislative enactments. One of them was the Social Security Act of 1935 with its provisions for unemployment insurance, old age benefits, and aid for the needy. Another major law passed under the Roosevelt administration was the Fair Labor Standards Act of June 1938, which established a minimum legal wage and decreed a work week of 40 hours effective in June 1941. Judicial views also became more favorable to organized labor in the 1930s. In *Thornhill* v. *Alabama*, the Supreme Court held that peaceful picketing was a legitimate form of free speech and was therefore protected as such by the Constitution of the United States.

The New Deal labor legislation spurred the organization of labor in the country. By 1941, 10.5 million people were union members. In the mid-1930s, many of the American Federation of Labor leaders remained as insensitive to the changing labor scene as the Knights of Labor had been in the early 1880s. It is to be noted that the large strikes of 1934, those of the longshoremen on the Pacific Coast and those of the cotton textile workers in the eastern states, were led by non–AF of L radicals. Too many American Federation of Labor leaders remained uninterested in organizing unions on other than a pure craft basis. Their apprehension that a large number of new unions, possibly industrial unions, resulting from the organization of workers in the mass-production industries, could successfully challenge their leadership was to divide the American labor movement into two large federations for 20 years. Neither the traditionalists within the American Federation of Labor nor the challengers of the Committee for Industrial Organization showed any interest in political reform or in political revolution.

The American Federation of the Labor tried to organize the mass-production industries by issuing charters to "federal unions," which were to represent, at least temporarily, workers in such industries. The understanding was that craftsmen in such industries would in time be transferred to pertinent craft unions. Most of the federation's leaders still supported the principle of "exclusive jurisdiction," the idea that only one union could be authorized to recruit workers in a given craft. An exception to the generally followed principle was made in 1901 when the United Mine Workers of America was authorized to organize all workers in and around the coal mines. As of 1903, resolutions favoring the establishment of industrial unions were introduced at the federation's conventions. The federation responded by creating "federal unions," but the latter came under bitter attack by the leaders of the craft unions. At the federation's convention in Atlantic City in 1935, a minority report was introduced that favored the creation of industrial unions. A majority of the delegates voted against this report. The men who signed the minority report were John L. Lewis, David Dubinsky, Charles P. Howard, A. A. Myrup, Frank B. Powers, and J. C. Lewis.

THE FORMATION OF THE CONGRESS OF INDUSTRIAL ORGANIZATIONS

Representatives of eight unions met at the headquarters of the United Mine Workers of America in Washington, D.C., just a few weeks after the convention in Atlantic City in order to organize a Committee for Industrial Organization. The unions represented in Washington were the United Mine Workers of America, the International Typographical Union, the Amalgamated Clothing Workers of America, the International

Ladies' Garment Workers' Union, the United Textile Workers of America, the Oil Field, Gas Well and Refinery Workers of America, the United Hatters, Cap and Millinery Workers' International Union, and the International Union of Mine, Mill and Smelter Workers (Taft 1964, pp. 471, 472). John L. Lewis of the United Mine Workers of America was elected temporary chairman, and Charles P. Howard of the International Typographical Union was elected temporary secretary.

The Committee for Industrial Organization (CIO) established as its aim the "encouragement and promotion of organization of the unorganized workers in mass production and other industries upon an industrial basis..." (Taft 1964, p. 472). The founders of the CIO claimed that they wanted to remain loyal to the American Federation of Labor and that their endeavor should cause no alarm to the federation's leadership. President Green of the AF of L, however, voiced his fear that the establishment of the CIO would lead to a division of the labor movement. One of his associates echoed the feelings of many AF of L leaders about the men in the CIO when he described them as "a gang of sluggers, communists, radicals and soap box artists, professional bums, expelled members of labor unions, outright scabs" (Kirkland 1951, p. 616).

The American Federation of Labor convention in Tampa, Florida, in November 1936, approved the suspension of unions that belonged to the CIO; these unions were later expelled. Financial help extended largely by the United Mine Workers of America allowed the Committee for Industrial Organization to survive and to achieve successful organization drives in the mass-production industries of the nation. Under the strong leadership of John L. Lewis, the CIO formed new unions of automobile workers, steelworkers, radio and electrical workers, rubber workers, and so on. By 1938, the CIO had attained its major objectives. Having severed their ties to the AF of L, CIO unions had to create a new labor federation. The establishment of such federation, however, was opposed by David Dubinsky and his International Ladies' Garment Workers' Union on the grounds that it would divide organized labor into two large groups. Nevertheless, a permanent Congress of Industrial Organizations was founded on November 14, 1938, at Pittsburgh, Pennsylvania. John L. Lewis became its president and Sidney Hillman and Philip Murray its vice-presidents.

When the Congress of Industrial Organizations met in San Francisco in October 1939, it had become a labor federation representing 4 million members organized into 35 internationals and into a multitude of other state and local organizations. At that time, World War II had already started in Europe. John L. Lewis took an isolationist stance and cautioned against American involvement in the war. He denounced a third Roosevelt term as an inevitable move toward American participation in the hostilities. Lewis then announced that a reelection of Franklin D.

Roosevelt would make him give up the presidency of the CIO. True to his word, Lewis resigned his position at the convention in Atlantic City in November 1940. Philip Murray, vice-president of both the CIO and the United Mine Workers of America, was unanimously elected to the presidency of the CIO.

Ill feelings soon developed between Lewis and Murray. Lewis drew up a plan of "accouplement" for the AF of L and the CIO without first consulting the president of either organization. In turn, Murray persuaded President Roosevelt to keep Lewis off the War Labor Board. Lewis retaliated by having Murray ousted from his position as vice-president of the United Mine Workers of America. When Murray accused Lewis of having impeded the nation's war effort, Lewis withdrew his miners from the CIO in October 1942.

John L. Lewis was certainly interested in the political events of his time, but he was not a politician. Lewis and most of the CIO leaders were, above all, organizers and the developers of industrial unionism in the United States. Lewis's support of the Republican party shows how far he stood from entertaining any revolutionary or radical political ideas. The fact that most CIO leaders in the 1940s shared Lewis's views is best revealed by the efforts taken by these men to purge their labor federation of Communist infiltration. It was indeed the action of these leaders rather than the impact of the Taft-Hartley Act of 1947 that succeeded in eradicating from the CIO unions acting according to Soviet guidance.

Communists had succeeded since 1938 in obtaining major positions in the CIO administrative apparatus; they were influential in the federation's legal and publicity departments and controlled a dozen CIO unions. They dutifully followed Moscow-dictated political strategy. Until August 1939, when the Nazi-Soviet nonaggression pact was signed, Soviet-inspired political planning had emphasized the formation of Popular Fronts that purported to join in a single alliance all groups opposed to the spread of Fascism. Communist trade union leaders in America embraced the Popular Front concept. Once the German-Soviet treaty was signed, and after hostilities had begun in Europe, the Communist strategy changed, at least up to the time when Hitler's troops invaded the Soviet Union. In conformity with the new line of propaganda, Communist-dominated unions in the United States attacked the war as "an imperialist war for profits, markets and colonies," and denounced Roosevelt's lend-lease program of help to England. Harry Bridges, the head of the International Longshoremen's and Warehousemen's Union, stated in April 1940:

> It is generally recognized that the present administration's policies in regard to the international situation, its pro-allied sympathizers, the endorsement of millions of dollars being sent abroad while millions of

Americans suffer unemployment and poverty can result in the embroiling of America into a foreign war in which she can have no concern except the protection of the investments of the large bankers and industrial interests of the country. (Taft 1964, p. 622)

The Communist tune quickly changed when Germany invaded the Soviet Union on June 22, 1941. Reversing himself, Bridges started calling the American war effort "a vital concern to the labor movement" and asked for a speedy declaration of war by Congress. Communist trade union leaders suddenly became major supporters of war against the Axis Powers. They denounced John L. Lewis as "the single most effective agent of the Fascist powers within the ranks of labor" (Taft 1964, p. 622).

Following the end of the war, the Communist-controlled unions once again changed the nature of their political attacks and directed them against American capitalism and imperialism.

As of 1946, the Executive Board of the CIO started taking action to weaken the Communist voice in the CIO. A Declaration of Policy was adopted by the board that rejected "efforts of the Communist Party or other political parties and their adherents to interfere in the affairs of the C.I.O." (Taft 1964, p. 625). In 1948, the CIO leadership dismissed Harry Bridges from his positon as CIO regional director for northern California. At its 1949 convention, the CIO delegates resolved that Communist unions would no longer be tolerated within the federation. This resolution led to the expulsion of the Communist-dominated United Electrical, Radio and Machine Workers of America and of the International Longshoremen's and Warehousemen's Union. The CIO leadership demonstrated that, just as its AF of L counterpart, its main commitment was to improve the standard of living of its members within the existing politicoeconomic system.

LABOR DURING AND SINCE WORLD WAR II

President Roosevelt, fearful that any labor turmoil during the years of war could weaken the American war effort, established a National War Labor Board by executive order. This board was to be concerned with "adjusting and settling labor disputes which might interrupt work which contributes to the effective prosecution of the war." The board, which became operative in January 1942, was also given the power to stabilize wages in order to contain inflationary pressures in the economy.

In July 1942, the Steel Workers Union, representing workers in "Little Steel"—Bethlehem Steel Corporation, Republic Steel, Youngstown Sheet and Tube Company, and Inland Steel Company—demanded a wage increase of one dollar a day or 12.5 cents an hour. The board rejected this demand. It found that the cost of living between January 1941 and May 1942 had risen by about 15 percent and that workers had already received wage increases of 11.8 percent since January 1, 1941, and should therefore only be granted a wage raise of .032 cent an hour. This "Little Steel formula" became the board's basis for wartime wage regulation. The enactment of the Economic Stabilization Act in October of that year bound the board to follow the Little Steel formula in all cases except where serious substandard pay conditions existed.

Organized labor protested what it considered to be a limitation imposed by the government on the process of collective bargaining. A number of strikes followed in 1943. Most of these were of short duration with the exception of those launched by John L. Lewis's United Mine Workers. Upon the expiration in April 1943 of its contract with the coal mine operators, the United Mine Workers, ignoring the Little Steel formula, demanded a wage increase of two dollars a day. The miners' demand was to be heard by the National War Labor Board, but the board refused to examine the case as long as miners went on striking. Meanwhile, Lewis accused the AF of L and the CIO, which had accepted the government's wage stabilization program, of being guilty of "cringing toadyism" (Taft 1964, p. 554).

A general strike in the bituminous fields was started on May 1, 1943. The government responded by taking control of the mines. On May 25, the board rejected the miners' demand, and they continued to engage in intermittent work stoppages. It was only in October that Lewis ordered his men to resume work regularly.

The little concern Lewis had shown for the national war effort induced Congress to pass the first antilabor measure enacted in the days of the Roosevelt administration. This measure, jointly sponsored by Representative Howard Smith of Virginia and Senator Tom L. Connally of Texas, gave power to the president of the United States to take control of any economic activity where a work stoppage constituted a threat to the war effort. The bill was passed by Congress over the veto of the president and became law on June 25, 1943. The Smith-Connally Law provided penalties for anyone who instigated a strike after government had taken control of the operations of a given activity.

In spite of this law, both the AF of L and the CIO continued to support the Roosevelt administration and its war activity. In preparation for the 1944 elections, most of the AF of L leaders campaigned in favor of the president's reelection. The CIO formed a Political Action Committee to work for a Democratic victory. The two large labor federations remained loyal to the New Deal government whose legislation had induced organized labor in America to rise to nearly 15 million people representing about 36 percent of the nonagricultural labor force by the end of the war.

President Harry S. Truman did not receive such dedicated support from organized labor. The end of the war had brought numerous layoffs as industry prepared to reconvert its productive facilities to peacetime use. With a return to a 40-hour work week for most workers in manufacturing, the disappearance of overtime pay, and rising prices, wages started falling behind prices. Aware of the existence of high wartime profits, organized labor claimed that wage increases could be granted by employers without need for prices being raised. Unable to reach an agreement at the collective bargaining table, unions in 1945 launched strikes in a number of industries. By January 1946, about 2 million workers were out on strike in the nation. CIO unions organized major strike campaigns in the mass-production industries. Following a renewal of intermittent strikes by coal miners, government once again took control of the coal mines.

The strike activities of 1945 and of 1946 caused the public to turn against labor. The Republicans obtained control of Congress in 1946, and this political change facilitated the enactment of the Taft-Hartley Act in 1947, a law viewed as hostile to it by organized labor.

If the early post–World War II period imposed the restrictive terms of the Taft-Hartley Act on trade union activity, it also found American unions more strongly established in society than ever before. The trade union had become in the 1940s as much a part of the American capitalist system as the business corporation. Successful collective bargaining by union officials enhanced the appeal of unions to workers, and the rising numbers of organized workers verified the fact that American workers gave greater importance to rising wages and to contractual fringe benefits than to industrial democracy. As of 1948, the United Automobile Workers signed long-term contracts with the companies, two- or five-year contracts that assured employers long periods of labor peace and granted workers automatic cost of living wage adjustments, wage increases tied to gains in productivity, and benefits such as health schemes, paid holidays, and retirement plans, which, in the 1920s, constituted mere privileges extended at the pleasure of the employer. The organized American labor force went on expanding until 1954, when, at the peak of the Korean War, its size attained 18 million, representing 35 percent of the nonagricultural labor force.

The failure of Congress to repeal the Taft-Hartley Act and the Republican victory in 1952 induced leaders in both major labor federations to consider seriously the benefits of increased labor strength through the unification of the AF of L and the CIO. Differences that had driven the two organizations apart in the past appeared inconsequential in the early 1950s. Both federations accepted the validity of industrial unions and entertained similar views regarding the government's foreign policy: The two organizations supported the foreign policies of Presidents Truman and Eisenhower, and both organizations took a strong anti-Communist stance; they backed the government's attempts to contain the expansion of Soviet power in the world through the extension of economic and military foreign aid; and they approved American participation in NATO and justified Truman's military intervention in Korea.

In November 1952, William Green of the AF of L and Philip Murray of the CIO died a few days apart. George Meany became the new leader of the AF of L; the CIO selected as its new president Walter Reuther of the United Automobile Workers, a man whose pragmatic ideas made him accept the existing political system. The two new presidents headed a Joint Unity Committee, a committee whose task was to study the possibility of fusion between the two labor federations. This committee announced on February 9, 1955 that an agreement had been reached on the establishment of a new, unified AF of L-CIO labor federation that recognized the need for labor to organize on the basis of both craft and industrial unions.

The first convention of the new organization took place in December 1955. It elected George Meany as president and Walter Reuther as vice-president in charge of the organization's Industrial Union Department. Embracing the traditional goal of American trade unionism, Meany asserted: "We do not seek to recast American society in any particular doctrinaire or ideological image. We seek an ever rising standard of living. Sam Gompers once put the matter succinctly. When asked what the labor movement wanted, he answered, 'More'..." (Dulles and Dubofsky 1984, p. 361).

During the three decades from 1955 to 1985, neither recession, nor the adverse impact of automation on employment in the basic industries, nor the advent of stagflation changed the strategy of the major American labor federation. The policy of the AF of L-CIO in the post–World War II period was strongly influenced by the values and attitudes of those workers who remained employed in the 1950s and the 1960s. For those workers, the real wage increased by 50 percent between 1945 and 1955 and by another 50 percent between the mid-1950s and the late 1960s. The employment contracts of these workers provided them with accident, sickness, and death insurance, unemployment benefits, pension plans, and other benefits. Most of these workers now identified with the middle class.

The story was different, however, for those who lost their jobs either because of economic recession or because of the effects of automation in production and distribution. The 1960s had started with an unemployment rate of 6.8 percent. Unemployment was to remain high in the 1960s and in the 1970s. At the same time, automation made for a reduction in the number of jobs in many industries. *Time* magazine noticed as early as 1961 that:

> In the highly automated chemical industry, the number of production jobs has fallen 3% since 1956 while output has soared 27%. Though steel capacity has increased 20% since 1955,, the number of men needed to operate the industry's plants—even at full capacity—has dropped 17,000. Auto employment slid from a peak of 746,000 in boom 1955 to 614,000 in November . . . since the meat industry's employment peak, 28,000 workers have lost their jobs despite a production increase of 3% . . . . (1961, p. 69)

The 1970s brought to the industrial nations of the West the end of the post–World War II boom and serious energy crises. The affluent decades of the 1950s and the 1960s had become history, and the new decade brought inflation, overproduction, and mass unemployment. By the end of the decade, the United States suffered from double-digit inflation, declining industrial productivity, and high rates of interest. The rate of unemployment was climbing to its highest level since the years of the Great Depression. By December 1982, this rate had attained 10.8 percent.

The AF of L-CIO's membership had already experienced losses in the early 1960s. The expulsion of the Teamsters' Union, the Laundry Workers, and the Bakery and Confectionery Workers from the federation after its Ethical Practices Committee found that the leaders of these unions were guilty of corrupt practices constituted a major loss of members for the federation—a loss made even greater when Walter Reuther withdrew the United Automobile Workers in 1967.

The growth of the federation's membership continued to suffer in the 1970s because the increasingly adverse economic conditions affected mostly manufacturing and consequently the workers in that sector of the economy and their unions. Between 1974 and 1978, these unions lost more than a million members. In the service and in the high-technology industries where employment was expanding, employers, championed by the National Association of Manufacturers, reverted to antiunion tactics and succeeded in dissuading many of their employees from joining a union through effective personnel policies.

The 1980 election of Ronald Reagan to the presidency of the United States was a further blow to organized labor. Reagan chose as his secretary of labor Raymond Donovan, a business executive with little experience in industrial relations. The new president did not consult any labor leaders before announcing his choice.

The president's program of trying to boost economic activity by helping the stronger and wealthier elements in society through generous tax cuts while imposing on the masses substantial reductions in general welfare expenditures was not very promising for the American worker. While large corporations used their newly found wealth to acquire control over other corporations, their investment for employment expansion remained negligible. As unemployment continued to rise in the early 1980s, the economic future did not look very bright for the American trade union movement.

CONCLUSION

The AF of L-CIO did not represent the entirety of the American organized labor movement in 1980. Affiliated and nonaffiliated unions in the early 1980s did not give evidence of entertaining views based on a strong class consciousness and on the desire of being politically represented by their own party. In spite of acute inflation and of high unemployment, in spite of renewed hostility against organized labor by corporate employers, and in spite of the failure of Congress to introduce new prolabor legislation, American unions continued to accept the existing politicoeconomic system. The major labor federations had retained their strong anti-Communist positions; after joining the International Confederation of Free Trade Unions in 1949, the AF of L-CIO later withdrew from this organization because of its weak opposition to the Soviet bloc nations. American trade unions continued to center their attention on the pursuit of Gompers's goal of "more." In the process, many union members voted in favor of the Republican candidates in both 1980 and in 1984. Most of them totally ignored Socialist thought and Socialist goals in both election years.

NOTES

Dulles, F. R., and M. Dubofsky. 1984. *Labor in America: A History.* Arlington Heights, Ill.: Harlan Davidson.

Droz, J. 1979. *Historia General del Socialismo.* Vol. 2. Barcelona: Ediciones Destino.

Kirkland, E. C. 1951. *A History of American Economic Life.* New York: Appleton-Century-Crofts.

Taft, P. 1964. *Organized Labor in American History.* New York: Harper & Row.

Time. 1961. February 24, p. 69.

Ware, N. J. 1929. *The Labor Movement in the United States, 1860–1895: A Study in Democracy.* New York: Vintage Books.

BIBLIOGRAPHY

Beard, M. R. *The American Labor Movement.* New York, 1969.

Bernstein, I. "The Growth of American Unions, 1945-60." *Labor History* 2, no. 2 (1961): 131-57.

Bimba, A. *The History of the American Working Class.* New York, 1968.

Blackman, J. L. Jr. *Presidential Seizure in Labor Disputes.* Cambridge, 1967.

Commons, J. R. *History of Labor in the United States.* New York, 1935.

Dubofsky, M. ed. *American Labor Since the New Deal.* New York, 1971.

Laslett, J. H. M. *Labor and the Left, A Study of Socialist and Radical Influences in the American Labor Movement, 1881-1924.* New York, 1970.

Miernyk, W. H. *Trade Unions in an Age of Affluence.* New York, 1962.

Perlman, S. and P. Taft. *History of Labor in the United States, 1896-1932.* New York, 1935.

Pierson, F. *Unions in Postwar America.* New York, 1967.

Rayback, J. G. *A History of American Labor.* New York, 1966.

Thompson, F., and P. Murfin. *The I.W.W., the First Seventy Years, 1905-1975.* Chicago, 1976.

9
Concluding Remarks

It is not possible to synthesize the global evolution of social ideas. Class consciousness, as a fraternal feeling that developed among the propertyless classes of industrial societies and became the foundation of trade union movements, evolved slowly. At the national or regional level, it responded differently to the different visions of the phenomenon of social transformation as perceived by individual theoreticians influenced by different historical times, by different institutions and conditions that characterized their particular socioeconomic environment. To try to explain the evolution of labor thought in terms of schools or of politicoeconomic systems presents the risk that the analysis may ignore a number of fortuitous or exogenous political, social, and economic factors that affected this thought in a unique way.

Should we insist on finding a given direction to the evolution of social thought, we may base our study on one of several methodologies. We may want to observe change in social terms in the context of historical stages. In this case, we could identify a "pre-Socialist" stage, the stage of "scientific socialism," and a third stage covering the practical application of "scientific socialism."

Another approach could follow a different type of historical stage analysis. In this case, an initial stage could be identified during which social thought would be essentially shaped by the relative degree of industrialization of the particular national or regional scenario and by the politicosocial positions of the pertinent social reform theorists. Social ideas and labor movements then acquire international dimensions during a second stage, to retrogress perhaps to an emphasis on pragmatic nationalism in the course of a final stage.

Another taxonomic approach will attempt to explain the evolution of social ideas in terms of the different industrial evolutions, of four or five nations or geographic areas. We may identify an Iberian-French type of social analysis, which was marked by a strong emphasis on sociopolitical ideas, a Germanic line of thought, which manifested itself initially in terms of a great interest in philosophical analysis and which became transformed in the course of rapid industrialization into pragmatic trade unionism; and Anglo-American thought stressing economic reformism.

Compared with British Chartism or Fabianism, French and Spanish social thought was from the outset more politically oriented. The French and Spanish labor movements had a more pronounced revolutionary character than those of other countries in Europe. In Gracchus Babeuf we find the first modern social revolutionary and the first martyr of social insurrection. The people Babeuf fought for were not only limited to the working class; they also included small landowners, small manufacturers, and small businessmen. The nebulous distinction between the low middle class and the class of wage earners appeared in the writings of numerous French critics. Influenced by the Enlightenment, they became the champions of the rights and interests of *le petit peuple* in general and did not address themselves exclusively, in a Marxian way, to an industrial proletariat. They recognized the fact that in their time the great majority of the French working class was constituted by artisans and craftsmen, peasants owning small plots of land, and small shopkeepers still tied to the institutions of the preindustrial era and strongly attached to the preservation of individual rights in small property. Nevertheless, Babeuf was the first to formulate the concept of the "dictatorship of the proletariat" and to preach economic communism and total social reform.

Etienne Cabet's communism was more utopian than that of Babeuf. Cabet, also under the influence of Enlightenment writers, believed that the social transformation he wanted could be obtained peacefully by the simple rational superiority of the concept of the collectivized society, an idea that had to appeal necessarily to the natural goodness of people.

The recognition of the exploitative nature of capitalism appeared also in the thinking of the disciples of Saint-Simon, such men as Saint-Amand Bazard, Barthélemy-Prosper Enfantin, Pierre Leroux, and Philippe-Joseph Benjamin Buchez. Charles Fourier and Pierre-Joseph Proudhon also opposed capitalism for both political and economic reasons. For both, the cooperative organization of production and of distribution could bring an end to capitalism without the use of violence.

French revolutionary syndicalism emerged at the end of the past century as a reaction to the harshness of the repression of the Paris Commune. More than a theoretical manifestation, it represented a movement based on action. Fernand Pelloutier opposed any parliamentary reformism and believed that the trade unions should become the leaders of revolutionary action. Inspired by Bakunin's anarchism, the French revolutionary syndicalists wanted to overthrow the existing politico-economic system by means of strikes, boycotts, sabotage, and worker occupation of factories. The anarchist movement divided into two directions. A "direct action" group advocated the use of the general strike and individual acts of terrorism to bring capitalism to its end. A more moderate group accepted the transformation of the existing society by way of a number of transition stages. In Spain, the "direct action" group was represented by the FAI, whereas the more evolutionary position was taken by the leaders of the CNT. With the establishment of the French CGT, Communists were able to implant firmly their ideology on the French labor movement. In Spain, it was only the civil war that was able to sap the strength of anarchism.

The various political entities that constituted the linguistic area known as Germany at the start of the nineteenth century were generally economically poorer than England and France. The misery of the German masses of small craftsmen was probably greater than that of their counterparts in the other countries. Until 1848, German social thought essentially mirrored the French example, with a few exceptions. Freidrich Hegel's dialectics and Ludwig Feuerbach's social materialism constituted the first steps leading to Marxist thought. On the whole, pre-Marx social thinking centered more on theory than on practical considerations. This type of thought may be explained in part by the fact that most German political entities were still governed by neofeudal institutions that kept the bourgeoisie out of political power.

The *Communist Manifesto* of 1848 and *The Capital* of 1867 brought to the world a materialist theory of historical evolution according to which the triumph of Socialist ideas was to emerge out of an increasing concentration of economic power in capitalist society and the eventual expropriation of the monopolistic class by the masses of workers. Marx presented to the proletariat a well-developed and coherent explanation of the breakdown of capitalism that included the concept of the class struggle and the vision of an international political alliance of all workers whose efforts to obtain political control of the state would succeed. The workers' revolution would lead to a new society in which there would be no exploitation of man by man.

Marx's message was well received by the early leaders of the German labor movement. Next to Friedrich Engels, Karl Kautsky in Germany did more to disseminate Marxism throughout Europe than any other writer. Between 1880 and the beginning of World War I, Kautsky, as the unofficial but most important theoretician of the German Social Democratic party, tried to reconcile the activities of the German labor movement with the theory of Karl Marx. Before him, Ferdinand Lassalle,

August Bebel, and Wilhelm Liebknecht, the early leaders of this movement, had been deeply influenced by Marx's ideas.

And yet, the Socialist delegates in the imperial parliament voted in
favor of war credits on August 4, 1914, and Carl Legien, the leader of the
Socialist trade unions signed the *Burgfrieden* agreement with the minister of the interior. In spite of Bismarck's earlier "antisocialist" laws, the
German labor movement embraced at the end of the nineteenth century
not merely a "revisionist" interpretation of Marxist theory but a "reformist" ideology that ignored Marxist theory entirely.

The interest of German workers in political and social change waned
as the empire of Wilhelm II became one of the leading industrial nations
of the world. The rapid industrialization of Germany after 1870 was indeed remarkable. In 1882, the number of people working in agriculture
and forestry was about equal to the number of workers in industry and
commerce. By 1907, there were nearly twice as many people employed
in industry as in agriculture. A rapid increase in the output of Ruhr coal
in the 1890s had allowed a dramatic expansion of the industrial sector.
Ruhr coal supplied the fuel needs of the new steelworks, the new gas-
works, the chemical plants, the railways, and the new mercantile fleet.
As John M. Keynes correctly observed, the economic power of Wilhelmine Germany was built "more truly on coal and iron, than on blood and
iron." Rapid industrialization was the reason for a rapidly climbing national income and for rising living standards. Per capita consumption of
commodities such as meat, sugar, coffee, rice, and cotton increased—a
trend indicating that workers participated in the rising standard of living. Advancing levels of employment, coupled with an improved living
standard, rapidly transformed the German worker into a *Kleinbuerger*, a
small bourgeois who lost interest in any type of social revolution.

This correlation between the industrialization of a particular economy
and the *embourgeoisement* of its labor movement was repeated in the
American case. Inspired by the business orientation of the British trade
unions, the leaders of the AF of L and the CIO accepted the politicoeconomic system in which they acted, became militant foes of Marxism and
of Soviet-dominated labor organizations, and centered their efforts on the
attainment of nonrevolutionary, limited economic objectives that satisfied the workers' demands for a higher standard of living and for greater
job security.

We started with the hypothesis that the pattern of evolution of social thought and the structure of national labor organizations are the product of the relative degree of economic backwardness and of the relative
pace of industrial advance of the economy in which a particular labor
movement operates. The more backward and poorer the economy, the
more solidly it is anchored to the traditional status quo, and the slower

its rate of growth, if any, as perceived by the workers, the greater the likelihood that the working class in that economy will center its attention on politicosocial theories of change and the greater will be the probability that such workers will form a number of labor organizations advocating different social and ethnic ideologies. In this case, the labor movement will show increasing fragmentation and will attach as much importance to political as to economic goals. The greater the perceived rate of economic growth and the more rapid the process of industrialization, the smaller will be the interest of workers in political and social change and the greater will be their effort to obtain a larger share of the rising national income. The history of the Spanish, French, German, and American labor movements supports this hypothesis.

Index

About the Author

Professor Lieberman is a native of France and lived for many years in Spain. He holds an LLM from Georgetown University and a PhD from the University of California at Berkeley. He is Professor of Economics at The University of Utah and has held appointments at Harvard University, The University of Auckland, New Zealand, and, most recently, at The Autonomous University of Madrid, Spain. He is the author of *THE INDUSTRIALIZATION OF NORWAY, 1800–1920*, (Scandia Books, 1970), *THE GROWTH OF EUROPEAN MIXED ECONOMIES, 1945–1970*, (Schenkman, 1977), *THE CONTEMPORARY SPANISH ECONOMY, A HISTORICAL PERSPECTIVE*, (Allen & Unwin, 1982) and the editor of *EUROPE AND THE INDUSTRIAL REVOLUTION* (Schenkman, 1972).